MULTINATIONALS: THEORY AND HISTORY

EUROPEAN SCIENCE FOUNDATION

The European Science Foundation is an international non-governmental organisation with its seat in Strasbourg (France). Its members are academies and research councils with national responsibility for supporting scientific research, and which are funded largely from governmental sources. The term 'science' is used in its broadest sense to include the humanities, social sciences, biomedical sciences, the natural sciences and mathematics. The ESF currently has 48 members from 18 European countries.

The tasks of the ESF are:

to assist its Member Organisations to coordinate research programmes;

to identify areas in need of stimulation, particularly those of an interdisciplinary nature;

to further cooperation between researchers by facilitating their movement between laboratories, holding workshops, managing support schemes approved by the Member Organisations, and arranging for the joint use of special equipment;

to harmonise and assemble data useful to the Member Organisations;

to foster the efficient dissermination of information;

to respond to initiatives which are aimed at advancing European science;

to maintain constructive relations with the European Communities and other relevant organisations.

The ESF is funded through a general budget to which all Member Organisations contribute (according to a scale assessed in relation to each country's net national income), and a series of special budgets covering additional activities, funded by those organisations which choose to participate. The programmes of the ESF are determined by the Assembly of all Member Organisations. Their implementation is supervised by an elected Executive Council, assisted by the office of the Foundation which consists of an international staff directed by the Secretary General.

Multinationals: Theory and History

Edited by
Peter Hertner
European University Institute
and
Geoffrey Jones
Business History Unit, London School of Economics

Gower

Published by
Gower Publishing Company Limited
Gower House
Croft Road
Aldershot
Hants GU11 3HR
England

Gower Publishing Company
Old Post Road
Brookfield
Vermont 05036
USA

Reprinted 1987

British Library Cataloguing in Publication Data
Multinationals: theory and history
1. International business enterprises
I. Hertner, Peter   II. Jones, Geoffrey, 1952-
338.8'8   HD 2755.5

Library of Congress Cataloging in Publication Data
Multinationals--theory and history. Papers originally presented at a conference held at the European University Institute, Florence, during 19-21 Sept. 1983 and sponsored by the European Science Foundation.
    Includes bibliographies and index
    1. International business enterprises--Europe--congresses.
2. International business enterprises--Europe--congresses.
I. Hertner, Peter. II. Jones, Geoffrey.   III. European Science Foundation.
HD2755.5M86 1986   338.8'8   85-24955

ISBN 0 566 05078 1

Printed in Great Britain by Blackmore Press, Shaftesbury, Dorset.

Contents

Preface

This book originated at an international conference held at the European University Institute, Florence during 19-21 September 1983. The Conference was organised by Peter Hertner and Geoffrey Jones, and sponsored by the European Science Foundation. The group of scholars which assembled in Florence included historians, business historians, economists and political scientists from 11 countries. Some presented papers, others intervened in the discussions. The papers selected for publication in this volume were extensively rewritten in the light of the Conference exchanges. The editors would therefore like to thank all who took part in the 1983 Florence Conference for their contribution to this book.

The participants at the Conference were Dr Stephen J. Nicholas (Australia), Professor Niels Amstrup, Professor Bjarke Fog and Professor Kristof Glamann (Denmark), Professor Jorma Avenainen and Dr. Riitta Hjerppe (Finland), Professor Albert Broder, Professor Patrick Fridenson and Professor Charles-Albert Michalet (France), Professor Peter Hertner and Professor Ehrenfried Pausenberger (Federal Republic of Germany), Professor Yair Aharoni and Professor Zeev Hirsch (Israel), Professor H. de Haan (Netherlands), Dr Even Lange (Norway), Dr Ragnhild Lundström, Professor Ulf Olsson and Dr Klaus Wohlert (Sweden), Mr John Cantwell, Professor Mark Casson, Mr T.A.B. Corley, Professor Leslie Hannah, Dr Geoffrey Jones, Dr William J. Reader, Professor Alice Teichova, Professor Charles Wilson (United Kingdom), and Professor Mira Wilkins (United States).

We would like also to thank Mr E.N. Shaw for his editorial assistance and Susan Crawshaw for the index.

Peter Hertner and Geoffrey Jones

1 Multinationals: Theory and History

Peter Hertner and Geoffrey Jones

The study of the multinational enterprise (MNE) has suffered, like so many subjects, from artificial divisions erected by academics between disciplines. There has been an enormous amount written by economists and other social scientists about multinationals in recent years.[1] One estimate is that on average at least five books appear on the subject every month. The attraction of the theme is obvious. Multinationals are very visible and important features of the contemporary world economy. It is a well-known, if rather misleading, fact that the total assets of some of the world's leading MNEs exceed the GNPs of various countries. Yet many studies of contemporary MNEs seem very abstract. Even empirical evidence on the motives, behaviour and performance of contemporary MNEs is often based on the analysis of aggregate published data and occasional interviews with senior management. This situation is hardly surprising since MNEs are unlikely to disclose their inner workings to outside researchers. However, this does mean that despite the quantity of the academic literature, a great deal that is written about MNEs is essentially speculative.

Business historians find this situation frustrating. Although some economists still seem unaware of the fact. MNEs have been around a long time. One scholar has traced their origins to the international activities of medieval bankers.[2] Some aspects of the international trading companies of the seventeenth and eighteenth centuries, the British, Dutch and French East India Companies and the Hudson's Bay Company had similarities to today's MNEs. By the second half of the nineteenth century firms owning and controlling manufacturing or extractive facilities in more than one country—the basic definition of a MNE—were active in the world economy. By the Second World War there were thousands of MNEs. Potentially, therefore, there is a great deal of historical information about MNEs. Moreover, information can often be drawn from detailed studies of the internal records and accounts of companies, as many firms are willing to allow outside

1

researchers to examine their affairs of several decades ago. Such historical data would appear to offer rich opportunities to test theories about contemporary MNEs, or to refine and develop new theories. In practice, however, the different methodologies and languages of theorists and historians have kept their work apart.

A further feature of the literature on MNEs is its Anglo-Saxon bias. The concept of the MNE began to be widely used by economists in the 1960s, at a time when companies based in the United States still dominated the international economy. The early theories of multinational growth, such as Raymond Vernon's product-cycle hypothesis, were devised during this period of American pre-eminence. Subsequently American and British economists came to dominate the study of multinationals, as they did most of post-war economics as a whole. Coincidently, the more advanced state of business history in the United States meant that more reliable historical data emerged on the development of American multinationals than on those of any other country. As a result American concepts and data have dominated most of both the theoretical and historical research on MNEs. This situation is unfortunate. Before 1914 there were more European than American multinationals.[3] The post-war era of American multinational pre-eminence was challenged after 1960, when European-owned MNEs began a further period of rapid expansion. During the 1970s a new generation of Japanese, Brazilian and South Korean MNEs emerged. It seems very likely that these non-American MNEs often grew, organised and behaved in different patterns to United States companies.

In September 1983 a conference, held at the European University Institute at Florence and sponsored by the European Science Foundation, assembled a group of leading European, American and Australian economists and business historians interested in the MNE. The aim was to initiate a dialogue between theorists and historians, and to introduce into that dialogue a Continental European perspective. This volume contains a selection of essays which originated as papers presented at the conference. All the essays have been completely revised in the light of conference discussions.

The contributors to this book examine a variety of aspects of the relationship between the theory and history of MNEs. The first two essays are by leading economists in the field of multinational studies. Dunning, Cantwell and Corley trace the origins of modern theories of the MNE. Casson critically reviews recent general theories of the MNE and considers the problems of their application to business history. Nicholas, a business historian specifically concerned with the application of theory to history, uses the concept of transaction costs, currently the most widely accepted general theory of the MNE, to explain the different modes in British multinational growth before 1939. Wilkins discusses a range of definitional problems which have emerged from her empirical work on the history of European MNEs in the United States. Jones presents a study of the performance of British MNEs before 1945. The remaining four essays are by continental European business historians, and examine aspects of the theory-history relationship in the study of MNEs using empirical evidence from the neglected Continental experience. Hertner and Lundström present surveys of early German and Swedish multinational growth respectively. Broder examines the inward flow of foreign MNEs into the French electrical industry, while Fridenson surveys the multinational expansion of the French automobile industry. The essays naturally vary widely in methodology and in perspective. Nevertheless, they offer fresh views and evidence on their field, and they share a common interest in suggesting the need for collaboration between theorists and historians of the MNE, to the mutual benefit of both sides.

The following sections of this Introduction attempt to place the essays in this volume in perspective by briefly examining recent developments in the work on MNEs by economists and historians. The concluding section suggests some problems in bringing the two sides together.

Theory and the MNE
The last 20 years have seen great advances in understanding the economics of the MNE. There have been major contributions to the field by economists such as S. Hymer, C.P. Kindleberger, Richard E. Caves, Raymond Vernon, John Dunning and Mark Casson. The Cantwell, Corley and Dunning essay in this volume traces the evolution of the place of international production in economic theory, while Casson reviews the attempts to formulate 'general theories' of the MNE. These two essays, and the regular reviews of MNE literature published elsewhere, made it unnecessary to use this Introduction for a further 'state of the art' review. Instead, attention is focused on a number of general points relevant to the theory and history theme.

A first point is that there is still no generally accepted definition of the MNE. One recent textbook by a leading expert defines a MNE 'as an enterprise that controls and manages production establishments—plants—located in at least two countries'.[4] But other economists widen their definition to include all 'income-generating assets', including presumably sales subsidiaries,[5] while others have preferred more rigorous definitions, raising, for example, the qualifying number of foreign countries to two or even six.[6] There are also severe problems in defining 'own' and 'control' for purposes of quantification.

3

Definitions of foreign direct investment, the instrument through which MNEs invest overseas, vary between countries and over time. The United States Department of Commerce until the 1960s defined foreign direct investment as an investment that controlled 25 per cent or more of the equity of an overseas business.[7] Subsequently the figure was reduced to 10 per cent.[8] A recent writer on British overseas investment before 1914 suggests 30 per cent as the appropriate figure.[9] In any case, shareholding percentages are a poor measure of control, and it is *control* over a foreign business which is the essential basis of the concept of the multinational.

Secondly, given the lack of general agreement on definitions, it is not surprising that there is no consensus amongst economists concerning the theory of the MNE. As Casson observes in this volume, none of the recent general theories of MNEs is really satisfactory. This is partly because the study of the MNE draws on so many different parts of macro- and microeconomic theory. Moreover it is well known that neoclassical economics, given its focus on the market, is deficient in explaining such subjects as the entrepreneur and management. Some of the most widely accepted concepts in the theory of the MNE have yet to be rigorously examined. As Casson argues, this criticism applies even to the transaction-cost explanation of MNE growth which has found wide acceptance in recent years among both economists and business historians.

A third general point is that theorists have examined many issues concerning the MNE, apart from explaining its appearance and growth. A glance at the recent textbook by Richard E. Caves suggests the range of matters which have come under scrutiny.[10] One set of questions concerns the dymanics of MNE growth. How are MNEs organised? Why do some MNEs enter foreign markets by acquiring a local firm, and others by making a greenfield investment or participating in a joint venture? Again considerable attention has focused on the consequences of MNEs. How do they affect the market structure of an industry in which they operate? What is the correlation between MNEs and levels of seller concentration in a market? How do MNEs affect wage structure and employment in their home and host economies? Do MNEs investing abroad 'export' jobs from their country of origin? A further set of questions concerns the behaviour of MNEs. How are their investments financed? How do the international transactions of MNEs affect national balance of payments? How do MNEs develop and transfer technology? Does the presence of MNEs in a market lead to a faster or slower rate of technological diffusion? How do MNEs affect national economic policies? Such concerns lead on to discussions of the overall impact of MNEs on their home and host economies.

The upshot for this volume is that there is no neat and selfcontained body of economic theory of the MNE waiting for testing or application by business historians. The picture is rather of a range of theoretical insights, some in conflict with one another, used to explain a variety of aspects of the MNE.

History and the MNE

Research on the history of MNEs was slow to get off the ground, with American researchers taking the lead. A number of the pioneering American business histories were of firms such as Standard Oil of New Jersey and Ford which had substantial international investments. Consequently the studies contained valuable information about the growth of American multinationals.[11] Applied economists, however, pioneered the explicit historical study of MNEs. In 1965 Raymond Vernon launched a Multinational Enterprise Project at Harvard University. This project assembled a wide range of statistical information on the historical evolution of American MNEs, focusing on the activities of a sample of 187 MNEs selected from a list of the largest 500 US industrial firms in 1967.[12] Subsequently Mira Wilkins assembled an enormous amount of information about the evolution of American multinationals in a two-volume study published in 1970 and 1974.[13]

This American work had a spillover effect in Europe. In the early 1970s two economists involved with the Harvard Project, John Stopford and Lawrence Franko, applied Vernon's methodology to the growth of British and continental European MNEs.[14] In 1977 Mira Wilkins wrote a *cri de coeur* in a leading European economic history journal calling for European business historians to investigate the history of European-based MNEs.[15] Wilkins, for her part, launched a major research project on the growth of European MNEs in the United States. Her paper in this volume reflects some of the conceptual questions which her new research raised.

In Europe, the United Kingdom has attracted most attention from students of the MNE. This was appropriate insofar as Britain has been the leading European home and host economy for MNEs in the twentieth century. The pattern of research had many similarities to the American experience. During the 1950s academic business historians began to appear. Charles Wilson's study of the Anglo-Dutch conglomerate Unilever was followed by histories of such leading British manufacturing firms as Imperial Chemical Industries, Courtaulds, Pilkington, Bowater and Metal Box.[16] Such histories all contained information on the overseas as well as the domestic activities of the firms. Recent years have seen the publication of several major studies of

British-based extractive multinationals, including British Petroleum, Burmah Oil and Rio Tinto.[17]

General studies of British-based multinationals were slower to emerge. Applied economists have done most of the pioneering. An article by John Stopford on the history of British MNEs was in this sense a turning-point. Unfortunately, Stopford's approach, and in particular his restriction of his database to those pre-1914 British MNEs which were amongst the 100 largest British manufacturing firms in 1970, limited the usefulness of his conclusions. Stopford discovered 14 such pre-1914 British manufacturing multinationals. He concluded that British manufacturers were slower than their American equivalents to become multinational. 'When war broke out in 1914', observed Stopford, 'most British manufacturers were viewing the world at a distance.'[18]

Over the last ten years it has become clear that this view of British multinational enterprise before 1914 cannot be sustained. The composition of the vast British foreign investment in the nineteenth century has been recalculated using modern definitions of foreign direct and portfolio investment. As a result the traditional image of British foreign investment before 1914 as overwhelmingly portfolio has been qualified. Svedberg has argued that over 40 per cent of British overseas investment in the Third World and South America by 1914 was direct.[19] Aggregate studies of British foreign investment in particular regions, such as Latin America, have supported this view,[20] although D.C.M. Platt has recently cast doubts on the accuracy of all British nineteenth-century foreign-investment statistics.[21] The most ambitious re-computation of British foreign direct investment, however, has been undertaken by John Dunning. Dunning has estimated that the stock of accumulated British foreign direct investment was $6,500 million in 1914 and $10,500 million in 1938, representing 45.5 per cent and 39.8 per cent of the world total respectively.[22] Dunning's data suggest that British foreign direct investment exceeded that of the United States throughout the pre-Second World War period. By implication, Britain was probably the world's leading home economy of MNEs in this period.

Business historians have gone some way in explaining who and what these British MNEs were, although no work of synthesis comparable to the Wilkins volumes exists. The role of British multinationals in particular countries before 1950, notably in the United States and India, has been examined.[23] In 1982 Nicholas published a survey of the motives and direction of British multinational investment, using a sample of 119 British manufacturing firms which made foreign direct investments betwen 1870 and 1914.[24] On a less aggregate level, business historians have produced archivally-based case studies of the international growth of British MNEs. These include David Fieldhouse's study of the growth and performance of Unilever in selected countries and Geoffrey Jones's case studies of a number of British manufacturing MNEs, including Cadbury, Dunlop and the Gramophone Company (later part of EMI).[25]

In a decade the wheel has apparently turned full-circle on Stopford's original propositions. It is now generally accepted that many British manufacturing firms made multinational investments before 1939. Any 'failure' may need to be detected not in the propensity to undertake foreign direct investment, but in the management and performance of such investments. Geoffrey Jones's essay in this volume explores this theme, though a great deal of basic research on individual companies needs to be undertaken before this kind of failure hypothesis can be generally accepted.

Elsewhere in Europe research on the historical origins of the MNE is less advanced. In the mid-1970s Lawrence Franko attempted a general survey of the development of Continental European multinationals.[26] This study has been to date the only attempt to view on a Continent-wide basis the activity of these firms. Unfortunately, like the Stopford study, Franko's work gave a very incomplete picture of the origins and growth of Continental multinationals. The study was based on secondary sources, and given the dearth of reliable information on the subject, major inaccuracies and misapprehensions arose.

The research on the multinationals of individual Continental European economies has been mixed. In Germany, which like Britain was a major home of manufacturing MNEs, histories of firms such as Siemens and AEG have provided some evidence on their multinational growth.[27] A number of studies of German foreign investment contained useful data for the student of MNEs, but did not deal with the subject specifically.[28] In 1979, however, Peter Hertner published an essay on German MNEs before the First World War, where he tried to show the multinational expansion of German business in Europe by means of a series of case studies of German locomotive factories in Italy and Russia, Mannesmann Tube factories in the United Kingdom, Austria-Hungary and Italy, and German electrical investments in Italy and Russia.[29] In the meantime further research by Walter Kirchner and Fritz Blaich on German firms in Russia, by G. Jacob-Wendler on Siemens and AEG in South America, Thomas R. Kabisch on German captial in the United States, and Peter Hertner on German companies and banks in Italy, have elucidated the dynamics of German multinational investment before 1914.[30] In his essay in this volume, Peter Hertner extends his examination of pre-1914 German MNEs to include samples from the previously-neglected consumer goods sector, and shows at the same time that international production was not limited to large companies. However, there is still no comprehensive survey of German multinational business for the pre-1945 period, nor are there any reliable statistics on either portfolio or foreign direct investment. Practically all the global figures rely on estimates calculated before 1914 or during the early 1920s.[31]

The small economies of Europe produced a disproportionally large number of MNEs before, and indeed after, the Second World War. Swiss chemical companies such as CIBA and Geigy, electrical-goods firms such as Brown Boveri, medical-goods firms such as Hoffman La Roche, and dairy-goods manufacturers such as Nestlé and the Anglo Swiss Condensed Milk Company, had made multinational investments before 1914.[32] The Netherlands shared with Britain the parentage of the Shell group and Unilever, and owned entirely such pioneer multinationals such as Enka and Philips. Sweden was also the home of many early multinationals, such as SKF, ASEA, L.M. Ericsson, Alfa-Laval and the Swedish Match Company, Lundström's essay in this volume reflects the impressive extent of research on the history of Swedish multinationals. In contrast, the history of Swiss and Dutch MNEs remains largely unknown. There is also the special case of Belgium, which before 1914 made substantial foreign direct investments, especially in public utilities in Continental Europe. On some definitions at least part of this investment was 'multinational', although it has not been studied in this context.[33]

The history of MNEs in two larger European economies, France and Italy, has been little studied. In the case of France, there has been considerable research on French foreign investment before 1914, but little specifically on the multinational aspect. Three different groups of historians have analysed aspects of French foreign investment. First, there are representatives of the French school of diplomatic history who have traditionally seen the history of French international relations in a wider context covering its economic and financial aspects. This category would include the work of René Girault on French investment in Russia, Raymond Poidevin on French investment in Germany and German investment in Russia, and J. Thobie on French capital in the Ottoman Empire.[34] Second, French economic historians have written on French overseas investment. Bertrand Gille's study of French investments in Italy and Albert Broder's work on French investment in Spain are examples of this approach.[35] Third, French business historians have made a significant contribution in this area. Patrick Fridenson's study of Renault includes an account of that firm's multinational growth.[36] In his essay in this volume Fridenson extends his coverage to French multinational automobile manufacturers as a whole. In addition to these studies of French investment, the role of foreign direct investment in France has attracted some attention.[37] Albert Broder's essay in this volume makes a contribution in this area by examining the role of foreign multinationals in the French electrical industry before the First World War.

There has been no serious study of Italian-based multinationals. Despite its late start in industrialisation, several Italian manufacturing companies had made multinational investments before 1914, and this trend increased in the inter-war years. Pirelli had factories in Britain, Spain and Argentina before 1914, while Fiat had built up a large network of factories in Europe and the United States by 1930. In 1983 a research project was launched at the European University Institute at Florence concerned with 'the Early Phase of Multinational Enterprise in Italy, France and Germany 1900–1929', and this study is providing the first real evidence on the nature and extent of early Italian multinational enterprise. The project is also providing new insights into the activities of French and German MNEs, such as Saint Gobain, Schneider (Le Creusot) and firms in the German iron and steel, chemical and electrical industries.[38]

What have been the main conclusions of business historians on European multinationals? The first is that it is now accepted that, despite the many gaps in our knowledge, there were many European-owned MNEs by 1914. The First World War provided a temporary check to European multinational growth, especially for German firms whose subsidiaries in Allied countries were sequestrated. During the 1920s certain European countries, such as the United Kingdom, Sweden and Italy, appear to have experienced a considerable surge in multinational activity, although the current state of research means that the dimensions of this growth remain unclear. In the German case, however, the chronic shortage of capital after 1918 prompted many firms to consider other strategies of international expansion, such as licensing, participation in cartels and joint ventures. Siemens and AEG in the 1920s, for example, attempted to combine their technology with American capital, a strategy which was often not successful.[39] Both European and American multinational expansion slowed in the 1930s. The depressed markets, exchange controls and political uncertainties of the period largely explain this phenomenon.

Secondly, considerable research by business historians has concentrated on establishing the causes of multinational growth. It is perhaps in this area that there has been the greatest interplay between theorists and historians. The concepts developed by economists to explain multinational growth have found wide acceptance by historians. It is now accepted that the firms which became multinational in the nineteenth century and afterwards generally possessed some kind of 'ownership-specific advantage', in the form of technology, marketing skills, access to financial sources or oligopolistic market structure, although, as both Casson and Lundström argue in their essays in this volume, the concept of 'advantage' is imprecise. It has also emerged that many firms which became multinational before 1914 preferred exporting to, rather than investing in, foreign markets. This strategy, however, was blocked by a variety of 'location-specific' factors. The spread of protectionism from the late 1870s was a major influence in this context, but patent legislation and other non-tariff trade barriers were also significant, and it is clear that no single 'location-specific' factor explains multinational growth. American manufacturers before 1914, for example, preferred to locate subsidiaries in free-trade Britain rather than the protectionist Continent, suggesting a higher priority to transport costs and scheduling problems than tariffs.[40] The matter, however, is complex. The establishment of a factory in Britain in 1910 by the Swedish match manufacturer Jönköping and Vulcan, for example, was a direct response to the introduction of an import duty on matches to Australia, with the accompanying preferential rate for goods of British origin.[41] The decision of the German Mannesmann company to establish a firm foothold in Britain in 1899 was influenced by similar considerations.

The specific application of the transactions approach to understanding multinational growth has only been used for British MNEs. Nicholas has employed the model to explain the growth of pre-1939 British MNEs.[43] He further develops this approach in his essay in this volume, where he suggests a dynamic model of alternative mode choice in the growth of British MNEs. Hertner's essay in this volume attempts to apply the transactions concept to the German experience. There has been no attempt to examine rigorously the reasons why MNEs opted for different strategies once the decision to undertake foreign direct investment had been made. The reasons why some firms made greenfield investments and others purchased going concerns, and why some firms established wholly-owned subsidiaries and others joint ventures, remain the realm of speculation. In the case of the United Kingdom, firms in the armaments sector, such as Vickers, Armstrong, Whitworth and John Brown, often opted for joint ventures with local or other foreign firms, probably for political reasons.[44] Leading British firms in the consumer goods sector, such as Lever Brothers and J. & P. Coats, seem to have preferred wholly-owned subsidiaries.

A third conclusion of recent research has been to confirm suspicions that European MNEs in certain vital respects grew, organised and behaved in different ways than American MNEs. Lundström shows that Swedish firms, for example, often made their first foreign direct investments much earlier in their corporate life than American firms. This was clearly a function of the small size of the Swedish home market. This generalisation also probably holds true for the Swiss and Dutch cases. It helps to explain, for example, the investments of Swiss textile firms in Northern Italy in the last third of the nineteenth century.[45] Again, Hertner shows that banks played a greater role in the spread of German MNEs before 1914 than in their American—or British—equivalents, especially in the case of the electrical-goods industry. Political factors were more influential with Continental than Anglo-Saxon MNEs. Recent case studies of German MNEs in inter-war central Europe have demonstrated their willingness to cooperate with their parent government.[46]

Business historians have, as yet, showed little interest in many of the topics of concern to theorists of the MNE. Clearly a major reason why economists rarely use historical evidence is that historians have provided so little evidence.

The whole area concerned with the behavioural characteristics of MNEs, for example, has attracted little attention from business historians. There has been little systematic investigation by business historians of the financing of investments, although one area where this has been explored in some depth is the case of German direct investment in Italy before 1914. Recent research has shown the importance of the financial ties between the affiliates of German firms and their parent companies.[47]

The role of MNEs in transferring technology across natural boundaries has also been little studied. A path-breaking article by Mira Wilkins in 1974, discussing the role of companies in transferring technologies, has elicited little response by business historians, although some archivally-based studies on this theme, particularly using German and American business archives, have been undertaken by economic historians and historians of science.[48] James Foreman-Peck has also explored the role of American multinationals in the European motor industry before 1939, and concludes that arm's-length licensing was at least as effective a means of transferring technology as transfer through MNEs.[49]

Historians have also had almost nothing to say about the costs and benefits to home and host economies of MNEs. It is extraordinary, given the United Kingdom's historical role as a major home and host economy for MNEs, that there has been no research on the balance-of-payments, employment, resource-transfer or market-structure effects of this multinational activity before 1939, or indeed afterwards. Even if

11

data limitations make discussions of such macroeconomic matters a hard task, there remains a list of related micro-issues which could be readily explored in business archives. One obvious area of research would be the use of transfer pricing by MNEs, but comparatively little has been published on this theme.

A third area which has been conspiciously neglected by European business historians concerns the relations of MNEs to their home and host governments. The sovereignty effects of MNEs have been much discussed by economists, political scientists and politicians. Allegations of abuse and of corporate power in the Third World, fuelled by events such as ITT's overtly political behaviour in Chile in the early 1970s, are widespread. Yet research by business historians on this theme has been very limited. Perhaps the examination of government-MNE relations has progressed further in the oil industry, where T.A.B. Corley, R.W. Ferrier, Geoffrey Jones and Maurice Pearton have discussed aspects of British (and Anglo-Dutch) oil companies' relations with government in the early twentieth century. [50] In addition, a few company studies—for example, of Vickers in inter-war Romania, British-American Tobacco in China and British oil and armaments firms in Russia between 1910 and 1930—have shed light on this theme.[51] A general discussion of the question, however, is badly needed.

Theory and History

The previous two sections have reviewed recent theoretical and historical work on the MNE, with particular focus on the neglected European perspective. This section examines some of the rewards in bringing theorists and historians together, and also some of the obstacles facing such a dialogue.

First, what can business historians contribute to theory? One basic answer is 'facts'. It is a regular complaint of historians that the 'data' used by economists is inaccurate and used out of context. Business historians are aware that secondary sources are often inaccurate and published accounts misleading. A particular minefield is the vast number of 'commemorative' company histories, many of which were written with little regard for scholarly precision. Economists seeking to 'test' models with historical data often seem to have a cavalier approach to 'facts'. The kind of empirical research in business archives which is reported in the essays in the second half of this volume can provide properly-documented accounts of corporate motives and performance rather than aggregate assumptions. The prima-facie case for a fruitful interplay between theory and history, with historians setting the record straight and providing accurate data for economists, seems overwhelming.

Inevitably, however, the matter is not as simple as it might seem. Economists and historians have different approaches to the use of evidence. Economic theory, as Casson observes, is concerned with the representative economic unit. A single firm, unless it is a complete monopolist, is never fully representative from this perspective and therefore case studies of individual companies are seen as providing, at best, anecdotal evidence. 'Case studies, in the nature of things, are of limited value', one economist, Richard E. Caves, has commented, 'because they represent small and non-random samples'.[52] Such views are reinforced by, for example, the tendency of business historians to write about large and successful MNEs rather than small and unsuccessful ones. Large firms commission histories, or maintain good archives. Business historians see matters in a different light. The difficulties of gaining access to archives inevitably make case studies 'non-random'. Moreover, the concept of 'representative' samples seems odd to many historians. Courtaulds and Dunlop, for example, dominated the inter-war British rayon and rubber goods industries respectively. Many business historians would argue that the performance of these two firms is more 'representative' of the industry as a whole than a random sample of the clustering of small and insignificant firms which were left with residual shares in the industries. No business historian, however, has yet suggested an answer to the question of how many case studies are required to make a case. Fortunately the numbers of pre-1939 multinationals are, at least compared to the post-war period, limited, and therefore some hope may be entertained that future research will cover almost all the cases.

In the meantime Casson's essay in this volume suggests one way forward in this methodological problem. A 'matrix' of case studies—such as a profitable multinational and a profitable non-multinational—meets the economist's desire for representativity and the business historian's need for some criteria to limit the number of case studies needed to make a case. The suggestion also helps to focus attention on 'failure', and the need to study it. Why did some firms not develop as MNEs? Why did some smaller European countries not spawn MNEs in the way of Sweden or the Netherlands?

If business historians seek to contribute to theory they also need to expand their horizons beyond 1945. The exchange controls, totalitarian regimes and depreciating currencies of the inter-war years led MNEs to act in different ways in this period than in the post-war era. Economists, therefore, may be forgiven for disregarding pre-1945 evidence as irrelevant. Some British company histories already go beyond 1945.[53] The raw material for general surveys of British MNEs in the post-war era is already in existence, and the period should no longer be the preserve of applied economists. Elsewhere in Europe, few serious business historians have gone beyond the 1945 watershed, and access to business archives in this period is still virtually impossible.

A second area where business historians might contribute to the theory is by emphasising the need for a dynamic view of MNEs. It would, of course, be quite misleading to describe all theory of MNEs as static. Raymond Vernon's product-cycle theory certainly captures some of the dynamic element. Yet, as Nicholas argues in Chapter 4, the market-hierarchy internalisation approach is essentially a static concept. Business historians emphasising, for example, alternative modes as stages in overseas involvement, can introduce a more realistic view of the business process. Historians can, in the same way, remind economists that corporate behaviour is related to time and place. For example, after the loss of all their assets in two world wars German banks were extremely reluctant to go abroad after 1945, and only made substantial multinational investments from the late 1960s. The apparent international retardation of the German banking sector can only be fully understood by appreciating these banks' historical experience. Again, it seems clear that post-1945 American MNEs only went abroad after they had reached a certain size in their domestic market. 'The successful firm', Caves observes, 'runs out its successes in the domestic market before incurring the transaction costs of going abroad'.[54] Yet, as Lundström demonstrates in her paper, this generalisation does not hold for Swedish MNEs, at least before the 1930s, many of which went abroad extremely early in their corporate careers.

What can theory contribute to historians of the MNE? Business archives contain a mass of disparate information. Theory nominates the variables which need to be isolated and examined. Microeconomists, in order to be rigorous in their analysis, are accustomed to enumerate all the variables, even if they subsequently use partial analysis when constructing their models. In contrast, historians, often flooded by empirical material, tend to overlook those factors not immediately present in their material. Moreover, their perspectives are often those of the economic agents themselves. Theory can help the historian to be liberated from this narrow perspective. The historian can only profit from adopting many of the concerns of economists, such as the crucial problem of the size of the market in explaining the performance of a firm.

Again, however, there are dangers. Economists often seem to use history as a quarry to 'test' theory. The preferred method of some business historians would be to let the evidence suggest generalisations. This has been essentially the approach of Alfred D. Chandler Jnr in his studies of the emergence of the large American corporations.[55] The widespread acceptance of Chandler outside the world of business historians suggests that this approach can be highly productive, provided the obvious dangers are avoided. There has to be, as Casson observes in this volume, a frank recognition of the limits of theory, but also a recognition of the limits of the aggregate empirical data often used by economists to test models. Business history can and should contribute empirical evidence that incorporates the dimensions of both space and time.

Notes

1. See, for example, the bibliography in R.E. Caves, *Multinational Enterprise and Economic Analysis* (Cambridge, 1982).
2. C. Wilson, 'The Multinational in Historical Perspective' in K. Nakagawa (ed.), *Strategy and Structure of Big Business* (Tokyo, 1977), pp. 265-303.
3. L. Franko, *The European Multinationals* (London, 1976), pp. 8-10. On this point see also M. Wilkins, 'Modern European Economic History and the Multinationals', *Journal of European Economic History* (1977), pp. 575-95.
4. R.E. Caves, op. cit., p. 1.
5. N. Hood and S. Young, *The Economics of Multinational Enterprise* (London, 1979).
6. R. Vernon, *Sovereignty at Bay* (London, 1971) prefers six foreign subsidiaries.
7. U.S. Department of Commerce, Office of Business Economics: *US Business Investments in Foreign Countries. A Supplement to the Survey of Current Business* (Washington, 1960), p. 76.
8. U.S. Department of Commerce, Office of Foreign Direct Investments: *1971 Foreign Direct Investment Program* (Washington, 1970); M. Wilkins, *The Emergence of Multinational Enterprise* (Cambridge, Mass., 1970), pp. x-xi.
9. M. Edelstein, *Overseas Investment in the Age of High Imperialism: The United Kingdom, 1850-1914* (London, 1982), p. 33.
10. R.E. Caves, op. cit.
11. R.W. and M.E. Hidy, *Pioneering in Big Business. The History of the Standard Oil Company (New Jersey), 1882-1911* (New York, 1955); M. Wilkins and F. Hill, *American Business Abroad: Ford on Six Continents* (Detroit, 1964).
12. R. Vernon, op. cit.
13. M. Wilkins, *The Emergence of Multinational Enterprise;* M. Wilkins, *The Maturing of Multinational Enterprise* (Cambridge, Mass., 1974).
14. L. Franko, op. cit.; J.M. Stopford, 'The Origins of British-based Multinational Manufacturing Enterprises', *Business History Review* (1974), pp. 303-35.
15. M. Wilkins, 'Modern European Economic History and the Multinationals'.
16. C. Wilson, *Unilever*, 3 vols (London, 1954); W.J. Reader, *Imperial Chemical Industries*, 2 vols (Oxford, 1970, 1975); D.C. Coleman, *Courtaulds: An Economic and Social History*, 3 vols (Oxford, 1969, 1980); T.C. Barker, *Pilkingtons* (London, 1977); W.J. Reader, *Bowater: A History* (Cambridge, 1981).
17. T.A.B. Corley, *A History of the Burmah Oil Company*, vol. 1 (London, 1983); R.W. Ferrier, *The History of the British Petroleum Company*, vol. 1 (Cambridge, 1982); C. Harvey, *The Rio Tinto Company* (Penzance, 1981).
18. J.M. Stopford, op. cit., p. 321.
19. P. Svedberg, 'The Portfolio-Direct Composition of Private Foreign Investment in 1914 Revisited', *Economic Journal* (1978), pp. 763-77.
20. I. Stone, 'British Direct and Portfolio Investment in Latin America before 1914', *Journal of Economic History* (1977), pp. 690-722.

21. D.C.M. Platt, 'British Portfolio Investments Overseas before 1870: Some Doubts', *Economic History Review* (1980), pp. 1-16; D.C.M. Platt, *Foreign Finance in Continental Europe and the USA 1815-1870* (London, 1984).
22. J.H. Dunning, 'Changes in the Level and Structure of International Production: the Last One Hundred Years', in M. Casson (ed.), *The Growth of International Business* (London, 1983).
23. B.R. Tomlinson, 'Foreign Private Investment in India 1920-1950', *Modern Asian Studies* (1978) pp. 655-77. For the United States see P.J. Buckley and B.R. Roberts, *European Direct Investment in the USA before World War One* (London, 1982), which, however, relies completely on secondary sources and provides an incomplete picture.
24. S.J. Nicholas, 'British Multinational Investment before 1939', *Journal of European Economic History* (1982), pp 605-30.
25. G. Jones, 'The Growth and Performance of British Multinational Firms before 1939: The Case of Dunlop', *Economic History Review* (1984), pp. 35-53; G. Jones, 'Multinational Chocolate: Cadbury Overseas, 1918-1939, *Business History* (1984), pp. 59-76; G. Jones, 'The Gramophone Company: An 'Anglo-American' Multinational 1889-1931', *Business History Review* (1985), pp. 76-100; D. Fieldhouse, *Unilever Overseas* (London, 1978).
26. L. Franko, op. cit.
27. G. Siemens, *Geschichte des Hauses Siemens*, 3 vols (Munich, 1947-52); *50 Jahre AEG* (printed for private circulation by AEG, Berlin, 1956).
28. See the bibliography given in P. Hertner, 'Fallstudien zu deutschen multinationalen Unternehmen vor dem Ersten Weltkrieg' in N. Horn and J. Kocka (eds), *Law and the Formation of the Big Enterprises in the 19th and early 20th Centuries* (Göttingen, 1979), pp. 388-419.
29. Ibid.
30. W. Kirchner, 'Russian Tariffs and Foreign Industries before 1914: The German Entrepreneur's Perspective', *Journal of Economic History* (1981), pp. 361-79; W. Kirchner, 'Russian Entrepreneurship and the "Russification" of Foreign Enterprise', *Zeitschrift für Unternehmensgeschichte* (1981), pp. 79-103; F. Blaich, 'Produktions und Absatzbedingungen für deutsche Unternehmer in Russland 1897-1915. Das Beispiel der Zellstoffabrik Waldhof' in J. Schneider (ed.), *Wirtschaftskräfte und Wirtschaftswege. Festschrift für Hermann Kellenbenz* (Suttgart, 1978), vol. 3, pp. 549-59; G. Jacob-Wendler, *Deutsche Elektroindustrie in Lateinamerika. Siemens und AEG (1980-1914)*, (Stuttgart, 1982); T.R. Kabisch, *Deutsches Kapital in den USA. Von der Reichsgründung bis zur Sequestrierung (1917) und Freigabe* (Stuttgart, 1982); P. Hertner, 'Das Auslandskapital in der italienischen Wirtschaft, 1883-1914: Probleme seiner Quantifizierung und Auswertung' in H. Kellenbenz (ed.), *Weltwirtschaftliche und währungspolitische Probleme seit dem Ausgang des Mittelalters* (Stuttgart and New York, 1981), pp. 93-121; P. Hertner, *Il capitale tedesco in Italia dall Unità alla Prima Guerra Mondiale. Banche miste e sviluppo economico italiano* (Bologna, 1984).
31. See the lists of estimates in J.M. Keynes, *Collected Writings of John Maynard Keynes*, vol. 2 (London, 1971), p. 106ff, and in C.E. McGuire, *Germany's Capacity to Pay. A Study of the Reparation Problem* (New York, 1923), p. 257ff. Among the optimistic contemporary estimates see P. Arndt, *Deutschlands Stellung in der Weltwirtschaft*, 2nd edn. (Leipzig, 1913) p. 29, who pleads for a total sum of 'at least 35 billion marks'. K. Helfferic, *Deutschlands Volkswohlstand 1888-1913* (Berlin, 1913), p. 112, indicates probably too low a figure by giving an estimate of 20 billion marks, because he seems to have neglected totally German direct investment in European countries. An acceptable estimate of 31 billion marks in 1914 is offered by F. Lenz, 'Wesen und Struktur des deutschen Kapitalexports vor 1914', *Weltwirtschaftliches Archiv* (1922), pp. 42-54.
32. Some of these firms have company histories which shed light on their multinational

activities. These include *75 Years Brown Boveri 1891-1966* (Baden, 1966) and J. Heer, *World Events, 1866-1966. The First Hundred Years of Nestlé* (Rivac, Switzerland), 1966).

33. J.P. McKay, *Pioneers for Profit: Foreign Entrepreneurship and Russian Industrialisation 1885-1913* (Chicago, 1970) has useful information on Belgian enterprises in Russia. See also M. Dumoulin, 'Italie-Belgique: 1861-1915; Relations Diplomatiques, Culturelles et Economiques' (unpublished thesis, Catholic University of Louvain, 1981) part 3, vol. 2.

34. R. Girault, *Emprunts russes et investissements français en Russie 1887-1914* (Paris, 1973); R. Poidevin, *Les Relations économiques et financières entre la France et l'Allemagne de 1898 à 1914* (Paris, 1969); J. Thobie, *Les Intérêts Economiques, Financiers et Politiques dans la Partie Asiatique de l'Empire Ottoman de 1895 à 1914* (unpublished thesis, Lille, 1973).

35. B. Gille, 'Les Investissements Français en Italie (1815-1914), (Torino, 1968); A. Broder, 'Les Investissements Etrangers en Espagne au XIX siècle: Méthodologie et Quantifications', *Revue d'histoire economique et sociale,* vol. 54 (1976), pp. 29-63; A. Broder, 'Le rôle des intérêts étrangers dans la Croissance de l'Espagne 1768-1920', (unpublished thesis, Paris, 1981).

36. P. Fridenson, *Histoire des Usines Renault: Naissance de la Grande Enterprise 1898-1939* (Paris, 1972). See also the excellent study by Jean-Pierre Daviet, *La Compagnie de Saint-Gobain de 1830 à 1939, une enterprise française à rayonnement international* (doctoral thesis, Paris, 1983).

37. F. Caron, 'Foreign Investments and Technology Transfers: The case of the French Chemical Industry in the 1950s and 1960s as Viewed by the Direction des Industries Chimiques' in A. Okochi and T. Inoue (eds), *Overseas Business Activities* (Tokyo, 1984) pp. 261-80.

38. The project is financed by the European University Institute, Florence, and directed by Peter Hertner. Its results will be published during 1985 and 1986.

39. This is one of the conclusions emerging from the research project mentioned in note 38. See also H. Schröter, 'Siemens and Central and South East Europe between the World Wars' in A. Teichova and P.L. Cottrell (eds), *International Business and Central Europe, 1918-1939* (Leicester, 1983) pp. 173-92.

40. A.D. Chandler, 'The Growth of the Transnational Industrial Firm in the United States and the United Kingdom: A Comparative Analysis', *Economic History Review* (1980), p. 401.

41. H. Lindgren, *Corporate Growth. The Swedish Match Industry in its Global Setting* (Stockholm, 1979), p. 56.

42. P. Hertner, 'Fallstudien zu deutschen multinationalen Unternehmen vor dem Ersten Weltkrieg', pp. 202-3.

43. S.J. Nicholas, op. cit.

44. C. Trebilcock, *The Vickers Brothers* (London, 1977), p. 133-9.

45. Georges Bonnant, 'Les Colonies Suisses d'Italie à la Fin du XIX siècle', *Schweizerische Zeitschrift für Geschichte* vol. 26 (1976), pp. 134–76. See also, especially for the Swiss electrical and engineering industries, Ernst Himmel, 'Industrielle Kapitalanlagen der Schweiz im Auslande' (University of Zurich thesis, Langensalza, 1922).

46. See the essays on Mannesmann, IG. Farbenindustrie and Siemens in A. Teichova and P.L. Cottrell (eds), op. cit.

47. P. Hertner, *Il capitale tedesco in Italie dall'Unità alla Prima Guerra Mondiale.*

48. M. Wilkins, 'The Role of Private Business in the International Diffusion of Technology', *Journal of Economic History* (1974). The three volume study by A.C. Sutton, *Western Technology and Soviet Economic Development* (Stanford, 1968, 1971 and 1973) uses German and American business archives. See also J.M. Liebenau, *Medical Science and Medical Industry 1890-1929* (unpublished PhD thesis, Pennsylvania, 1981), especially pp. 313-30.

17

49. J. Foreman-Peck, 'The American Challenge of the Twenties: Multinationals and the European Motor Industry', *Journal of Economic History* (1982), pp. 865–881.

50. T.A.B. Corley, *A History of the Burmah Oil Company,* vol. 1; R.W. Ferrier, *The History of the British Petroleum Company,* vol. 1; G. Jones, *The State and the Emergence of the British Oil Industry* (London, 1981); M. Pearton, *Oil and the Rumanian State* (Oxford, 1971).

51. S. Cochran, *Big Business in China: Sino-Foreign Rivalry in the Cigarette Industry 1890-1930* (Cambridge, Mass., 1980); R.P.T. Davenport-Hines, 'Vickers Balkan Conscience: Aspects of Anglo-Romanian Armaments, 1918–1939', *British History* (1983), pp. 287-319. G. Jones and C. Trebilcock, 'Russian Industry and British Business 1910-1930: Oil and Armaments', *Journal of European Economic History* (1982), pp. 61-103.

52. R.E. Caves op. cit., p. 145.

53. W.J. Reader, *Bowater: A History* (Cambridge, 1981); W.J. Reader, *Metal Box: A History* (London, 1976); D.C. Coleman, *Courtaulds,* vol. 3 (Oxford, 1980); D.K. Fieldhouse, *Unilever Overseas* (London, 1978) all discuss the multinational investments of their firms up to the mid-1960s. W.J. Reader, *Imperial Chemical Industries,* vol. 2 (Oxford, 1975) deals with ICI's foreign relations and investments until the early 1950s.

54. R.E. Caves, op. cit., p. 14.

55. A.D. Chandler, *Strategy and Structure: Chapters in the History of American Industrial Enterprise* (Cambridge, Mass., 1962); A.D.Chandler, *The Visible Hand: The Managerial Revolution in American Business* (Cambridge, Mass., 1977).

2 The Theory of International Production: Some Historical Antecedents

John H. Dunning, John A. Cantwell and T.A.B. Corley

Introduction

This chapter represents an attempt to resolve an apparent paradox in the theory and history of international production. Until recently, most economists have believed that international production, by which we mean production in more than one country under a common nationality of ownership or control, was of little importance in the world economy before 1960. If this were so, it would explain why it is only in the last two decades that we have seen the emergence of a separate theory of the multinational enterprise (MNE), the major institution through which international production is organised.

However, historical research now suggests that international production was both absolutely and relatively more important before 1914 than at any time until at least the 1960s.[1] Why, then, was it not incorporated into theoretical discussion before 1914? As we mention below, there was some discussion, around the turn of the century, of international cartels, and of the export of capital in general. Yet this lay largely outside the mainstream economic literature, in which international production was not treated as an issue worthy of separate attention.

We shall argue that a closer inspection of the theory and history of international production helps us to answer this question. On the historical side, there has been a major shift in the geographical and industrial composition of international production, as well as in the organisational capacities of the MNE, which now make it impossible to treat as a 'special case' of certain more general economic phenomena. On the theoretical side, as illustrated by Table 2.1, the development of neoclassical theory after 1870, at the time when the modern MNE had begun to emerge, meant that most economists treated the firm as a 'black box' which could be subsumed within a general analysis of markets.

Now the strength of the modern theory of international production is that it enables us to contrast the approach of earlier economists to this topic with more recent views, and thereby to situate each in its historical context. Modern theories of the MNE are comprehensively surveyed by Caves;[2] however, their elements may be summarised within the structure of an eclectic framework as set out by Dunning.[3] This suggests that firms will engage in international production under the following conditions. Firstly, there must be *location* advantages to foreign production in a given host country compared with exporting to the host country from the home country. These have to do with the costs of organising production in different countries, as well as the international structure of taxes, tariffs, and so on. Secondly, MNEs must have *ownership* advantages *vis-à-vis* other firms wishing to supply a similar market, which represent a range of competitive strengths that are essential to their continued growth, and ultimately to their survival. It is helpful to distinguish two categories of such advantages. The first are the unique intangible assets possessed by each firm which consist of new product and process innovations, as well as managerial and marketing skills; these have been called asset or production cost advantages.[4]

The second category of such advantages are generally known as governance of transaction cost advantages, and refer essentially to economies of integration within the firm, achieved, that is, through the common ownership of production activities located in more than one country. Since these latter advantages have no market outside the MNE they must be internalised. The term *internalisation advantage* embraces these gains from multinationality as well as the benefits of replacing the markets for the first kind of advantage relative, for example, to the licensing of intangible assets for use within independent foreign firms.

In terms of economic theory, as set out in Table 2.1, we may try to explain the existence of *location* advantages for a given pattern of international production through the theories of capital movements, trade or location; *ownership* advantages through the theories of industrial organisation, innovation, and the firm; and *internalisation* advantages through theories of the firm and markets. It follows that different schools of economic thought, partly conditioned by the different historical circumstances surrounding their origins, may be expected to have varying approaches to explaining international production (insofar as they consider it worthy of attention).

In the earliest days of the expansion of commerce between the sixteenth and eighteenth centuries, what international production there was followed the trading companies and their associated colonial settlements. At this time, international trade and production was

TABLE 2.1: DEVELOPMENT OF THE THEORY OF INTERNATIONAL PRODUCTION: MERCANTILIST PERIOD

Factors underlying international production:

May follow the pattern suggested by the:

				LOCATION ADVANTAGES		OWNERSHIP ADVANTAGES		INTERNALISATION ADVANTAGES
Central concerns of period	Main features of international production	Period	THEORY OF CAPITAL MOVEMENTS	THEORY OF TRADE	THEORY OF LOCATION	THEORY OF INDUSTRIAL ORGANISATION	THEORY OF INNOVATION	THEORY OF THE FIRM
International commerce and exchange.	Trading companies especially in colonies.	MERCANTILIST PERIOD (16th century – 18th century)	Early mercantilists: prohibition on export of money needed to accumulate national wealth. Later mercantilists: flow of money regulated by balance of trade.	Later mercantilists (Mun): government sponsored stimulation of export industries and carrying trade to accumulate national wealth.	Later mercantilists: more expensive industrial manufactures at home, cheaper raw materials in colonies.			

TABLE 2.1: DEVELOPMENT OF THE THEORY OF INTERNATIONAL PRODUCTION: CLASSICAL PERIOD

Factors underlying international production:

May follow the pattern suggested by the:

				LOCATION ADVANTAGES		OWNERSHIP ADVANTAGES		INTERNALISATION ADVANTAGES
Central concerns of period	*Main features of international production*	*Period*	*THEORY OF CAPITAL MOVEMENTS*	*THEORY OF TRADE*	*THEORY OF LOCATION*	*THEORY OF INDUSTRIAL ORGANISATION*	*THEORY OF INNOVATION*	*THEORY OF THE FIRM*
Value, capital accumulation and income distribution.	Resource-based especially in dependent territories; manufacture by individual entrepreneurs or expatriate investors.	CLASSICAL PERIOD (1776–1870).	Regulated by differential profit rates. Ricardo, J.S. Mill: barriers to international capital movements. Hume's specie-flow mechanism equalised money prices.	Smith: absolute advantage conditioned by position in development cycle – manufactures traded for certain products of land. Free trade ensured profits productively re-invested. Ricardo: comparative labour cost. Free trade in wage goods meant higher domestic profits and continued accumulation.	Smith, von Thünen: early consideration of transport costs. Smith: advantages of natural circumstances, and acquired advantages through development. Ricardo, J.S. Mill: comparative advantages through natural endowments and technological capabilities.	Little analysis of market structure. Competition behavioural process of rivalry enforcing accumulation.	Smith: evolutionary view of technological progress with expansion of market. Marx: application of science to large scale manufacture through machine technology. Major and minor innovations incorporated.	Marx: concentration and centralisation of capital. Hierarchic organisation of labour process in firm.

TABLE 2.1: DEVELOPMENT OF THE THEORY OF INTERNATIONAL PRODUCTION: NEOCLASSICAL PERIOD

Factors underlying international production:

May follow the pattern suggested by the:

				LOCATION ADVANTAGES		OWNERSHIP ADVANTAGES		INTERNALISATION ADVANTAGES
Central concerns of period	Main features of international production	Period	THEORY OF CAPITAL MOVEMENTS	THEORY OF TRADE	THEORY OF LOCATION	THEORY OF INDUSTRIAL ORGANISATION	THEORY OF INNOVATION	THEORY OF THE FIRM
Static resource allocation.	Emergence of international production as an extension of the domestic activities firms: resource-based and import-substituting.	NEO-CLASSICAL PERIOD (1870–1920).	Regulated by differential interest rates. Fisher: human knowledge and physical capital distinguished.	Marshall: Reciprocal demand. Technology moves to where most appropriately used. Heckscher: comparative advantage of relative factor endowments.	Weber: industries transport-oriented, labour-oriented (i.e. decentralised or agglomerated in centres)	General assumption of perfect competition. Monopoly due to artificial restrictions.	Outside neoclassical tradition- Schumpeter: major (disequilibrating) innovations undertaken by individual entrepreneurs in accordance with expectations.	Marshall: 'trees in the forest' varying around representative firm. American institutionalist critics – Veblen: control of large businessmen decisive to direction of modern industry.

TABLE 2.1: DEVELOPMENT OF THE THEORY OF INTERNATIONAL PRODUCTION

Factors underlying international production:

May follow the pattern suggested by the:

Central concerns of period	Main features of international production	Period	THEORY OF CAPITAL MOVEMENTS	LOCATION ADVANTAGES		OWNERSHIP ADVANTAGES		INTERNALISATION ADVANTAGES
				THEORY OF TRADE	THEORY OF LOCATION	THEORY OF INDUSTRIAL ORGANISATION	THEORY OF INNOVATION	THEORY OF THE FIRM
Markets not perfectly self-adjusting (thus economics of disequilibrium or less than full employment equilibrium); as illustrated by Keynesian demand management and the theory of imperfect competition.	Increase in import-substituting investment. Later followed by rise in intra-industry investment, appearance of globally integrated MNE, and increase in joint venture and licensing activity.	MODERN PERIOD (1920 up to 1950s)	Regulated by differential interest rates. Short term capital movements may be destabilising.	H-O-S model: factor movements and trade may be substitutes. Later critical models: trade greatest between similarly endowed countries; attempts to explain intra-industry trade.	Ohlin: locational factors (e.g. transport costs) strongly influence pattern of inter-regional and international trade. Losch: Firms control spatial markets. Hotelling: Agglomeration of activities through locational inter-dependence.	Chamberlin, J. Robinson theory of monopolistic/imperfect competition. Bain: barriers to entry in concentrated industries.	Usher: emphasis on continuous minor technological improvements.	Sraffa, Kaldor, EAG Robinson: limits to the size of firm. Coase: transaction costs of participating in markets compared with costs of internal co-ordination of activities.

clearly locationally determined, and the theoretical explanation of Adam Smith captured this well, as we describe below. Later economic changes following in the wake of industrial revolution gave rise to business enterprises founded around ownership and internalisation advantages. The latter became increasingly important for the establishment of international production as firms matured in their organisation of economic activity.

However, while ownership and to some extent internalisation advantages were known to be critical to business success and failure, purely locational accounts of the aggregate pattern of international trade and production continued to predominate. This is because, until the 1950s, the bulk of international production was organised by developed-country firms in the less-developed world, while the industrial structure of each country's exports was significantly different from the structure of its imports. The incorporation of ownership and internalisation advantages in theoretical work had to await the massive growth of US foreign direct investment (FDI) in European manufacturing after 1945, based largely on technological ownership advantages, and the spread of globally integrated MNEs across the industrialised countries thereafter. The rapid growth of intra-industry trade between developed countries likewise gave rise to new theories of international trade after 1960. It was only when the ownership and internalisation advantages of firms were integrated into the analysis that a distinct theory of international production emerged.

With this in mind we will sketch out what earlier economists had to say about the state of international production in their day. We shall also occasionally show how their reasoning may be related to the modern theory of international production, as a relevant extension or application of their models in today's conditions. After an introductory discussion, three periods will be examined: the period to 1914; from 1914 to 1960; and from 1960 to 1980.

The Emergence of Theory with the Growth of International Production
Part of the explanation of the divergence between the history and theory of international production is that what became the theory of the firm was little developed before the inter-war period. As befitted his time, Adam Smith dealt with individual entrepreneurs rather than corporations, whose activities, he maintained were coordinated through markets. Most economists writing after 1870 adopted an analytical framework which assumed that entrepreneurial and productive activity depend upon the conditions of market coordination. They therefore chose to ignore the growing importance of the direct coordination of economic activities by firms without the

intermediation of markets.

Others, such as Marshall, despite their awareness of institutional facts, did not seem to believe the international firm worthy of separate theoretical appraisal. Technology transfer within the firm was probably seen as a special case of general international technology transfer. British economists especially regarded outward investment as an extension of domestic economic activity, not unreasonably as the colonies accounted for a good proportion of such investment before 1914, where the interests of investing countries and firms were assumed to coincide. Many British companies confined their overseas investments to the dominions prior to 1914, and it was only in the 1960s that they made the transition to the more diverse range of experience across quite disparate countries and markets.

British economists in particular, unlike the American institutionalists, chose to neglect the more rapid development of corporate structures in the US, which, together with Germany, had, by the turn of the century, become the home of a new group of dynamic industries and companies. Thus, although the US was more resource-sufficient than the UK, she had built up a significant stock of foreign direct investment by 1914, and by 1939 the value of her foreign manufacturing subsidiaries' output was twice that of her export of manufactures.

Yet, until the 1920s, no government regularly collected data on direct investment flows or stocks, or on the activities of either their own MNEs or foreign companies in their midst. Official inquiries, if held, were at irregular intervals, and usually into the stock of FDI. The US Department of Commerce published its first foreign investment study in 1929, and others followed in 1936, 1940 and 1950. Since 1950 annual figures have been published. Before the Second World War, only Canada published FDI flow data. Not until 1962 did the UK government start to publish a regular series of FDI flows, and only in 1963 were the activities of foreign companies separately identified in the UK Census of Production. As to world-wide data, even as recently as 1960 there was no overall estimate of the amount of foreign direct capital invested globally.

Moreover, theoretical and empirical research is interactive, and governments do not usually go to the trouble and expense of collecting economic data unless they are likely to be useful (e.g., for taxation or planning purposes) or unless the precise extent of a problem (e.g., for a royal commission) needs to be established. Even then, there seems to be a time-lag between new economic problems emerging and serious attention being paid to them. Until economists were obliged to adjust their theoretical frameworks to distinguish international production, empirical evidence on the topic was sparse.

International Production Before 1914

The Scope of MNE Activity in 1914

Dunning's estimates have revealed the extent and location of FDI in 1914.[5] Not surprisingly, it was the most developed countries that accounted for the bulk of FDI at that time: Britain, the US, Germany and France contributed nearly 87 per cent. As to the recipients, developing countries received nearly 63 per cent—mainly Latin America and Asia—but the US received over 10 per cent and Russia over 7 per cent; Britain's inward share was nearly $1\frac{1}{2}$ per cent.

In this FDI pattern were two separate but interlinked strands. The first were the mainly resource-based investments, to supply the home country with food and raw materials.[6] Typically, therefore, the host countries were colonial territories: either actual colonies or *de facto* ones such as the 'honorary dominions' of Latin America. Associated investment often took place on infrastructural projects, for example, railroad networks and public utilities. This type of FDI, leading to 'supply-oriented' MNEs, represented by far the greatest part, perhaps as much as 85 per cent, of total FDI in 1914. The second type, leading to 'market-oriented' MNEs, was import-substituting manufacturing investment, usually located in the most developed countries, but also in those on the brink of 'take off' such as Tsarist Russia and the white British dominions. This type became significant only in the period 1870-1914.

Between the 1870s and 1914, large multi-unit enterprises grew up, both in the United States and in Europe. Integrating mass production with mass distribution, they built up a coordinated system of goods flow from raw materials, via production, to the retailer and final consumer. From the outset such enterprises were associated with the possession of strong ownership advantages. Import-substituting production abroad was a response to increasingly rigorous tariffs and patent laws, especially in North America, France, Germany and Russia.[7] International cartel arrangements were also common by the 1900s. By 1914 MNEs, operating in conditions either of intense competition or of collaboration, were prevalent in many parts of the world.

Explanations of FDI by pre-1914 Economists

Practical men of affairs knew well the extent of MNE activity. Several British works published in 1901-2 on the 'American invasion' pointed out that many leading US firms had set up factories in Britain,[8] while in the US and continental Europe there was a widespread recognition of the role of FDI in scaling tariff barriers.

However, those economists who did consider the question of FDI before 1914 tended to think of it in terms of colonialist policies.[9] If the home country lacked the primary products concerned, it had to go out and

27

obtain them. The mercantilists (who flourished from the sixteenth to the eighteenth centuries) and the classical economists (from Adam Smith in 1776 to the 1870s) put their analyses in macroeconomic terms; for them international production would simply have been a special case of the theory of international trade.

Mercantilists. Perhaps the most noteworthy exponent of mercantilism—which proclaimed the doctrine that a favourable balance of trade was essential for a nation's prosperity—was Thomas Mun, a director of the East India Company.[10] To him international production, as for instance undertaken by the trading companies of his time, would help to provide raw materials for the home country and to give work to the domestic labour which made them up into finished goods for export. However, since the mercantilists saw national wealth as being created through international trade rather than production, the activities of trading companies were explained through the pattern of locational advantages of countries, in terms of their export potential. The ability of the companies to conduct such operations arose from the authority of the home country state rather than internally generated ownership advantages.

Adam Smith. Smith's treatment of the macroeconomic locational advantages was a more sophisticated one, and his theory of trade is more interestingly related to modern discussions of international production, once the theory of the firm is taken into account.[11] Smith put forward a dynamic theory of domestic and international trade as part of the development or growth process which lay at the root of his analysis. For Adam Smith, as for the mercantilists, trade occurred because of absolute advantage, arising from differences in climate, fertility and other natural and acquired location advantages of particular countries.[12] However, unlike the mercantilists, as trade was seen to be supportive of the growth of production rather than vice versa, Smith was able to view trade as mutually beneficial to the countries concerned. An undeveloped country was likely to have an advantage in some specific agricultural areas to which its fresh natural endowments could be adapted; while a development cycle led developed countries towards the production of more refined manufactures.

Smith seemed to believe that the development cycle for nations was an expansion of that followed by town and country. A surplus above the subsistence needs of producers first arose in agriculture, and the town afforded a market for this surplus produce, while, through the division of labour, providing manufactures for the countryside with a smaller quantity of labour than if they had been produced in the country itself. The emergence of the town was responsible for the appearance of good government and the accumulation of wealth by merchants and manufacturers, who, when under the pressure of competition, were parsimonious by comparison with the prodigal landlords.[13] Hence, by

28

redistributing the value of surplus produce, trade assisted in increasing capital accumulation.

Once a country became sufficiently rich and set on a course of rapid expansion, international trade and foreign investment were encouraged by a falling rate of profit arising from a surplus of capital rather than simply a surplus produce over subsistence needs. In the same way that the appearance of towns introduced law and good government in the older countries, colonial settlers were able to bring such benefits of experience with them to the newer countries. These might be thought of as internalisation advantages at a country level, assisting the agricultural development of colonies through trade and investment, with the colonial power receiving in return goods such as tobacco which could not be produced at home, for its own consumption or re-export. There is also an early consideration of ownership advantages here in that colonists took abroad with them the skills which had earlier been developed in the home country, and applied them on the more spacious fertile land of the colonies (i.e. combined them with the location advantages of producing abroad).

It was in the interest of the colony to concentrate its efforts on agriculture which set a greater productive labour into motion and laid the foundation of lasting improvement in national wealth. Refined manufactures could be imported from the home country, widening its market, furthering the division of labour in manufacturing, and strengthening capital accumulation in both trading participants.

If Smith's development process is translated into an expansion of firms, it parallels the early product-cycle view[14] of MNEs moving in accordance with the changing locational advantages of countries (from the US to Europe in the 1960s). It is likewise related to the current Kojima or Ozawa idea of a macroeconomic or trade-creating type of FDI, following what is perceived to be the dynamic comparative advantage of countries (from Japan to South East Asia in the 1970s).[15]

Although Smith's model incorporated only the rudimentary type of international production that existed in his day, its theoretical structure is thus highly relevant to recent discussions in international economics. The locational aspects of Smith's development cycle can also be linked with a view of dependent development later encompassed by Hymer.[16] According to Hymer, the MNE perpetuates an existing state of uneven development by locating its activities in a spatial hierarchy (from the urban centres of the developed countries to the rural less-developed countries). This is related to Smith's view that since merchants and manufacturers were better able to collude than other classes, they might succeed in obtaining an artificially high rate of profit, partly through colonial restrictions on trade in their interest, which had rendered a potentially beneficial increase in trade 'destructive to several unfortunate countries'. European countries were regarded as being equally hindered if they embarked upon trade, and the foreign activities required to support it, before establishing a firm agricultural base of their own. For this reason, Smith was sceptical of foreign investment, and he poured scorn on what he saw as the economically harmful activities of the chartered trading companies in erecting forts and garrisons which were often unnecessary and sometimes paid for by government subsidies.

However, Smith's formulation of a macroeconomic locational framework for the analysis of international trade deserves reappraisal by contemporary economists, in view of its capacity to accommodate the role of international production once the firm is more explicitly introduced into the discussion.

David Ricardo. Whereas Smith had based his theory of trade on absolute advantage and admitted to overseas capital movements, Ricardo's rested on comparative advantage, as he emphasised international factor immobility; or rather, he emphasised that the emigration of capital or labour was sufficiently limited or 'checked' for the proposition to hold.[17] Capital owners, he maintained—reasonably in the conditions of 1817—were loath to take the risk of allowing their capital to go out of their immediate control, and equally disinclined—should they contemplate accompanying their capital—to forsake their homeland and submit themselves to strange regimes and unfamiliar laws, even with the prospect of more favourable returns.

He admitted that comparative advantages arose from technological differences as well as natural endowments.[18] However, he assumed that capital and labour moved together; differences arose in overall productivities rather than the varying availability of capital internationally, as in the much later Heckscher-Ohlin-Samuelson model of trade (see below).[19] Like Smith, Ricardo objected to outward investment, fearing untoward consequences for capital accumulation in Britain itself. Relying as he did on Say's law of markets, he could not accept the possibility of excess capital at home.

J.S. Mill. While adhering to the Ricardian international trade theory framework, Mill saw positive benefits for a home country (if relatively advanced) from investment overseas. To him such investment both absorbed part of the increased capital that was the cause of falling profitability, and provided for the home country cheap food and raw materials, thereby increasing opportunities for the lucrative employment of capital at home.[20] At the same time, he was dismissive of the supposed advantages, put foward by Smith, of extending the market, since he regarded the gains from trade (including enhanced efficiency) as the consequence of receiving imports advantageously in barter terms.

Like Ricardo, Mill assumed some degree of—but not complete—capital immobility. Capital could not move to remote parts of the world as 'readily and for so small an inducement' as to another quarter of the same town: hence the varying rates of profit on capital in different countries. However—writing in 1848—he accepted that there was already a tendency for capital to be shifted around the world, and as the capital itself became more cosmopolitan, customs and institutions began to converge in character and suspicion of foreigners diminished. Therefore, he continued, 'both population and capital now move from one of these (more developed) countries to another on much less temptation than heretofore'. *Alfred Marshall.* In his unpublished *Theory of Foreign Trade,* which probably dated from the late 1870s, Marshall discussed in realistic terms 'the migration of capitalists in company with their capital'. He cited Bagehot's comment that international capital movements had become one of the greatest instruments of world-wide trade.[21] He also spoke of 'a few prominent cases' where English capitalists had set up branch establishments for making textiles on the continent of Europe, and for iron manufacture in America.[22] Yet these instances did not lead him to shift his Ricardian views on international trade.[23]

The Role of Ownership and Internalisation Advantages in the Thinking of pre-1914 Economists

(i) Some Ownership Advantages. As shown above, the early classical economists stressed advantages in productive activity at a country or regional level within which a variety of firms were not differentiated. However, with the growing importance of technological change and mass marketing techniques, Marx, Schumpeter and other critics more clearly translated these into ownership advantages at the company level through companies' competitive adoption of innovations and differentiated products.

Clearly, locational considerations were still significant, but by the latter part of the nineteenth century they could not carry the weight of the whole analysis. Advantaged foreign firms were motivated to set up production facilities by high tariffs in the US and continental Europe, and by slow technical progress in Britain after 1870, which laid it open to technologically advanced US firms. In the rapidly industrialising pre-1914 Russia, entrepreneurs, sponsored by interested investors, commissioned home-based scientists and engineers to undertake detailed studies of indigenous industrial techniques in Russia. In contrast with the assumption of the conventional location framework, the factor they looked at was not so much the average profitability of the foreign industry, as what ownership advantages over indigenous competitors could be discovered.[24]

The origin of ownership advantages considered by economists before 1914 can be discussed under the headings of innovation and entrepreneurship.

Innovation In contrast with the disequilibrating theory of Schumpeter, Adam Smith's theory of innovation was an evolutionary one, in which all firms were expanding more or less in line with the growth of the market overall. The benign workings of the invisible hand would bring about an adaptation of industrial structure and emerging new technology to the fresh opportunities being created by the extension of the market.

Unlike Smith, Marx was perhaps the first to predict a trend towards the creation of large firms, enjoying ownership advantages based on the application of science in technology, especially machine technology. The motive for innovation he put forward was the social pressure of competition, in a world of rapid technical change; this was in contrast with the later view of Schumpeter, that innovations arose from individual decisions, based on expectations.

The neo-classical period after 1870, with its emphasis on optimisation with fixed resource endowments, gave little incentive for exploring the ownership advantages of individual firms. Even Marshall, who for the first time—in mainstream economics—devised a realistic theory of the firm by bringing together supply and demand aspects, did not explore the possibility that better-than-representative firms might possess ownership advantages useful for opening up production overseas to set alongside his strictly locational views.

Entrepreneurship. Like innovation, entrepreneurship is highly relevant to the formation of ownership advantages. Of the entrepreneur's functions, that of innovation, was initially set out by Schumpeter in 1911.[26] Those of organisation and the bearing of uncertainty had been covered by Say in the early nineteenth century.[27] By contrast, Adam Smith portrays only a rather shadowy entrepreneur, or 'undertaker', in line with his evolutionary process generally.

(ii) Internalisation advantages. We have to look to Marx and some institutional writers in the US and Europe—from very different perspectives—for any serious discussion of what we would now call the internalisation advantages within the firm. Marx gave a central place to the planning of the firms, mainly through the promotion of technical progress as a means of achieving higher productivity and hence higher profits. Marx was thus addressing the same issues of internalisation advantages as did the later Coasian theory of transaction costs, which has become such an integral part of the modern theory of international production.

A classical interpretation of internalisation advantages with reference to Marx is presented in Cantwell.[28] E.G. Wakefield was the only earlier classical economist to have insisted that if colonial settlers engaged in subsistence farming rather than combining to produce tradeable commodities, then they could not be regarded as expatriate investors as implicitly suggested by Smith.[29] Marx commended Wakefield on this point for seeing how the social productive power of labour on a large scale, to create profits, required the enforcement of a hierarchical organisation of the labour process.[30]

Meanwhile, in the US, the institutionalists were putting forward a rather different view of the capitalist process. Although Veblen and Mitchell wrote in this general area,[31] perhaps of greater interest is the contribution of J.R. Commons, whose basic ideas were formulated in the formative years of managerial capitalism. In his *Legal Foundations of Capitalism,*[32] he forcibly took the neoclassical economists to task for neglecting non-market transactions. Although the bulk of his work was descriptive and historical, Commons never ceased to emphasise a holistic approach to economic activity in general; in this sense he is a worthy antecedent to Coase, Williamson and Chandler.

On the continent of Europe, the movement in German industry towards concentration and cartels between 1880 and 1910 gave rise to a remarkable series of studies on monopolies and their activities, notably by Liefmann, Levy and Hilferding.[33] As a precursor to the later literature on the theory of the firm and its transaction cost minimising functions there was a lively recognition that in the pre-1914 developed world, international production was an alternative to the (almost as important) international agreements as 'attempts to draw back the destructive forces of international competition'.[34]

Hilferding argued that the gradual rise of tariffs would facilitate international cartels as much as MNEs, especially those cartels based on the allocation of geographical markets and price agreements. These were combinations of national cartels already well established behind protective barriers. This is a valuable argument, as it offers a partial explanation of the spread of international cartels with the increasing importance of tariffs up to 1939, but their absence after 1945 in a freer trading environment.

While Hilferding's general explanation of the export of capital was a traditional locational one of equalising national rates of profit, he did distinguish FDI by cartels and MNEs which, by producing in two protected countries, could earn higher prices and profits than if they exported from just one country under free trade. Liefmann's contribution was to show how international cartels both help to prevent dumping and permit overseas firms in a high tariff country and are therefore imperfect substitutes for international concerns.

International Production 1914-60
The Growth of MNE Activity 1914-60
The radical changes that took place in the composition of international production during this period were largely confined to its two final decades. In 1938, nearly two-thirds of FDI was still going to developing

countries, once again Latin America and Asia in particular.

By 1960, the share provided by the US had leapt to 49 per cent, while that of Britain was down to 16 per cent. The recipient areas had also changed markedly, with developed countries now accounting for two-thirds of global FDI, due largely to the substantial growth of US manufacturing investment in Canada and Western Europe in the 1950s.

Analysis by Economists

Throughout this period, ownership and internalisation advantages were essential to those firms engaged in business activity abroad. However, it was only in the 1950s when the locational pattern of FDI (and trade) underwent a major shift towards the industrialised world, that it became clearer how these advantages affected not just the fortunes of individual firms, but were an integral part of any general explanation of international production. Ownership advantages were obviously crucial in the rise of technology-intensive FDI, which could not be described in purely locational terms. However, until 1960 economists continued to focus on locational factors since it appeared possible to them to treat FDI as a special case of international capital movements.

Location advantages. The most comprehensive work on international production in the inter-war period is to be found in various mainly descriptive studies such as that of Southard,[35] which listed a wide range of locational advantages enjoyed by US firms producing in Europe. In his review of the period Dunning has emphasised the role of import restrictions in explaining much of US direct investment in European manufacturing industry in these years.[36]

The main development in trade theory was the evolution of what became the Heckscher-Ohlin-Samuelson (HOS) model, in which trade is held to arise from the fact that different countries have different factor endowments: countries that are rich in capital will tend to export capital-intensive goods, while those with abundant labour will export labour-intensive goods. For trade to follow this pattern, the Ricardian factor-immobility condition is essential. Yet if we examine the antecedents of the model, namely the separate works of Heckscher, Ohlin and Stolper and Samuelson,[37] none of them provides a convincing analysis of why international production takes place (as an alternative to trade) in the absence of frictions. In a later work, Ohlin[38] recognised that the weakness of seeing factor movements across frontiers and trade as simple substitutes—e.g., in the HOS model as developed by Mundell[39]—is that factor movements alter the pattern of production and trade through time. He now accepts that he should also have considered differences in technology of the type retained only in certain countries or firms.

In his 1933 book, Ohlin did take location theory into the area of international trade and production. J.H. von Thünen, acknowledged to be the father of location theory, evolved his ideas from a similar standpoint to the trade theorist, in seeking to establish where each commodity would be produced with a given distribution of resources.[40] As in any simple model of import-substituting FDI, he looked at substitution between transport and non-transport costs, so that agricultural goods (on which he concentrated his analysis), cheaply cultivated with a high transport cost, would be produced close to the market (the town), while goods with high production costs but easy to transport would be produced in more distant locations.

Weber generalised that location theory, making allowances for variations in real wages and productivity between locations.[41] Industries could be placed in one of three categories: transport-oriented, labour-oriented, and those relying on more integrated operations with agglomerating advantages in the town or centres of activity. In the first two cases, there were decentralising tendencies, leading to mutliple production locations: a vital prerequisite of any international production theory.

Hotelling postulated that the interdependence of economic agents' activities could influence the pattern of location, and thus create a further motive for Weber's case of the agglomeration of certain types of firm at the centre of a market area.[42] This parallels the argument of modern oligopolistic explanations of the MNE.

The firm was brought more specifically into location theory by the market area school, notably by Lösch,[43] who sought to determine the spatial features of a firm's market through a process similar to imperfect or monopolistic competition (see below), but using spatial rather than product differentiation.

Ownership advantages. J.H. Williams, in citing an 'impressive' array of basic industries, from oil to match manufacture, which had expanded 'in disregard of political frontiers', remarked that sometimes they were the consequence of one country's projection into others of tangible and intangible capital 'along the lines of an industry and its market, as against the obvious alternative of home employment in other lines'.[44] In other cases these industries represented an 'international assembling of capital and management for world enterprises ramifying into many countries': very striking examples of 'an organic interconnection of international trade, movement of productive factors, transport and market organisation'. Even then, he did not attempt to incorporate these ideas into a new theory of international trade organised by firms with ownership advantages.

The development of the theory of the firm by Chamberlin and Robinson at last provided a basis for exploring ownership advantages, which had been more or less lost sight of in the earlier preoccupation with the market as the sole organiser of economic activity.[45] In particular, the concept of market power was brought firmly into the analysis, while the work of Bain, both on barriers to entry[46] and on industrial economics generally,[47] helped to work out the implications of these theories on an industry-wide scale.

Penrose's theory of the growth of the firm brought back the entrepreneur (of the Schumpeterian innovative kind) into the analysis with her twin concepts of managerial limits to growth and managerial slack as a springboard for growth.[48] Moreover, her analysis of corporate diversification has analogies with international involvement as firms gain experience of transferring ownership advantages across national frontiers just as they do across industries.

Internalisation advantages. Coase contrasted how resources were transferred through the market by relative prices, with the way in which the price mechanism was superseded within the firm, so that resources move by the fiat of the entrepreneur.[49] This theme was first clearly applied to international production by Buckley and Casson.[50]

For the subsequent development of the theory, Coase's key achievement was to introduce into the analysis the costs of coordinating marketing and management across different activities, namely, relating costs to the structure and extent of the firm's diversification.[51] Williamson's *Markets and Hierarchies,* which has been the inspiration for much subsequent research on internalisation in MNEs, drew both on Coase and on the earlier emphasis by Commons on transactions as the fundamental unit of economic investigation.[52]

Although economists had not yet appreciated its significance for the theory of international trade and production, the transition of giant corporations from the unitary to the multidivisional form gave rise to organisation theory.[53]

International Production 1960-80
The Scope of MNE Activity 1960-80
Developments in international production since 1960 have been narrated by Stopford and Dunning.[54] Perhaps most notably, the rise of US FDI in the 1950s and 1960s has in the 1970s been matched by an increase in FDI by West Germany and Japan. Very recently, in the 1980s, MNEs have emerged from some of the newly industrialising countries, e.g., South Korea, Hong Kong and Singapore.

Related to the trend of FDI being largely between developed countries, cross-investment or intra-industry FDI has emerged: a comparatively rare phenomenon before 1945. Consequently, as between source countries, the industrial pattern of international investment (like trade) has tended to converge.

Analysis by Economists

These developments in the 1960s and 1970s have strongly influenced the direction of the growing body of research into international production. In particular, the increasingly prevalent phenomenon of cross-investment could not adequately explained by location advantages alone. The focus of discussion therefore shifted to ownership advantages, first clearly articulated in the work of Hymer, who laid the foundations of the modern theory of international production.[55]

Vernon helped to show the interaction of the two advantages in his product-cycle model.[56] This drew on a theory of innovation to demonstrate the ownership advantages of firms alongside the location advantages of countries. An interpretation of the product-cycle model in the eclectic framework is discussed by Dunning and Cantwell.[57]

This novel emphasis on the ownership advantage of firms in international economics drew in some authors who had started from trade theory[58] and some who started from industrial economics.[59] It also fitted in with the arguments of those who feared the 'American challenge' to Europe, in contending that US firms were engaged in monopolistic rent-seeking through the exploitation of their ownership advantages.[60]

During the 1970s, internalisation advantages were incorporated into the main analysis of international production. This reflected the growth of FDI taking place in high-technology-intensive manufacturing industries, where firms became increasingly dependent on the integration of research and development with production and marketing. A further development in the 1970s was the emergence of global multinationality through rationalised investment, which integrated the activities of its subsidiaries within the regional blocs such as the EEC, or sometimes across greater distances. The historical trend in international production, away from that based upon the privileged possession of a specific intangible asset, and towards that based on the common control of a set of interrelated activities, is described by Dunning.[61]

Conclusions

Our survey of the views (mainly since 1776) of interested authors on international production suggests that those who were most aware of this activity were men of affairs—such as Bagehot—, businessmen or civil servants such as consular officials. Not until the 1950s, when US firms began to undertake massive FDI in Europe, were economists compelled to revise their purely locational approach towards international trade and capital movements, with international production as a special case.

Up to 1870 economists used a macroeconomic approach, in line with classical economic thought generally, and locational considerations were naturally of the greatest interest as long as the bulk of FDI was resource-based and often located in colonial or dependent territories, regarded often as offshoots of home production. Outside these areas, international production was organised by individual entrepreneurs, again attracted by the advantages of foreign locations.

From the 1870s onwards, both the composition of FDI and the tenor of economic thought underwent a change. The modern MNE began to evolve and increasingly undertook, as well as resource-based investments, market-oriented and import-substituting investments to supplement their domestic activity. A corresponding theory of microeconomic location advantages was therefore required: this took a number of decades to be formulated.

In the freer trading conditions after 1945, when cross-investment on a vast scale grew up between countries, the ownership advantages specific to firms have become clearer. More recently, the fall in the share of import-substituting investment, owing to the rise of joint ventures in developing countries, on the one hand, and of internationally integrated investment in industrialised countries on the other, has helped to focus attention on internalisation advantages.

The modern theory of international production has thus moved away from a reliance on country-oriented advantages in production towards firm-specific (ownership and internalisation) advantages. Dunning and Norman suggest that this is also related to a maturing of firms whose ownership advantages are now less dependent on the characteristics of their home country, and more dependent on their degree of multinationality.[62] This is associated with intra-industry FDI, and a new organisational efficiency of MNEs, which leads them to seek international expansion in its own right.

These factors help to explain why a distinct theoretical framework for the analysis of international production has only grown up recently. Economists attempt to adapt existing paradigms to explain new developments, and it is only when the adaptations required are so drastic as to undermine the original framework that new paradigms emerge. This stage appears to have been reached in international economics: neoclassical models grounded on the assumption that the technical conditions of production are everywhere the same cannot hope to account for current trends in the international division of labour.

In this chapter we have stressed the growing importance of the theory of the firm to an understanding of international trade and production.

However, given that the modern MNE is increasingly mobile in its allocation of economic activity, we have also moved back towards a Smithian world with regard to the international location of production.[63] Smith's locational framework is thus once again relevant, as we described earlier.

We hope, therefore, that we have thrown some light on a hitherto inadequately explored aspect of the history of economic thought, international production theory, into which the present paper represents a preliminary inquiry.

Notes

1. J.H. Dunning, 'Changes in the Level and Structure of International Production: the Last One Hundred Years' in M. Casson (ed.), *The Growth of International Business* (London, 1983), pp. 84-139; P. Svedberg, 'The Portfolio-Direct Composition of Private Foreign Investment in 1914 Revisited', *Economic Journal* (1978), pp. 763-77.
2. R.E. Caves, *Multinational Enterprise and Economic Analysis* (Cambridge, 1983).
3. J.H. Dunning, *International Production and Multinational Enterprise* (London, 1981).
4. J.H. Dunning, 'Changes in the Level and Structure of International Production'; D.J. Treece, 'Technological and Organisational factors in the Theory of the Multinational Enterprise' in M. Casson (ed.), *The Growth of International Business*.
5. J.H. Dunning, 'Changes in the Level and Structure of International Production', pp. 85ff.
6. M. Edelstein, *Overseas Investment in the Age of High Imperialism: The United Kingdom, 1850-1914* (London, 1982), pp. 9, 33ff.
7. Alfred D. Chandler, 'Institutional Integration: An Approach to Comparative Studies of the History of Large Scale Business Enterprise' in K. Nakagawa (ed.), *Strategy and Structure of Big Business* (Tokyo, 1977), p. 135; M. Wilkins, *The Emergence of Multinational Enterprise: American Business Abroad from the Colonial Era to 1914* (Cambridge, Mass., 1970); J.M. Stopford, 'The Origins of British-based Multinational Manufacturing Enterprises', *Business History Review* (1974), pp. 303-35.
8. M. Wilkins, *The Emergence of Multinational Enterprise* (Cambridge, Mass., 1970), pp. 215, 273.
9. P. Svedberg, 'Colonial Enforcement of Foreign Direct Investment', *Manchester School of Economics and Social Studies* (1981), pp. 21-38.
10. T. Mun, *England's Treasure by Forraign Trade* (1664; reprinted in London, 1928).
11. A. Smith, *An Inquiry into the Nature and Causes of the Wealth of Nations* (London, 1776; reprinted in E. Cannan (ed.), New York, 1937)
12. A.I. Bloomfield, 'Adam Smith and the Theory of International Trade' in A.S. Skinner and T. Wilson (eds), *Essays on Adam Smith* (London, 1975), p. 458.
13. N. Rosenberg, 'Adam Smith on Profits: Paradox Lost and Regained' in Skinner and Wilson (eds), *Essays on Adam Smith*.
14. R. Vernon, 'International Investment and International Trade in the Product Cycle,' *Quarterly Journal of Economics* (1966), pp. 190-207.
15. K. Kojima, *Direct Foreign Investment: a Japanese Model of Multinational Business Operations* (London, 1978); T.Ozawa, 'A newer type of foreign investment in Third World resource development', *Rivesta Internazionale di Scienze Economiche e Commerciali* (1982) pp. 1133-51.
16. S.H. Hymer, 'The Multinational Corporation and the Law of Uneven

Development' in J. Bhagwati (ed.), *Economics and World Order from the 1970s to the 1990s* (Ontario, 1972), pp. 113-40. (Reprinted in H. Radice, (ed.), *International Firms and Modern Imperialism* (Harmondsworth, 1975),) pp. 37-62.)

17. D. Ricardo, *On the Principles of Political Economy and Taxation,* (London, 1817; reprinted Harmondsworth, 1971).
18. D.P. O'Brien, *The Classical Economists* (Oxford, 1975), p. 181.
19. For a further discussion of the relevance of Ricardo on trade theory to the modern theory of international production see J.A. Cantwell, 'The Relevance of the Classical Economists to the Theory of International Production', *University of Reading Discussion Paper in International Investment and Business Studies*, No. 79 (1984).
20. J.S. Mill, *Principles of Political Economy* (London, 1848; reprinted 1909), p. 73.
21. N.S. Stevas (ed.) *Collected Works of Walter Bagehot: Vol.XI, Economic Essays* (London, 1978), pp. 275-9.
22. J.K. Whitaker, (ed.), *The Early Economic Writings of Alfred Marshall, 1867-1890* (London, 1975), pp. 27-8.
23. A. Marshall, *Money, Credit and Commerce* (London, 1923), pp. 7-11.
24. J.P. McKay, *Pioneers for Profit: Foreign Entrepreneurship and Russian Industrialisation, 1885-1913* (Chicago, 1970).
25. A. Marshall, *Industry and Trade,* (London, 1919), p. ix.
26. J.A. Schumpeter, *Theorie der wirtschaftlichen Entwicklung* (1911), translated as *The Theory of Economic Development* (Cambridge, Mass., 1934), p. ix.
27. G. Koolman, 'Say's Conception of the Role of the Entrepreneur', *Economica,* (1971), pp. 269-86.
28. J.A. Cantwell, op. cit.
29. E.G. Wakefield, *England and America: A Comparison of the Social and Political State of Both Nations,* 2 vols, (London, 1833).
30. K. Marx, *Capital,* vol 1 (1867; reprinted London, 1970), pp. 765-74.
31. T.B. Veblen, *The Theory of Business Enterprise* (1904; reprinted New Brunswick, NJ., 1978); W.C. Mitchell, *Business Cycles* (Berkeley, Cal., 1913).
32. J.R. Commons, *Legal Foundations of Capitalism* (Madison, 1924)
33. R. Liefmann, *Die Unternehmerverbände,* (1897), later enlarged upon in Liefmann, *Cartels, Concerns and Trusts* (London, 1932); H. Levy, *Monopoly and Competition: a Study in English Industrial Organisation* (English Translation, London, 1911); R. Hilferding, *Finance Capital: a Study of the Latest Phase of Capitalist Development* (1910; English translation, London, 1981).
34. H. Levy, op. cit.
35. F.A. Southard, *American Industry in Europe* (Boston, Mass. 1931; reprinted New York, 1976).
36. J.H. Dunning, 'Changes in the Level and Structure of International Production'.
37. E.F. Heckscher, 'The Effect of Foreign Trade on the Distribution of Income', *Economisk Tidskrift* (1919), pp. 497-512, reprinted in AEA *Readings in the Theory of International Trade,* (London, 1950), pp. 272-300; B. Ohlin, *Inter-regional and International Trade* (Cambridge, Mass., 1933); W.F. Stolper and P.A. Samuelson, 'Protection and Real Wages', *Review of Economic Studies* (1941), pp. 58-73.
38. B. Ohlin, 'Some Aspects of the Relations between International Movements of Commodities, Factors of Production and Technology' in B. Ohlin, P.-O. Hesselborn and P.M. Wijkman (eds), *The International Allocation of Economic Activity* (London, 1977), pp. 25-56.
39. R.A. Mundell, 'International Trade and Factor Mobility, *American Economic Review* (1957), pp. 321-35.
40. J.H. Von Thünen, *Der Isolierte Staat* (1826); English translation in P. Hall (ed.), *Von Thünen's Isolated State* (Oxford, 1966).
41. A. Weber, *Über den Standort der Industrien,* translated as *Alfred Weber's Theory of Location of Industries* (Chicago, 1929).

42. H. Hotelling, 'Stability in Competition', *Economic Journal* (1929), pp. 41-57.
43. A. Lösch, *Die räumliche Ordnung der Wirtschaft* (1940), translated as *The Economics of Location* (New Haven, Conn., 1954).
44. J.H. Williams, 'The Theory of International Trade Reconsidered', *Economic Journal* (1929), pp. 195-209.
45. E.H. Chamberlin, *The Theory of Monopolistic Competition* (Cambridge, Mass. 1933); J. Robinson, *The Economics of Imperfect Competition* (London, 1933).
46. J.S. Bain, 'Economies of Scale, Concentration and the Condition of Entry in Twenty Manufacturing Industries', *American Economic Review* (1954, pp. 15–39) J.S. Bain, *Barriers to New Competition* (Cambridge, Mass., 1956).
47. J.S. Bain, *Industrial Organisation* (New York, 1959).
48. E.T. Penrose, *The Theory of the Growth of the Firm,* (Oxford, 1959).
49. R.H. Coase, 'The Nature of the Firm', *Economica* (1937), pp. 386-405.
50. P.J. Buckley and M.C. Casson, *The Future of the Multinational Enterprise* (London, 1976).
51. M. Casson, 'Introduction: the Conceptual Framework' in M. Casson (ed.), *The Growth of International Business,* pp. 1-33.
52. O.E. Williamson, *Markets and Hierarchies: Analysis and Antitrust Implications* (New York, 1975); J.R. Commons, *Institutional Economics: its Place in Political Economy* (Madison, 1934; reprinted New York, 1951).
53. See for example the analysis of functionalisation in the United States by W. Robinson, *Fundamentals of Business Organisation* (New York, 1925); of coordination in the United States by J.D. Mooney and A.C. Reiley, *Onward Industry!* (New York, 1931); and of organisational principles by L. Urwick, *Management of Tomorrow* (London, 1933) and L. Urwick, *Scientific Principles and Organisation* (New York, 1938).
54. J.M. Stopford and J.H. Dunning, *Multinationals: Company Performance and Global Trends* (London, 1983).
55. S.H. Hymer, *The International Operations of National Firms: a Study of Direct Foreign Investment* (PhD thesis Massachusetts Institute of Technology, 1960; reprinted Cambridge, Mass., 1976).
56. R. Vernon, 'International Investment and International Trade in the Product Cycle'.
57. J.H. Dunning and J.A. Cantwell, 'Inward Direct Investment from the U.S. and Europe's Technological Competitiveness', (University of Reading, 1981).
58. C.P. Kindleberger, *American Business Abroad: Six Lectures on Direct Investment* (New Haven, Conn., 1969).
59. R.E. Caves, 'International Corporations: The Industrial Economics of Foreign Investment' *Economica* (1971), pp. 1-27.
60. J.J. Servan-Schreiber, *Le Défi Américain* (1967), translated as *The American Challenge* (New York, 1968).
61. J.H. Dunning, 'Changes in the Level and Structure of International Production; J.H. Dunning, 'Market Power of the Firm and International Transfer of Technology: a Historical Excursion,' *International Journal of Industrial Organisation* (1983), pp. 333-51.
62. J.H. Dunning and G. Norman, 'Intra-industry Production as a Form of International Economic Involvement: An Exploratory Paper, *University of Reading Discussion Paper in International Investment and Business Studies,* no. 74 (1983).
63. This issue is further discussed in J.H. Dunning and J.A. Cantwell, 'The emergence of multinationals in the organisation of international production', *IFCU Conference on Codes of Conduct of Multinationals and their impact on Third World Countries.* (Lisbon, October 1983).

41

3 General Theories of the Multinational Enterprise: Their Relevance to Business History[1]

Mark Casson

Introduction

In the past few years there has been a spate of new theories which claim to be general theories of the multinational enterprise (MNE).[2] The object of this chapter is to assess the logical coherence of these theories and to examine their relevance to the history of the MNE. It is suggested that there are several weaknesses that are common to all the theories. To begin with, they are far too steeped in the special institutional forms of foreign involvement which have prevailed in the post-war period. As a result, the concept of the MNE which underpins current theories remains too narrow to make analytical study of the economic history of the MNE an especially rewarding subject. Thus the theories presuppose a static configuration of independent nations, each with a liberal constitution, and with its production organised largely by private companies and corporations. The theories do not consider in detail the position of nations with colonial or dominion status, nor the consequences for international business of political instability caused, for example, by international territorial disputes. Neither do they take account of the fact that throughout history there has been unappropriated frontier territory, such as that represented today by the Antarctic, the oceans and the atmosphere.

Theories of the MNE, being themselves the product of liberal thought applied to economics, presume a liberal political framework. This means that, if applied uncritically, they give a distorted view of MNEs' economic relations with illiberal economies—whether the socialist countries of Eastern Europe, or fascist dictatorships elsewhere.

The legal privileges afforded by a liberal constitution encourage business leaders to clothe their activities in a corporate 'shell'. The legal shell provided by incorporation may well, however, disguise the true locus of economic power within the firm.[3] The theories' preoccupation with the firm and its arm's-length contractual alternatives make them difficult to apply to earlier times in which the extended family, the partnership, the merchant guild and the cartel were also important forms of economic organisation (as some still are today).

The Concept of Ownership Advantage

The current economic theory of the MNE began mainly as an attempt to explain post-war US corporate investment in Western European industry. The theory was mainly concerned with manufacturing industry rather than services such as banking. Initially, two main analytical questions were posed: Firstly, why do the investing firms produce in Europe rather than in the US? Secondly, how can they compete with indigenous producers, given the additional costs of doing business abroad?

The answer to the first question is that the investments were import-substituting. Sourcing the foreign market by local production was made profitable by the avoidance of transport costs and tariffs. In some cases it also provided access to cheaper labour. Although labour productivity may have been lower in Europe—due partly to the lower scale of production—labour was relatively cheap in Europe, because the combination of the dollar shortage and nominal wage stickiness in the US[4] made the US own-product wage very high. The answer to the second question lies in the technology gap: the cost to US firms of doing business abroad was offset by lower production costs and better product quality achieved through superior technology and more professional management practices. This is the essence of the Hymer-Kindleberger theory of the MNE: it synthesises what Dunning calls the location and ownership advantages of international production.

Both Hymer and Caves emphasised the monopolistic nature of the ownership advantage,[5] Hymer pointing to privileged access to proprietary technology, and Caves to special skills in the design and marketing of differentiated products. Other writers emphasised non-monopolistic advantages, e.g. Aliber, who argued that stockholder preferences for strong currency assets gave an advantage to all firms whose parent company was based in a strong currency area.[6]

The importance of the distinction between monopolistic and non-monopolistic advantages is not always recognised in applications of the Hymer-Kindleberger theory. 'Advantage' is a relative concept—someone always has an advantage *relative* to someone else—and it is important to specify who that someone else is. When a foreign firm enjoys a monopolistic advantage, such as a proprietary technology, it enjoys an advantage not only over indigenous firms but over all firms everywhere. On the other hand, a foreign firm which enjoys a non-monopolistic advantage may enjoy an advantage only over indigenous firms. This means, for example, that in an industry where there are no indigenous firms, none of the foreign firms need have any kind of advantage relative to the other firms actually operating in the industry. In applied work on multinationals, therefore, it is incorrect to assume that each multinational in the industry must have some kind of advantage relative to the other others. This is true if the advantages are monopolistic, but untrue of they are not.

A third question was also posed by Hymer and Kindleberger,[7] namely, Why do US firms not license their ownership advantages to European firms? Consideration of this question showed that ownership and location factors were not themselves sufficient to explain international production: some disincentive to license is also required. A number of disincentives have been suggested; though different, they are related to each other. First, if the advantage is advertised for sale, it will attract attention: imitation will be encouraged, and the appropriation of monopoly rents made that much more difficult.[8] Secondly, buyers will be reluctant to pay the full value of the advantage as they will be uncertain of exactly what is on offer, or what its quality is.[9] Thirdly, transfers of technology between employees of the same firm may be less costly than transfers of technology between employees of different firms, because the employees share a common corporate culture, and this makes it easy for them to learn from one another. This last idea is rarely articulated, but underpins much of the discussion in the literature.

Buckley and Casson went further by suggesting that this question was merely a special case of the question of why multinational firms exist anyway. In other words, why is multinational organisation of economic activity preferred to a network of arm's-length contractual arrangements between individual factor-owners and individual consumers in different countries? Following McManus, Buckley and Casson appeal to the Coase theorem for the answer.[10] They show that a necessary and sufficient condition for the existence of an MNE is that there is a net benefit to internalising an intermediate product market linking activities located in different countries.[11] In this context, the concept of an intermediate product market is a very broad one. It includes markets in raw materials, semi-processed products, components, and also wholesale products ready for final distribution. It includes markets in technology and all kinds of know-how. Finally, it includes markets in price commitments and production commitments; these commitments are used both to establish collusion in oligopolistic industries, and to reduce costs through rationalisation in industries utilising indivisible assets. Different motives for internalising lead to different patterns of backward, forward, horizontal and conglomerate integration. It is the relation between the motive for internalisation and the resulting pattern of integration that yields the major predictions of internalisation theory.

An immediate consequence of this result is that a monopolistic advantage is not necessary to explain why an MNE exists, any more than it is necessary to explain why a uninational firms exists. For example, when profit-tax rates are not harmonised between two countries, firms in an industry whose product is mined in one country and processed in another have an incentive to internalise the raw material market in order to minimise tax liabilities through transfer pricing. The same result would ensue if tax rates were harmonised but economies from vertical integration were operating. In neither case is monopolistic advantage required.

In a definitive statement of his recent work, Dunning[12] asserts that three different types of advantage are necessary to explain the behaviour of MNEs: ownership advantage, internalisation advantage and location advantage. Some writers identify Dunning's ownership advantage with a monopolistic advantage, but this is incorrect. It was established above that a monopolistic advantage is not always necessary where MNEs are concerned. Dunning's ownership advantage concept includes any advantage that an MNE possesses over rival indigenous firms. It includes, for example, the advantage of transfer pricing referred to above. Ownership advantage thus includes some of the advantages of internalisation. This means that in some cases, Dunning's statement that both ownership and internalisation advantages are necessary becomes almost a tautology. By grouping together under the one heading both monopolistic and non-monopolistic advantages, and internalisation and non-internalisation advantages, the ownership advantage concept is in danger of obscuring the crucial analytical issues.

The problem seems to be that internalisation was first introduced into the theory to explain the disincentive to licensing a monopolistic advantage[13] and some writers continue to regard this as the only role of internalisation. They speak of 'internalising an advantage, as though internalisation had its everyday connotation of 'keeping to oneself'. They fail to recognise that in the theory of the firm it is markets that are internalised and not the advantages themselves. The internalisation of a market for a monopolistic advantage is a special case of the internalisation of markets in general. Internalisation is nothing if it is not a general theory of how market failure leads to the creation of firms.[14] From this perspective, internalisation theory does not leave any gaps that an ownership advantage is needed to fill.

Nevertheless a paradox arises here. Empirical work on the MNE regularly points to the importance of ownership advantages—even in pre-war investments, where vertical integration was an important factor too. The evidence also suggests that managers rarely perceive licensing as a crucial issue—the advantages of internalising the market for know-how are usually believed to be heavily outweighed by the costs. The resolution of this paradox may lie in identifying another question, namely, why it is that certain firms are persistently successful and grow large while other firms are only short-lived or always remain small.

Dunning is on firmer ground when he argues that the *success* of MNEs *vis-à-vis* non-MNEs rests on their possession of ownership advantages. The question of success and failure is, in fact, absolutely crucial, and the discovery of a convincing answer would have major policy implications. According to our interpretation, therefore, the major contribution of Dunning's theory is its assertion that possession of an ownership advantage is a necessary condition for sustained profitability and growth.

This interpretation of Dunning is supported by a reconsideration of the two questions posed at the beginning of this section. It is worth noting that while the first question of the Hymer-Kindleberger theory concerns managerial choice between two alternative strategies of sourcing a foreign market, the second question is not directly concerned with managerial choice, but with the ability of the firm to survive in a foreign market environment. The fact that the latter question is concerned specifically with competition from indigenous producers does not alter the fact that the basic issue is the survival of the firm. Questions of managerial choice and questions of survival are logically quite distinct. Internalisation theory represents an extension of the theory of choice to encompass the choice, within each market, of the appropriate contractual arrangement. Ownership advantage, however, is not concerned with choice, but with the performance of the firm once managerial choices have been made. Its proper place is not within the subdivision of the theory that deals with choice, but with the subdivision that deals with the success, and the consequent growth, of the firm.

The Concept of Internalisation

It might appear that our critique of the ownership advantage concept indicates support for Rugman's view that internalisation alone constitutes the general theory of the MNE.[15] Rugman's work is notable for its lively and readable presentation of the major analytical concepts. Unfortunately, however, Rugman's use of the internalisation concept is not always consistent. Internalisation has different connotations in different branches of economics. *Internalisation of a market* refers to the replacement of an arm's-length contractual relationship (i.e. the external market) with unified ownership (i.e. the internal market), while *internalisation of an externality* refers to the creation of a market of any kind where none existed before.

The first concept of internalisation is used in industrial organisation theory and the second in the economics of welfare. Writers who discuss the welfare implications of alternative forms of industrial organisation need always to keep this distinction in mind. Rugman, unfortunately, confuses the two concepts at crucial points in his analysis.

There is some disagreement in the welfare literature as to whether the internalisation of an externality involves the creation of a market of *any* kind[16] or whether it involves the creation of a market specifically through the unification of ownership.[17] If the former interpretation is used then internalisation of an externality does not imply the creation of an internal market, whereas if the latter interpretation is used then it does. However, *neither* interpretation implies that the internalisation of a market removes an externality. It *may* do so, but equally it may not. Only if the external market is missing altogether is the creation of an internal market practically certain to lead to the avoidance of an externality.

It is possible that the replacement of external markets by internal ones may increase efficiency, but there is no guarantee that it will do so. Rugman defines an externality as a divergence between private and social costs, and it is quite possible that internalisation may increase this divergence and not reduce it. Thus an MNE which maximises monopoly profits by restricting the output of high-technology goods, or uses vertical integration as a barrier to entry, may well *create* externalities, according to Rugman's definition. Internalisation of a market is not, therefore, equivalent to the removal of an externality.

Although Rugman is seeking a general theory, he is actually very restrictive in his interpretation of the internalisation of a market. He identifies internalisation of a market with centralisation of control, failing to recognise that when ownership is unified, control can still be decentralised using shadow prices or other kinds of flexible budgetary control within the ownership unit. He also claims that research and development must be centralised within the MNE, a claim that seems contrary to his emphasis elsewhere upon the benefits of the international division of labour within the MNE.

In recent work, Rugman discusses applications of internalisation theory to the oil and drugs industries.[18] His examples suggest that the distinctions drawn above may be unduly pedantic, since in these cases markets internalised within the firm are indeed missing altogether outside it. This, however, is an empirical issue, and further research must be done before support can be given to Rugman's policy recommendations on such practical grounds.

It is quite possible, in fact, to extend internalisation theory in new directions, but not along the lines that previous authors have suggested. There is one particular extension that is of special interest to the economic historian, and which also illustrates vividly the way in which multinational organisation may damage social efficiency. By internalising collusive agreements on price and output, the MNE may render collusive arrangements more readily enforceable, and so provide a more powerful mechanism for exploiting international monopoly power than an international cartel.[19]

Suppose, for example, that, in the absence of anti-trust policy, it is planned to create a world monopoly through collaboration between oligopolistic firms producing in different countries. A suitable arm's-length contractual arrangement would be a collusive agreement between the oligopolists; if the arrangement were long-term it could lead to the institution of an international cartel. The main administrative problem for cartel members would be the avoidance of covert price-cutting and the violation of production quotas by the others. Unified ownership effected through an MNE would reduce the incentives to default on the collusive agreement, and would also make it easier to effect adjustments in prices and quotas, as protracted negotiations would be avoided. The main disadvantage of the MNE would be that, being a more overt use of monopoly power, it would be more likely to attract political hostility. Additionally, the agglomeration of capital would be so large that shareholdings would be highly diversified and it would therefore be difficult for the owners to discipline the management.

It may be objected that, in the absence of entry barriers, neither the cartel nor the MNE could exploit its monopoly power in the long run. This is correct, but there are sufficient industries characterised by natural monopoly stemming from economics of scale to render this objection a fairly weak one. The issue of the transition from international cartel to MNE in naturally monopolistic industries is a subject that has so far received little attention, and one that should repay further study.

Modelling Transaction Costs
Internalisation is a powerful analytical concept, but to render it operational it is necessary to make specific assumptions about the costs of alternative institutional arrangements. Very little effort has been made in this direction. The appropriate methodology is to specify transaction cost functions, and then to determine which institutional

arrangement has the lowest cost under given circumstances.[20] Given profit maximisation, rational transactors will choose the arrangement with lowest cost.

The specification of transaction cost functions is not, however, an easy matter. To set up a transaction, traders must invest in acquiring information. Some of the information is needed simply to make contact, some to secure the most favourable terms in the bargain, and some to reduce the risk of default. Information, once acquired, may prove useful in subsequent trades. This means that transaction costs—or some component of them—represent an investment; not all transaction costs are a recurrent cost. Matters are further complicated by the fact that not only is information required for trade, but trade itself generates information. This means that each trade reduces the marginal transaction cost incurred by a subsequent trade in the same product, or with the same person, i.e. there are economies to repeated trade.

Because of 'learning by trading', two traders seeking a long-term relationship will normally commence with a trial or one-off trade. If this is mutually satisfactory they will progress to recurrent spot trade, which may increase in regularity as mutual confidence grows. If the traders are looking for a long-term partner at the outset then, where the initial transaction is concerned, the value of the commodity itself may be very small compared with the value of the information that the initial trade conveys.

Another feature of transaction costs is that it is often difficult to quantify the variables on which they depend. 'Psychic distance'—generated by differences in language and culture—raises transaction costs by impeding information flow between the two parties, but an adequate measure of psychic distance is difficult to devise.

The concept of psychic distance is usually applied to *direct* communication between two parties. It must be recognised, however, that information relevant to trade can also be obtained at second hand. For example, information about product quality may be obtained through social contacts with people who have prior experience of the product; information about a trader's integrity and his ability to pay may be obtained from people with personal knowledge of him. Of course, the value of second-hand information is very much a matter of confidence in the person who acts as the contact: respect for a contact is required before one can accept his assessment of someone else. Thus psychic distance is essentially a social phenomenon, in the sense that it depends not only upon channels of direct communication between the two parties, but also upon indirect channels mediated by other people. This suggests that a major factor reducing the psychic distance between transactors is common membership of a social group.

An important corollary relates to the role of reputation in promoting trade. Reputation is achieved when a favourable opinion percolates widely through the network of social contacts, so that many people are willing to place confidence in the person or the product. As a result, people are willing to trade without further acquisition of information, so that the marginal cost of transacting is reduced. Effective creation of a reputation involves skilful use of social contacts, and an astute knowledge of how the network of social communication is structured, so that contacts can be developed at crucial points. Reputation, in other words, tends to be acquired by people with a good understanding of the structure and the customs of the group (or groups) to which they belong. They can achieve this reputation either for themselves, personally, or for the product that they supply.

Reputation reduces the relative cost of arm's-length trade. If buyer and seller have great confidence in each other, there is little reason for one to acquire control over the other in order to monitor product quality or to guard against default. The converse of this is that the need for internal markets is greatest where reputation is lacking. In a new industry, for example, producers may have little confidence in the quality of the inputs they are purchasing, and so may integrate backwards to secure quality control. They may also have little confidence in the ability of retailers to promote their product effectively, and so may resort to direct selling in place of wholesale supply. Similar reasoning suggests that arm's-length trade will be most common in countries with strong cultural homogeneity. Thus for example, the relatively high ratio of wholesale to retail sales in Japan compared to Western Europe and the US may be attributed in part to a greater degree of trust—coupled with the cultivation of personal reputation—that seems to exist amongst the Japanese.

As an industry matures and reputations are built up, arm's-length trade becomes easier to organise. The firms that survive will have acquired a reputation. As a result, intermediate products can be traded between the subsidiaries of different firms: markets that were closed against outside suppliers become opened up, even though outside suppliers may be used only to 'top-up' intra-firm supplies. Individual managers may even be able to acquire reputations within their firms, sufficient to allow them to 'buy out' their subsidiaries and operate on an arm's-length basis with the parent establishment.

The analysis of reputation also has a bearing on our earlier discussion of ownership advantage. The fact that MNEs internalise markets should not obscure the obvious fact that they are involved in arm's length trade in both final product and factor markets. Where customers are concerned, a reputation for product quality may be the basis for a monopolistic advantage—especially where a brand name is used to indicate quality. Where factor suppliers are concerned, reputation may confer an important ownership advantage in the capital market. The typical MNE enjoys an international reputation, and is therefore able to borrow funds from sources in several countries. When the cost of capital differs internationally, the MNE's reputation gives it an important advantage over purely indigenous firms.

The Synthesis of Internalisation and the Orthodox Theory of Trade
The current economic theory of the MNE has developed independently of orthodox trade theory. Attempts by trade theorists to develop a theory of the MNE by grafting capital movements onto the Heckscher-Ohlin-Stolper-Samuelson (HOSS) model have signally failed. This is because the HOSS model stands firmly in the neoclassical tradition. There are no transaction costs in the HOSS model, and so there are no grounds for distinguishing between direct and indirect investment. This is a point altogether ignored by Kojima.[21] Yet it is clearly unsatisfactory for the theory of the MNE to remain divorced from mainstream trade theory, and a number of efforts have been made to integrate them.

The simplest way to integrate the theory of transaction costs—i.e. internalisation theory—with the HOSS model is to recognise that the case for multinational operations rests upon the relative and not the absolute costs of transacting.[22] Suppose that, apart from transaction costs, the HOSS assumptions apply. If it is assumed that, although certain institutional arrangements may be costly, the cheapest method of transacting is always a costless one, then the HOSS approach to the location of production remains valid. So long as the MNE plans efficiently, it will mimic the location of production that would prevail under arm's length contracts, as described by the HOSS model. (This result is analogous to the theoretical equivalence of competitive general equilibrium and idealised central planning that was discovered in the 1930s.)

The result is, of course, of limited interest because of the strong assumptions upon which it is based. It becomes more interesting when the HOSS model is modified to allow for technology gaps and for intermediate product trade. With these modifications, the basic insight of the HOSS model—that trade in final products can substitute for factor movements—is augmented by two further insights: (1) that technology transfer can substitute either for trade in final products or for factor movements; and (2) that intermediate product trade can substitute for trade in final products and also for technology transfer and factor movement.

51

Insight (1) encompasses the case where the export of technology through foreign direct investment substitutes for the export of high-technology products, as occurs in the 'maturing product' phase of the product cycle.[23] In this way the modified HOSS model can shed light on the global implications of import-substituting high-technology investment, as discussed in the section on ownership advantage.

Insight (2) encompasses the case of internationally rationalised production, exemplified by an assembly line supplied with components from a number of different locations. The potential for rationalised production in manufacturing has existed since the development of mass production and interchangeable parts in the early part of the century, but because of political instability and obstacles to trade in the inter-war period, it was not until the creation of customs unions and free trade areas in the 1960s and 1970s that the potential has been fully exploited.

It is not difficult to integrate the modified HOSS model with the modern theory of international finance. Both theories, being neoclassical, emphasise that markets facilitate functional specialisation. Each new market that is created permits a further separation of functions. The introduction of an international market in risk capital and an international market in loanable funds demonstrates that the provision of risk-bearing and the provision of 'abstinence' or 'waiting' can be separated from the organisation of production and trade.[24] This result has two important consequences.

Firstly, it demonstrates that a firm can obtain a controlling equity stake in a foreign plant merely by exchanging its debenture debt for equity debt in the foreign country. As a result, what is called foreign direct investment may involve no international movement of capital at all. Foreign direct investment may occur simply at the expense of foreign indirect investment, leaving the total stock of foreign investment completely unchanged.

Secondly, it means that when financial markets are globally integrated, a firm may produce in one set of countries, be funded by debenture-holders in another set of countries and have its risks borne by equity-holders in yet another set of countries. This has serious implications for people who wish to talk of 'US' multinationals or 'British' multinationals, since an important element in multinationality is that ownership, funding and production operations can each have quite distinct patterns of multinationality.

The main problem with the attempted synthesis of transaction costs and neoclassical theory is that the synthesis concedes too much to the neoclassical position. The focus in neoclassical theory is upon markets, and upon the functional specialisation that markets permit: the firm is of no intrinsic interest. All the theory requires is a representative firm that can be regarded as a 'black box'. The 'black box' must have an upward-sloping long-run supply curve of output and downward-sloping long-run derived demand curves for factors, and that is all.

The synthesis achieved with transaction cost theory makes it possible to predict, in principle, the institutional arrangement that will prevail within the black box, but only at the expense of assuming that the institutional arrangement will be one in which the management function is totally trivial. The triviality of management follows both from the fact that the institutional arrangement is by assumption costless, and also from the fact that since the firm's environment is purely neoclassical, all relevant information about the environment is encapsulated in freely available market prices (or a fully known demand curve in the case of product monopoly). In the neoclassical world, the invisible hand of the market does practically all the managing that is required. One cannot have an economic theory of the MNE that includes both the neoclassical theory of location and a realistic theory of management.

The neoclassical theory has enjoyed the undivided attention of a majority of British and American economists for well over a century. It would seem most fruitful at this stage to embrace the idea that the management and the organisation of the firm are of such intrinsic interest that the neoclassical approach should be put to one side for the moment, so that research can be focused more closely upon the firm.

Entrepreneurship and the Dynamics of Ownership Advantage

The moral of our review of the literature is that there is no really satisfactory general theory of the MNE. The best way to further enhance the relevance of the theory seems to be not to 'purify' or 'generalise' it, but to focus upon specific gaps in it.

This section and the next discuss two such gaps in the theory, and outline possible ways in which they could be filled. This section raises the question of how ownership advantages are created, and what factors determine the pace at which they are dissipated. The next section discusses political factors, and in particular the role of source-country governments acting as 'protectors' of their MNEs.

It is a commonplace that, where entrepreneurship is concerned, there is a gap in conventional economic theory.[25] Theories of the MNE are no exception to this. The entrepreneur fills the gap labelled 'fixed factor' in the neoclassical theory of the firm. Entrepreneurial ability is analogous to a fixed factor endowment because it sets a limit to the efficient size of the firm. The fact that neoclassical theory reduces the entrepreneur to a mere 'fixed factor' illustrates well the essentially static nature of its approach.

The same criticism may be applied to the 'ownership advantage' approach. Ownership advantage may be interpreted as a measure of the net wealth accruing from past entrepreneurial activity[26] but it tells us nothing about how this entrepreneurial activity was actually carried on, and offers little clue about the circumstances under which it is likely to continue in the future. Why is it, for example, that in the past 500 years technological and commercial advantages have passed from Italy to the Netherlands, and then to England, Germany and the United States? Why did US advanced technology appear exactly when it did, and why has it diffused so slowly to developing countries as compared to Western Europe? Why has it diffused much more rapidly to Japan? Current theories are too static to handle issues of this kind.

It is possible to develop a dynamic theory of ownership advantage using the economic theory of the entrepreneur. The theory views the economy as an evolutionary system[27] whose future is very uncertain, so that decisions have to be made on the basis of mere speculations about their consequences. Even the *probable* consequences of decisions cannot be estimated objectively: there are often insufficient precedents with which to estimate the relative frequencies of different outcomes.[28] People therefore hold different opinions about what is the best policy to pursue. Decisions upon which opinions differ may be termed judgemental decisions, and a person who specialises in taking judgemental decisions is defined as an entrepreneur[29]. The entrepreneur is of importance to the historian because at turning points in the evolutionary process it is his judgement which most often prevails.

There is one aspect of this theory that is particularly relevant to the MNE, and that is the idea that the most crucial entrepreneurial judgements take place on 'the frontier'.

Schumpeter defines the entrepreneur as someone who innovates by carrying out 'new combinations'.[30] Leibenstein emphasises judgement in identifying 'gaps' to be filled, and Penrose in finding 'interstices' to explore.[31] Kirzner emphasises the importance of alertness to opportunity.[32] This activity of exploring new opportunities takes place on the frontiers of knowledge. Other activity takes place on the territorial frontier: voyages of discovery to new lands, for example, or expeditions to prospect for mineral deposits. In historical terms, the exploitation of the frontiers of technology and territory seem to have gone hand in hand. In eighteenth- and nineteenth-century Britain, the industrial revolution at home was accompanied by the commercial exploitation of new colonial territories abroad. In the late nineteenth-century United States, the exploitation of the mid-Western frontier was paralleled by inventive activity in the Eastern states. Several other examples could be given from earlier periods.

The historical parallel between territorial and technological frontiers is matched by a theoretical parallel. It is a feature of any frontier that the environment in which people operate is not properly mapped out or fully understood. Since people do not have a proper model of the 'frontier territory', it is difficult for them to make choices which are 'optimal' in the usual sense of that word.[33] People may not know exactly where the frontier is, nor how far it extends, nor how many rival 'prospectors' there are and where exactly they are 'located'. It is difficult for people to plan rationally under these circumstances, and even more difficult to imagine how any kind of equilibrium distribution of frontier activity could emerge.

Another feature of frontiers is that property rights are usually ambiguous and ill-defined. As the frontier moves forward, the law moves along behind. It usually consolidates the position that has already been attained. The theory of the entrepreneur analyses the kind of situation that frontiersmen—working in a legal vacuum—are likely to generate. Where people on the frontier are drawn from a unified social group, they will tend to appropriate the frontier in accordance with custom. Custom cannot, however, anticipate all eventualities. It may dictate, for example, that priority of discovery confers ownership, but fail to indicate just how much of a newly discovered territory may be fairly appropriated. Custom may recognise the rights of individuals to keep newly discovered information secret, but may equally recognise the rights of others to extract the information by subterfuge, if they can.

Where there is a mixture of social groups on the frontier, it is more likely that force and not custom will govern appropriability, and that the strongest group will consolidate its position through the laws that it finally imposes upon the others.

Neoclassical theory provides little guidance on the factors influencing the allocation of resources when neither law nor custom prevails. The theory of games[34] analyses some of the strategic issues involved, but does so in an essentially static manner.

Successful frontier activity requires a combination of skills: the ability to identify profit opportunities, the judgement to evaluate them, and the tactical awareness to exploit them properly.

The identification of profit opportunities involves synthesising information from diverse sources. Identifying a potential innovation, for example, requires the entrepreneur not only to make contact with the inventor, but also to know something about the activities which the invention may displace. Skill in making social contacts is invaluable in obtaining information of this kind, and to exercise this skill it is often important for the entrepreneur to gain entry to the right social group.

Judgement is required because imponderables always have a crucial effect on the profitability of an innovation. There are diminishing returns to collecting 'objective' information: sooner or later the entrepreneur must rely upon subjective assessments. Entrepreneurs who have acquired a varied background—through travel or migration, for example—are most likely to develop judgement of this kind.

Tactical awareness is important in securing exclusive rights to the opportunity, and thereby appropriating the maximum reward from it. Dynamic considerations suggest that a particularly successful appropriation strategy is likely to be the 'pre-emptive strike'. Once a discovery is made, the entrepreneur quickly extracts all the economically relevant information from what he has found, and uses it to guide him towards further discoveries before others learn of his find and draw similar conclusions for themselves. An entrepreneur with a good 'track record' may attract a following of potential imitators, and may have to resort to diversionary tactics to put them 'off the scent'. At the same time he will attempt to consolidate his position by erecting 'barriers to entry'—which in this context could be anything from physical defences to announcements of threatened reprisals against imitators. Where resources are difficult to defend, the entrepreneur may attempt to monopolise more easily defensible resources which are complementary to them, for example if the entrepreneur has discovered a new technology, he may attempt to monopolise the raw material sources on which the exploitation of the technology depends. This may be more effective than attempting to defend his know-how through a patent since, even if a patent is available, his patent application will merely advertise his discovery to potential imitators.

The theory of the entrepreneur makes it possible to identify the kind of skills which favour business success. The 'frontier' concept indicates that these skills are most likely to belong to the social extrovert, the migrant and the military officer. This in turn provides a link with the kind of cultural values most likely to encourage entrepreneurship.[35]

Cultures which promote entrepreneurship are most likely to prove viable in the long run. Cultural differences may explain, for example, why foreign entrepreneurs often persistently identify opportunities that are missed by indigenous entrepreneurs. The foreign culture may accord higher status to the skills that make for entrepreneurial success. Even when the indigenous population is inventive, it may be foreign entrepreneurs that adopt the inventions and appropriate the economic rewards. Cultural differences may also explain why in some countries indigenous entrepreneurs are so much slower to learn from foreign example than in others. The very narrow background of the indigenous entrepreneurs in some countries may make the practices of the foreign entrepreneurs seem quite alien to them: their inclination is to resist the innovations, rather than to imitate them.

Specific instances of the role of entrepreneurship in the growth of the MNE have been given elsewhere.[36] Tactical behaviour by MNEs is exemplified by their exploration activities in the oil and mineral industries, and by the way that they have used their control of transport networks to create barriers to the entry of rival firms. A number of studies have suggested that the cultural impact of the MNE has been one of the most enduring effects of foreign direct investment.

The MNE and the Nation-state

In current economic theories of the MNE the *multinational* aspect receives much less attention than the *enterprise* aspect. An extreme position on this is taken by Williamson, who discusses the theory of the MNE as though it were merely a special case of the theory of the firm.[37]

It was, in fact, political concern about the threat to national sovereignty that sparked off post-war interest in the MNE.[38] Economic theories of the MNE assume a fixed configuration of nation-states. Taking the nation-state for granted, they inquire into the viability of the enterprise. This is the thrust of the Hymer–Kindleberger approach: given the costs of operating across national borders, what are the economic advantages of doing so? But this question can be turned around the other way. Given the economic advantages of operating on a global scale, what is the rationale for continuing to split up the world into different nation-states? Is the nation-state really viable in a world where the barriers to organisation over distance have been substantially reduced by jet travel and modern telecommunications?

With the world split up into different nation-states, each claiming sovereignty over some particular territory, an individual entrepreneur may, within limits, choose the state from which he takes citizenship. Although he is likely to be born a citizen of one particular country, he does not necessarily have to remain a citizen of that country if economic incentives suggest otherwise. The same point applies to a legal entity such as a firm. Differences in legislation mean that the privileges offered to firms—joint stock organisation, limited liability and, above all, rights to confidentiality—may differ between states. A firm registered under one jurisdiction may change to another by arranging to be taken over by a holding company registered elsewhere.

With both individuals and firms having a choice of national allegiance, it seems reasonable to postulate an international market for the services of nation-states. The 'product' is the bundle of services provided by the nation-state. The 'payment' is principally the tax obligations imposed by the state. The 'price' is therefore the value of the services provided per unit of taxation.

The privileges of corporate organisation are just one element in the package offered by the government. Fair adjudication when the company is in the right—coupled, perhaps, with the opportunity for bribery and corruption when the company is in the wrong—is also very valuable. The private costs of the adjudication process are an important component of transaction costs, and so the minimisation of these costs is a major consideration. Freedom of contract, and immunity for *ad hoc* interventions by the government executive are important too; when the executive does intervene, for example by regulating markets, it should be in response to rent-seeking lobbying by the company.[39]

For the MNE, however, the quality of the protection afforded for its assets is almost certainly the paramount consideration. A colonial power, for example, is able to offer much better protection to firms in its dependent territories than are other nations. This suggests that an enterprising businessman seeking to operate in the colonies would seek citizenship of the colonising nation, if he did not have it already, and would register his company under the jurisdiction of the colonial government. Likewise, if sovereignty over a colonial territory changes, it may be advantageous for entrepreneurs to seek new protectors by changing their corporate identity.

The net benefits conferred by a protector cannot be assessed without taking account of the tax liabilities involved. When entrepreneurs can shop around for protection, protectors must compete for custom by offering protection on reasonable terms. Imperial or colonial powers may demand high taxes to support high levels of military spending. Nations with little economic strength must compete by offering important legal privileges and low taxation: for example, attracting banking by offering exceptional confidentiality, offering flags of convenience to shippers who wish to operate with low safety standards, tax havens for those who wish to exploit opportunities for transfer pricing, and so on.

It is inevitable that from time to time rival protectors come into conflict with each other. Protectors, for example, may make rival claims to the same territory. This is particularly likely on the frontier. As noted earlier, unappropriated frontier territory is especially attractive to entrepreneurs. To begin with, entrepreneurs are operating in a legal vacuum, being entirely self-reliant where protection is concerned. Secrecy, subterfuge and the rule of force determine the appropriation of frontier territory, especially where the rival entrepreneurs are drawn from different social groups. In due course, each entrepreneur will appeal to his protector to consolidate his position by helping him to defend the territory he has acquired. If the territory is valuable, for example rich in minerals, he can expect vigorous protection because of the potential tax revenues involved. There is, however, a clear incentive for each protector not merely to consolidate established positions but to attempt to expropriate property held under weaker protection. Where valuable resources are at stake, nations may easily be drawn into war. This is likely to lead to mutual expropriation of existing foreign investments even if these are nowhere near the frontier. Instability on the frontier may therefore spill over to raise protection costs elsewhere, and damage the climate for foreign investment as a whole.

This discussion of the economic role of the nation-state may seem somewhat fanciful but, in other contexts, economic theory already reaches well into the domain of public choice.[40] The view that nation-states operate in a market environment underlines the fact that nation-states are not permanent institutions. Like enterprises, some grow, while others survive only a short time. The recent economic history of Europe illustrates this very well. The break-up of the Austro-Hungarian empire made some European companies into MNEs overnight.[41] These MNEs promoted advances in armaments technology and the growth of strategic industries in the interwar period. Rival prospecting for raw materials to supply these industries led to international tension in the years before the Second World War. After the war, the map of Europe was redrawn again, and greater emphasis was placed on European political union under the aegis of the US as superpower. The conversion of military technology to civilian uses, when combined with US marketing skills, gave the US the economic power to sustain this role. It was under this protection that US companies acquired the confidence to invest in Europe on a large scale.

The Place of Theory in Business History

Although this chapter is critical of several aspects of current theory, theory is still of considerable relevance to the business historian. It is important, however, to appreciate its scope and limitations. It is obvious that economic theory cannot derive laws analogous to those in physics, which involve simple exact relationships between measurable quantities, which are valid throughout space and time.

In any economic situation—such as the growth of a particular firm—there are a multitude of specific factors at work, and these can obscure the influence of general factors. The influence of general factors can be easily discerned only when information on a number of different economic situations is pooled. The best way to isolate their influence is to identify for each factor two groups of cases: one group where theory predicts that the factor will have had a significance influence and the other group where theory predicts that it will not. It is then possible to compare the *average* behaviour in the two groups to see if the evidence reveals an effect of the magnitude and direction expected from the factor.

Another way of expressing the same idea is to say that economic theory is concerned with representative economic units, such as Marshall's representative firm. No single firm is ever fully representative: the only way of approximating representative behaviour is by taking a group of actual firms. Where the group has been selected from a larger population, the members of the group need to be selected so that the group reflects the same variety in behaviour as does the population as a whole. The historian needs to beware of the possibility that the kind of firms that make available archival material may be unrepresentative of firms in their industry as a whole—they may, for example, be more profitable, or longer-lived, than the typical firm. A statistician would say that a sample of firms selected on the basis of access to archives is unlikely to be a random sample of the firms in the industry, and that the results obtained from the sample may therefore present a biased picture of the population. For various reasons, business historians appear to be attracted to the study of successful firms, and this is sometimes justified on the grounds that the successful firms are the dominant firms in their industry. It should not be forgotten, however, that unless these firms enjoy a total monopoly of their respective industries, they will not be *representative* of the firms within them.

Research in business archives is very time-consuming, and it is therefore appropriate to inquire into the minimal number of cases that must be studied in order to put an economic theory to the test. A simple answer is that if the economic theory suggests that n distinct factors influence behaviour then 2^n cases should be studied. In the most elementary case, where just one factor is involved, the minimum number of cases is two. If, for example, theory asserts that higher profits leads to faster growth, then it is necessary to compare the growth of two firms, one of which is more profitable than the other. If the more profitable firm does indeed grow faster, then the theory is tentatively confirmed. If it does not grow faster, then the theory is tentatively rejected. With just two cases, however, specific factors may be masking the effects of profits, and the result may be spurious. To reduce this problem, additional cases must be considered.

If theory predicted that growth depends upon both profitability and the firm's degree of multinationality, then four cases would need to be studied: a profitable multinational firm, a profitable non-multinational firm, an unprofitable multinational firm, and an unprofitable non-multinational firm. Information on the non-multinational firm is necessary to provide a 'control' or 'norm' with which the behaviour of the multinational can be compared. Likewise information on the unprofitable firm is necessary to provide a 'control' for the profitable firm. The use of controls is developed further in the theory of experimental design and analysis of variance.[42]

To summarise, it is evident that in the history of any particular business, specific factors exert an important influence upon its development. If, for example, the founder of a British firm has a cousin in Sydney, that may tip the balance in favour of locating his first overseas investment in Australia. It cannot be inferred from this, however, that in a sample of, say, twenty companies, the location of the initial overseas investment is determined by the migration of favourite cousins. It is likely that in a sample of twenty companies, factors such as transport costs, tariffs and the size of the market will appear more important, even though in any one case their effects may be only dimly discerned.

Conclusion

The economic theory of the MNE is a lively area of academic enterprise, and further developments can be expected to bring the theory closer to the needs of the business historian. In the meantime, there is enormous scope for applying the current theory to data generated by business historians. Once it is appreciated that economic theory is concerned with general influences on the behaviour of the representative firm, rather than with all the influences at work on each individual firm, it should be possible for business historians to gain new insights from application of the theory.

Notes

1. The author is grateful to John Cantwell, Tony Corley, John Dunning, Leslie Hannah, Geoffrey Jones, Steve Nicholas and Alan Rugman for their comments on the earlier version; however, the author alone is responsible for the views expressed.
2. The theories are related, though by no means identical. They include Dunning's eclectic theory as set out in J.H. Dunning, 'Trade, Location of Economic Activity and the Multinational Enterprise: a Search for an Eclectic Approach' in B. Ohlin, P.O. Hesselborn and P.M. Wijkman (eds), *The International Allocation of Economic Activity* (London, 1977) and J.H. Dunning, *International Production and the Multinational Enterprise* (London, 1981); Rugman's generalised internalisation theory, in A.M. Rugman, *Inside the Multinationals: The Economics of Internal Markets* (London, 1981); and Kojima's macroeconomic theory of foreign direct investment, in K. Kojima, 'A Macroeconomic Approach to Foreign Direct Investment', *Hitotsubashi Journal of Economics* (1973), pp. 1–21 and K. Kojima, *Direct Foreign Investment: A Japanese Model of Multinational Business Operations* (London, 1978). Kojima's approach is rather different from the other two, and as it has already been critically examined by P.J. Buckley, 'A Macroeconomic versus International Business Approach to Direct Foreign Investment: A Comment on Professor Kojima's Interpretation', *Hitotsubashi Journal of Economics* (forthcoming), only

passing reference is made to it here. There is also the synthesis between internalisation theory and neoclassical location theory originally proposed by P.J. Buckley and M. Casson, *The Future of the Multinational Enterprise* (London, 1976) and elaborated in M. Casson, *Alternatives to the Multinational Enterprise* (London, 1979). Finally, Williamson appears to suggest that his markets and hierarchies approach, as outlined in O.E. Williamson, *Markets and Hierarchies: Analysis and Antitrust Implications* (New York, 1975), already embraces the MNE as a special case, see O.E. Williamson, 'The Modern Corporation: Origins, Evolution and Attributes', *Journal of Economic Literature* (1981), pp. 1537–68. This does not by any means exhaust the list of contending theories. However, there is sufficient variety in the theories already mentioned to bring out the most important issues involved.

There are now many reviews of the economic theory of the MNE: see particularly P.J. Buckley, 'A Critical Review of Theories of the Multinational Enterprise', *Aussenwirtschaft* (1981), pp. 70–87, and P.J. Buckley, 'New Theories of International Business: Some Unresolved Issues' in M. Casson (ed.), *The Growth of International Business* (London, 1983); A. Calvert, 'A Synthesis of Foreign Direct Investment Theories and Theories of the Multinational Firm', *Journal of International Business Studies* (1981), pp. 43–60; R.E. Caves, *Multinational Enterprise and Economic Analysis* (Cambridge, 1982); J.H. Dunning, *International Production and the Multinational Enterprise*; and J.-F. Hennart, *A Theory of Multinational Enterprise* (Ann Arbor, 1982). There is even a second-generation literature reviewing the reviewers: N.M. Kay, 'Multinational Enterprise: A Review Article', *Scottish Journal of Political Economy* (1983), pp. 304–12.

3. M. Wilkins, 'The Significance of Foreign Investment in US Development, 1879 to mid-1914', *University of Reading Discussion Papers in International Investment and Business Studies* (1982).

4. R.J. Gordon, 'Why US Wage and Employment Behaviour Differs from that in Britain and Japan', *Economic Journal* (1982), pp. 13–44.

5. S.H. Hymer, *The International Operations of National Firms: A Study of Direct Investment* (Cambridge, Mass., 1976); R.E. Caves, 'International Corporations: the Industrial Economics of Foreign Investment', *Economica* (1971), pp. 1–27.

6. R.Z. Aliber, 'A Theory of Direct Investment' in C.P. Kindleberger (ed.), *The International Corporation* (Cambridge, Mass., 1970).

7. S.H. Hymer, op. cit.; C.P. Kindleberger, *American Business Abroad* (New Haven, Conn., 1960).

8. S.P. Magee, 'Multinational Corporations, Industry Technology Cycle and Development', *Journal of World Trade Law* (1977), pp. 297–321.

9. P.J. Buckley and M. Casson, op. cit.

10. J.C. McManus, 'The Theory of the Multinational Firm' in G. Paquet (ed.), *The Multinational Firm and the Nation State* (Toronto, 1972); R.H. Coase, 'The Nature of the Firm', *Economica* (1937), pp. 386–405.

11. P.J. Buckley and M. Casson, op. cit.

12. J.H. Dunning, *International Production and the Multinational Enterprise*.

13. J.J. Boddewyn, 'Foreign Direct Divestment Theory: Is it the Reverse of FDI Theory?', *Weltwirtschaftliches Archiv* (1983), pp. 345–55.

14. R. Sugden, 'Why Transnational Corporations?', *Warwick Economic Research Papers*, no. 222 (1983).

15. A.M. Rugman, *Inside the Multinationals: The Economics of Internal Markets* (London, 1981); A.M. Rugman, 'Internalisation and Non-equity Forms of International Involvement' in A.M. Rugman (ed.), *New Theories of the Multinational Enterprise* (Beckenham, 1982).

16. This is suggested by E.J. Mishan, *Elements of Cost-Benefit Analysis*, 2nd edn (London, 1976), Chapter 16.

17. Y.-K. Ng, *Welfare Economics: Introduction and Development of Basic Concepts*, (London, 1983), p. 175.

18. A.M. Rugman, 'The Determinants of Intra-industry Direct Foreign Investment', *Dalhousie Discussion Papers in International Business*, no. 25 (1983); A.M. Rugman, 'Transfer Pricing in the Canadian Petroleum Industry', mimeo (1983).

19. M. Casson, 'Multinational Monopolies and International Cartels' in P.J. Buckley and M. Casson, *Theory of the Multinational Enterprise: Selected Papers* (London, 1984).

20. M. Casson, 'Foreword' in A.M. Rugman, *Inside the Multinationals: The Economics of Internal Markets* (London, 1981); S. Nicholas, 'The Theory of Multinational Enterprise as a Transactional Mode', Chapter 4, this volume.

21. K. Kojima, 'A Macroeconomic Approach to Foreign Direct Investment'; K. Kojima, *Direct Foreign Investment.*

22. M. Casson, *Alternatives to the Multinational Enterprise* (London, 1979).

23. R. Vernon, 'International Investment and International Trade in the Product Cycle', *Quarterly Journal of Economics* (1966), pp. 190–207.

24. M. Casson, 'The Theory of Foreign Direct Investment' in J. Black and J.H. Dunning (eds), *International Capital Movements* (London, 1982).

25. W.J. Baumol, 'Entrepreneurship in Economic Theory', *American Economic Review* (Papers and Proceedings), 58 (1968), pp. 64–71.

26. S. Hirsh, 'An International Trade and Investment Theory of the Firm', *Oxford Economic Papers* (1976), pp. 258–70; P.J. Buckley, 'New Theories of International Business: Some Unresolved Issues' in M. Casson (ed.), *The Growth of International Business* (London, 1983).

27. R.R. Nelson and S.G. Winter, *An Evolutionary Theory of Economic Change* (Cambridge, Mass., 1982).

28. F.H. Knight, *Risk, Uncertainty and Profit* (Chicago, 1921, 1971 ed. by G.J. Stigler).

29. M. Casson, *The Entrepreneur: An Economic Theory* (Oxford, 1980).

30. J.A. Schumpeter, *The Theory of Economic Development* (Cambridge, Mass., 1934).

31. H. Leibenstein, *General X-efficiency Theory and Economic Development* (New York, 1978); E.T. Penrose, *The Theory of the Growth of the Firm* (Oxford, 1959).

32. I.M. Kirzner, *Competition and Entrepreneurship* (Chicago, 1973); I.M. Kirzner, *Perception, Opportunity and Profit* (Chicago, 1979).

33. H.A. Simon, *Reason in Human Affairs* (Oxford, 1983).

34. J. von Neumann and O. Morgenstern, *Theory of Games and Economic Behaviour* (Princeton, NJ, 1944).

35. F. Redlich, 'The Military Enterpriser: A Neglected Area of Research', *Explorations in Entrepreneurial History* (1956), pp. 252–6.

36. M. Casson, 'Entrepreneurship and Foreign Direct Investment' in P.J. Buckley and M. Casson, *Economic Theory of the Multinational Enterprise: Selected Papers* (London, 1985).

37. O.E. Williamson, 'The Modern Corporation: Origins, Evolution and Attributes', *Journal of Economic Literature* (1981), pp. 1537–68.

38. J.J. Servan-Schreiber, *The American Challenge* (New York, 1968); R. Vernon, *Sovereignty at Bay: The Multinational Spread of US Enterprises* (New York, 1971).

39. A.O. Krueger, 'The Political Economy of the Rent-seeking Society', *American Economic Review* (1974), pp. 291–303.

40. D.C. Mueller, *Public Choice* (Cambridge, 1979).

41. A. Teichova, 'Outline of Certain Research Results concerning Multinationals in Interwar East-Central Europe', paper presented to the Florence Conference on Multinationals: Theory and History, 19–21 September 1983.

42. M.D. Intriligator, *Econometric Models, Techniques and Applications* (Amsterdam, 1978).

4 The Theory of Multinational Enterprise as a Transactional Mode

Stephen Nicholas

Transactional Model of MNE

The transactional model of the multinational enterprise (MNE) holds that international firms arise to internalise transaction costs in arm's-length markets.[1] Transaction costs arise when arm's-length markets fail to value and protect quasi-rents from firm-specific advantages in technology, management skills, product differentiation and brand name.[2] As a first step to making the internalisation concept operational, it is important to distinguish between the reasons firms transact abroad and the mode (contractual or institutional form) of transacting.[3] Firms transact abroad to transfer property rights in goods and to gain quasi-rents from firm-specific assets, most importantly knowledge related to technology. However, firm-specific advantages which allow firms to transact abroad do not explain the *form* of overseas involvement. This was immediately apparent in the cross-sectional statistical studies of US and UK MNEs where firm-specific advantage variables failed to differentiate between exports or foreign production as alternative choices of overseas activity.[4] Recognising the problem from a theoretical viewpoint, John Dunning has argued that 'without the incentive to internalise the production and/or sale of technology, foreign investment in technology-based industries would give way to licensing agreements and/or to the outright sale of knowledge on a contractual basis'.[5] In short, the form of international involvement depends on transaction costs. Transaction costs in arm's-length markets are attenuated by internal administrative markets in hierarchical firms. In his classic 1937 article on the nature of domestic firms, Coase gave the rule for internalisation: given transaction costs, firms would exist and 'tend to expand until the cost of organising an extra transaction within the firm becomes equal to the cost of carrying out the same transaction by means of an exchange in the open market'.[6] In the transactional model of the MNE, mode form is a choice between markets and hierarchy.

However, the market-hierarchy internalisation approach is a static concept. It fails to explain the transition from one mode (internal or external) to the other.[7] Further, the market-hierarchy dichotomy is too narrow. Firms are not islands of planned coordination in a sea of market relations.[8] Recent work on comparative institutional arrangements distinguishes discrete contractual forms, including markets, intermediate modes (contracts, franchises, licences, agents) and hierarchical firms, which attenuate transaction costs. This view has been endorsed by Oliver Williamson who analysed transaction costs in terms of 'the comparative costs of planning, adopting and monitoring task completion under alternative governance structures—whereby governance structure I have reference to the explicit or implicit contractual framework within which a transaction is located (markets, firms and mixed modes—e.g. franchising—included)'.[9]

Stages in Foreign Involvement

One of the major contributions of economic historians to the evolution of MNEs has been to emphasise alternative modes as stages in overseas involvement. For American MNEs, Wilkins discovered that American firms first exported, next employed the agency system, and then made a foreign direct investment in sales branches followed by a foreign direct investment in production.[10] In a study of 119 British MNEs before 1939, 70 per cent of the firms had overseas travellers and 99 per cent entered into agency contracts before making an initial foreign direct investment in a sales branch.[11] In almost all cases, overseas production by British manufacturing MNEs was preceded by sales subsidiaries. Eight case studies of European MNEs in the US before 1914 by Buckley and Roberts revealed a similar pattern of agents preceding sales subsidiaries and sales branches preceding production.[12] In a study of Swedish MNEs, Jan Johansen and Jan-Erik Valhne found that firms expanded their international commitments in small steps rather than by making a single large foreign production investment.[13] Based on a sample of specialist steel, pulp and paper and engineering firms, the typical Swedish pattern was to start exporting to a country via an agent, later to establish a sales subsidiary and finally to start production in the host country.

Stages of international involvement can be linked with familiar forms of domestic transacting. In the home market, British MNEs employed networks of agents, warehouses, depots and branch offices which were copied and transferred to overseas markets.[14] For example, by 1895 Peak Frean, the biscuit maker, had depots in Bristol, Leeds, Cardiff, Liverpool, Newcastle and Edinburgh, each controlled by managers with two clerks and supporting teams of home travellers. Before 1920,

Alex Morton Sons and Co had established showrooms at Carlisle, London, Manchester, Birmingham, Newcastle and Glasgow, and offices in Manchester, London and Bradford, a practice followed by other textile firms including Lawthiam Drake and William Jones. Gourock Rope Company had warehouses in Liverpool and London by 1880 and in Lowestoft, Yarmouth, Plymouth and Hull by 1901. In the carpet industry, at least 18 provincial carpet firms had London sales offices and warehouses by 1840. The large carpet makers by the 1880s had warehouses in all the main provincial centres which acted as a base for the firm's travellers and agents. Lever in soap, Wall Paper Manufacturers, Borthwicks in meat, Schweppes in mineral water and fruit drinks, W. & T. Avery, makers of precision weighing machines, and Lister in farm appliances, all established branch depots, warehouses and offices. Before firms had warehouses and depots an agency system where goods were stocked and displayed was utilised. The agency system was widespread in the engineering, food, textiles, metal products and chemical industries before 1900 and used by firms such as Linen Thread Company, Peak Frean, Pilkington, Courtaulds and Reckitt.

The experience with domestic agents, depots and sales branches meant MNEs could transfer abroad unique knowledge about serving markets gained at home. Caves's argument that MNEs abroad opted for familiar forms of business decisions developed at home is reinforced by the evidence that the same modes and stages were employed by British MNEs in domestic and foreign markets.[15] The experience with marketing and distribution modes at home created a firm-specific asset which provided the MNE with an advantage over foreign firms. Marketing skills allowed low-technology, food, textile and consumer goods firms to rank as major British MNEs in the pre-1939 period.[16] Most of these firms contained no technology or research-and-development-based advantages required by the traditional explanation that MNEs internalised technical know-how.[17]

Dynamic Approach to Mode Transition

The emphasis on stages of overseas involvement focuses attention on the need for a dynamic model of alternative mode choice. A dynamic model must recognise that MNEs are multi-product firms where only the final stage of overseas activity involves multi-plants. In both the agency system and the sales branch stage the MNE is a single-plant firm. But the sales branch transfers goods and services through internal administrative markets while in the agency mode arm's-length markets are used. While both sales subsidiaries and production branches employ hierarchy, only in production branches is the MNE a multi-plant firm. The dynamic model must explain why the move to internal markets and multi-plant production occurs in different modes.

The primary variable determining mode choice is the frequency of transactions.[18] Discrete transactions which involve no prospect of future conduct, such as one-off sales or purchases, are mediated through the market and do not generate intermediate contractual modes. However, when transactions are recurrent, both intermediate modes, such as agents, licensing and franchising, and hierarchical sales and production branches are likely to arise. Generally, a wholly-owned sales subsidiary incurs higher fixed costs of transacting (that is, higher costs of establishing the subsidiary independent of the volume of sales) but a lower marginal cost associated with an extension of the volume of sales relative to agents or licensing.[19] Therefore, the more frequent the transactions, *ceteris paribus*, the more likely a mode of transacting will be chosen with a high fixed but low variable cost.

The nature of the product is a secondary variable determining mode choice through transaction-specific investments.[20] The MNE undertakes investment in specialised capital, brand name and product differentiation the return on which is dependent on the transaction mode chosen. For example, the return on an agricultural machinery firm's investment in brand name and goodwill depends on each agent or franchisee providing a particular level of demonstration, service and repair. Not only does the nature of the product require the MNE to make transaction-specific investments, but it also requires the mode in the host economy to invest in specialised capital. For example, the demonstration, servicing and repair of agricultural machinery requires investment in specialised tools and shops by the agent or franchisee. The final variable determining mode choice centres around plant- and product-specific scale economies. It is well known that MNE plants will be smaller and more plentiful the larger transport costs are relative to production costs and the less densely packed are the consumers of the firm's products.

Agency as an Intermediate Mode

The agency mode is a cooperative relationship formed through periodically negotiated long-term contracts which specify behaviour for repeat- or frequent-transaction situations.[21] The repeat transactions are between the product maker (the MNE as principal) and the agent as seller of the product. The contractual relationship derives from the asymmetry of information about markets and products by the parties. The principal has product-specific knowledge which is imperfectly transferred to the agent, while the agent has market-specific information including language, local customs and laws, and advantages of continuous market contact through residency in the host economy. Within the agent-principal relationship conflict develops over stockholding, promotional effort, discretionary pricing and 'reasonable' levels of service.

Contractual arrangements between agent and principal are essentially decision problems under uncertainty. The principal specifies a feasible set of selling actions by the agent. The more complete the principal's knowledge of the agent the lower the risks of entering into the agency contract and the lower the costs of monitoring the agency agreement. Risks and monitoring arise since agency agreements are subject to post-contractual opportunistic behaviour by agents. By the avoidance of contractual performance, agents cheat the principal, maximising their wealth at the expense of the principal. Agency performance is highly prone to shirking because contracts requiring the input of human energy into task completion, such as working a sales area, are particularly costly to meter and enforce.

The likelihood of agent opportunistic behaviour increases when the nature of the product requires transaction-specific investments. By reneging on contractual performance, agents can appropriate quasi-rents from the MNE specialised assets such as brand name, product differentiation, product quality, and stock on consignment to the agent. Besides costly monitoring of the agent, the MNE attenuates opportunism by employing various forms of agent bonding. Bonding involves idiosyncratic investments by the agent in physical capital, such as warehouses and shops, or human capital, such as product knowledge, which locks the agent into the contractual arrangement with the MNE.[22] When the pecuniary loss from idiosyncratic investment is large, the threat to withdraw business by the MNE deters agent opportunism.

Monitoring Costs and the Transition between Modes

Elsewhere I have discussed the transition from agencies to sales subsidiaries for British manufacturing MNEs.[23] Here the basic outline of the transition is briefly discussed and extended. Agency contracts specified rules for the selling and payment for goods. Every agency contract contained vague (and unenforceable) provisions requiring the agents to 'push the sale' of the principal's products. Such promises to behave non-opportunistically were supplemented with monitoring arrangements by the principal. Agents could sit back and wait for orders. The demand for the principal's products coming from transaction-specific investment in brand name, goodwill and product differentiation, created an appropriable rent that opportunistic agents could capture at the cost of rudimentary paperwork. To strengthen vague performance clauses and to ensure service quality agents were paid on commission and contracts contain specific input requirements covering the amount of travelling, advertising, and showing the agent was required to do. The input requirements were a form of bonding, involving investments by the agent, which locked the agent into the contractual relationship. To ensure a competent sales staff, principals required agents to invest in engineers or special salesmen with specific technical knowledge of the principal's product. To enforce the contract requirements, principals commonly shared the expense of a technical representative or salesman, particularly when knowledge of the product was concentrated in the principal. Many firms, particularly in engineering, provided their own technical salesman or mechanic who lived with the agent.

Perhaps the most important bonding and monitoring arrangement was the requirement that agents carry stock of the goods to be sold. Stocks ensured prompt delivery, and also served as advertising when displayed in offices and showrooms. Idiosyncratic investment in machines, offices, warehouses, and showrooms effectively locked the agent into the contract. Stocks for sale purchased by the agent, however, tended to be carried at less than the optimum level; while consignment goods, which earned the agent commission but remained the principal's property, tended to be overstocked. Therefore, provisions for consignments in the contract were supplemented by a range of monitoring mechanisms. Stocks were monitored by weekly, monthly, or half-yearly stocklists provided by the agents. Alternatively, agents might be required to send terms of each sale to the principal. The arrangements were given teeth by rights to inspect the stock, to inspect the agent's books on demand, and to appoint the agent's bookkeeper or storekeeper. The most effective mechanism for monitoring sales behaviour and stock levels was to send directors or the firm's travelling representatives to check agents. Frequent trips by directors and travelling representatives were undertaken by every firm with an agency network.

The requirement to carry stock meant that the agent was utilised as part of the MNE's inventory system. MNEs insure against running out of stock, which lost customers and sales, by using agents as warehouses. The inventory management problem involved optimising plant production for stock replenishment, plant production for sales and safety stock kept with agents. Since agents tended to overstock, inventory management was not efficient. The magnitude of the costs depended on both the costs of holding excessive inventories and costs of suboptimal plant utilisation. Stocking abroad was considerable; in 1929 the agricultural machinery firm Fowler's had stocks valued at

£86,805 with their agents.

The second major area open to opportunism was the payments system. Of course, stock monitoring and the right to inspect the books also allowed the principal to monitor payments. Such methods were superfluous when the principal insisted on direct execution of orders to customers. But the agent, through misinforming the principal, could collect a commission by passing orders of non-creditworthy customers. As a result, contracts specified that the agent should take every precaution to pass orders only of creditworthy customers, or to advice the principal whether credit should be given. Peak Frean, the London biscuit firm, required the agent to share the loss from customers' bad debts. Contracts explicitly allowed principals to refuse orders or to make the final approval of orders. Despite such safeguards bad debts were common. One arrangement to avoid bad debts was the requirement that agents pay by bill of exchange or letters of credit drawn on a London or European merchant house. Principals also encouraged payment through charging interest on outstanding payments and offering a discount—usually 2 or 3 per cent—for cash within one to three months of the sale.

Agency costs, then, can be classified into contract specification costs, monitoring costs, costs attached to lost rent through opportunism and inventory costs due to overstocking. Agency costs increase with the frequency of transactions and the amount of transaction-specific investments. Increasing the frequency of transactions increases the opportunity for agent opportunism and increases the costs of monitoring. The greater the principal's transaction-specific investments, the larger the rent an opportunistic agent can appropriate. Vertical integration reduces monitoring costs, especially when appropriable quasi-rents from transaction specific investments are large. A sales branch replaces the agency system. However, vertical integration involves a switch to another mode making the costs of the alternative modes an explicit variable in the transition. Unfortunately, business historians have been slow to investigate the administration and fixed costs of hierarchical sales subsidiaries.

Costs of Sales Branches and the Transition Between Modes

Generally, fixed costs of a sales branch are much greater than the fixed costs involved in an agency system, but the costs of extending sales is less. Therefore, there has to be some mimimum frequency of transactions before a sales subsidiary is established. For example, the agricultural machinery firm of Ransomes calculated a £10,000 a year trade would be required before a Paris branch could compete with an agency system turning over £2000 a year. The relative total costs of an

Figure 4.1: *Mode Switch Points*

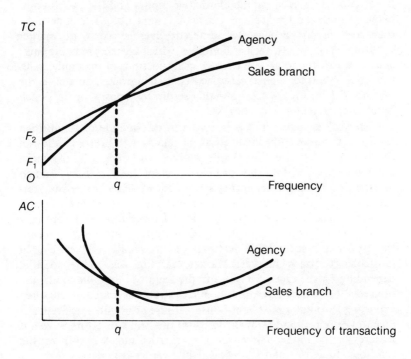

Figure 4.2: *Mode set-up costs*

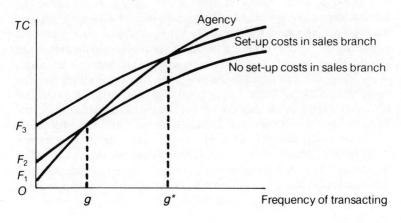

71

agency and sales system are shown in Figures 4.1. OF_1 and OF_2 are the fixed costs of establishing the alternative modes and the switch point between modes occurs at some transaction frequency q. The slope of the total-cost functions indicates different average costs of market servicing. Set-up costs, such as buildings, which are incurred only once, shift upwards the total- and average-cost functions of the mode. Sales branches involved higher set-up costs than agencies, therefore the distance F_1F_2 in Figure 4.2 shows that set-up costs postpone the switch point to transaction frequency g.

Historical evidence indicates that vertical integration by British MNEs not infrequently involved agent takeover.[24] Takeover allowed the MNE to capture the agent's market knowledge. In the more common case where the principal establishes a sales branch independent of the former agency system, the MNE had gained market-specific knowledge through the contractual agency system. Weekly and monthly stock and sales reports, reports from the firm's technicians resident with the agent and visits by representatives and directors meant the principal accumulated a stock of knowledge on servicing a particular overseas market. Market learning was mode specific, depending on the type of mode and the length of time the mode was utilised.[25] For example, market familiarisation was less complete when exporting through a merchant house because sales and stock reports, inventory control and frequent visits by the firm's directors were not features of the mode. The effect of market learning was to pivot the total-cost functions and shift down the average-cost curves for sales branches allowing the hierarchical firm to replace agents at a lower transaction frequency such as $\bar{g}$ (see Figure 4.3).

Two further factors need to be considered: the costs of internal administration in the branch mode and the absence of a multi-plant investment decision. Work on internal administration has tended to emphasise cost savings of hierarchical firms over arm's-length markets, largely ignoring administration costs. Internal administration reduced opportunism. With no claim to profit streams, the sales branch is less susceptible to opportunism.[26] Further, internal performance and stock monitoring are more comprehensive and less costly than external monitoring. Internal monitors have more freedom and experience less resistance than outside monitors.[27] Second, the hierarchical domestic firm developed internal monitoring, auditing and cost procedures which were transferred to sales branches.[28] The foreign sales branch could be integrated into the domestic firm's structure in much the same way as sales branches and warehouses at home. Inventory management could be rationalised, reducing overstocking which was a feature of the agency mode. Finally, internal organisation allowed disputes and

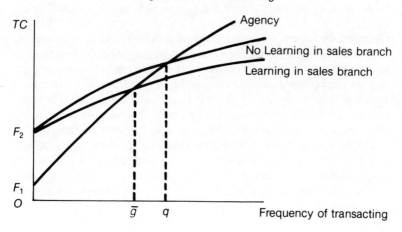
Figure 4.3: *Mode Learning*

conflicts to be mediated informally using the authority structure of the hierarchical firm.[29] These benefits need to be set alongside the costs of internal administration.

The costs of internal administration may explain sales branches which operate autonomously. The absence of internal organisational structure in the parent MNE conducive to the transfer and evaluation of information between branches allowed, by default, branch independence. At home, the holding-company form of control was widespread.[30] Holding-company structures only partially mediate internal administrative competition between branches. Further, in the holding structure only minimal policy and financial controls were exercised centrally. Not surprisingly some overseas sales companies such as Rowntree Mackintosh and Crosse & Blackwell were given a long and loose rein, delivering an annual report and only subject to an occasional visit from home.[31] In these cases, the flow of information may have declined after the establishment of a sales branch. How widespread autonomous branch transacting was remains an area for future research. However, in the inter-war years administrative costs arising from mergers were solved by British firms developing centralised and divisional structures with the head office auditing and assessing subsidiaries.[32] Many of these firms, including ICI, Reckitt, Fisons, Metal Box, and British Plateboard, were MNEs. Even without formal centralised and multi-divisional structures British MNEs developed *ad hoc* structures to monitor performance and assess information from abroad. In a sample of 119 British MNEs, 60 per cent had export departments usually controlled by one of the firm's directors while investing abroad.[33] Formal structures were developed by Holman Bros, Metal Box, Renold Chain, Marsh Bros, Baker Perkins Gourock, Beecham, Cadbury, BTH, and John Dickinson, to control sales subsidiaries. In other cases, the administrative structure created to coordinate a network of overseas travellers and receive sales and stock reports during the agency modes meant British parent firms had a structure adaptable to evaluating overseas subsidiaries. The sales branch mode provided valuable experience in administrative control and assessment and auditing procedures which were prerequisites to multi-plant production. Further, the sales branch allows assessment of a multi-plant investment decision. Aharoni emphasises the information and search costs in determining sites, labour and raw material inputs and government approval which are mediated as a sales branch gains market-specific knowledge.[34] The role of mode knowledge in the shift to multi-plant production is comparable with the role of knowledge in the shift from agents to sales branches.

Transition from Sales to Production Branch
The decision to invest in a sales branch does not involve a multi-plant investment decision. It is a decision to establish a hierarchical firm. The switch from a sales to a production branch is a multi-plant foreign investment decision. The importance of the sales branches as a source of information and experience has already been stressed. The frequency of transacting, impacting on the costs of transport, tariffs, and multiplant economies is the major factor determining the decision to make a direct foreign investment in a production subsidiary. Transport costs depend on commodity type, shipping medium, distance and whether transport costs can be passed on to customers. Since British MNEs typically produce in oligopolistic markets, price inflexibility limits their ability to pass on to customers higher transport costs. In the presence of transport costs, single-plant production will occur at less than minimum efficient size. The frequency of transactions (market size) is expanded only with increase in the distance the product travels. Markets are at first highly concentrated, then as a second step are extended into outlying areas. This implies that with increasing distance customers are less densely packed. With rising transport costs due to the increasing distances and declining customer density plants operated will be smaller and there will be more of them.[35] By relating transport cost to transaction frequency, we formalise the historical evidence that transport costs were a major factor determining foreign direct investment by British MNEs before 1939.

The multi-product nature of the MNE plays a crucial role in multi-plant decisions. Economies are embedded in the length of production runs for individual products. The production runs depend on the frequency of transacting. Large-lot production or long production runs for one product encourage learning-by-doing, reduce machines set-up and inventory costs, increase product quality control and save managerial costs involved in frequent shift between product runs.[36] Economic historians have neglected the multi-product characteristics of MNEs. While British MNEs supplied a large range of products to overseas markets, most revenue was accounted for by a few product lines. Production abroad for Coates, Dunlop, BOC, Gourock, Lever and Nobel occurred in small plants concentrating on a few products, offering product-specific scale economies.

Finally, the role of tariffs in multi-plant investment decisions can be related to the transaction frequency and to scale economies. Horst has analysed the impact of tariffs on multiplant investment decisions in terms of market size, real comparative advantages, scale economies in production and price constraints.[37] Depending on the mix of these factors tariffs can lead to production in two countries with exports, production in two countries with no exports, production in the foreign country with imports, continued home production with exports or home production and no exports. For British MNEs, tariff-induced multi-plant investment most frequently results in production in both markets and home exports continuing at a reduced level. Foreign plants were usually smaller than home plants and concentrated on a smaller range of products. From a sample of 119 British MNEs before 1939, over 30 per cent of the firms gave tariffs as a motive for overseas direct investment, ranking as a major factor in drink, vehicles, chemicals, textiles and metal goods.[38] However, much of this historical data is anecdotal, isolating tariffs from transaction frequencies, scale economies, comparative advantages and pricing policies. Recent statistical work hints that work in business archives to relate tariffs, scale economies, exports and comparative advantage might be fruitful. Horst and Swedenborg found exports and foreign investment related but industries characterised by capital-intensive production and plant scale economies exported more and invested less in small overseas markets.[39] Data does not exist for similar studies for pre-1939 MNEs. Further, the statistical studies are too aggregative and the results subject to such wide confidence intervals that the findings are suggestive rather than definitive. However, firm archives could be mined for sales figures (including local production and export) pricing lists and product mixes and combined with arguments for multi-plant production gleaned from letter books and board minutes. Such data could provide an important test for the role of tariffs in the multi-plant investment decisions.

75

Internal Administration and Investment Decisions

There also exists a haphazard or random factor in the foreign direct investment decision. When export markets are threatened or a competitor goes abroad, the MNE may react by making a multi-plant decision. This is borne out by the historical evidence that a foreign production decision to protect markets was a precipitating factor for pre-1939 British MNEs.[40] How the firm reacts to the random 'opportunity' for direct investment depends on transaction frequency, scale economies and market knowledge. It also depends on how the 'opportunity' is perceived in the hierarchy of the firm and the response by management. Aharoni emphasised the cumulative process of individual and organisational commitments which bring investment decisions to fruition.[41] Recently, Yves Doz has examined the relationship between decision processes and administrative coordination inside the MNE.[42] Administrative control mechanisms, such as data, information, and management control and conflict resolution procedures, determine the balance of power between branch and head office. Decisions to invest depend on the balances of power and the responsiveness of the administrative structure to change. Before the response to haphazard or random factors can be understood, the evolution of control and administration structures in the hierarchical sales branch requires study. As a first step, the link between levels of sales, branch autonomy and multi-plant investment decisions needs to be analysed. The development of internal sales branch management structures and their dependence on headquarters has been a surprisingly neglected area of historical enquiry. There is evidence that business historians, relying on board minutes and internal correspondence, can throw light on the negotiations and internal impetus for change within MNEs.[43] By tying random 'opportunities' to internal management and administration, the MNE will be seen as making an ordered response to historical accident. Second, management's response can be placed against the background of transaction frequencies, tariffs, and scale economies.

Conclusion

This paper has focused on the MNE both as a structure and a process. The structure is alternative mode forms (including exports, agencies, sales branches and multi-plant production) for mediating transactions internationally. By process, I mean the shifts between alternative mode forms. Internalisation theory in the transactional cost model is static. It provides no insight into the transition between alternative modes of transacting. I argue here that shifts between modes can be analysed in terms of the alternative costs of competing organisation forms. The frequency of transacting was seen as a major variable determining the costs of the alternative modes.

As transaction frequencies increase the costs of contrast specification, monitoring, opportunism and inventory control in the agency mode increase. Sales branches have higher fixed (and set-up) costs but a lower cost of extending sales than agencies. As transactions increase, a switch point between an agency and a branch depends on these relative costs. The switch point was also shown to depend on market knowledge gained by the MNE in the agency mode. The switch to a sales branch from an agency was a decision to replace arm's-length market contracting with a hierarchical firm. The shift from a sales branch to overseas production is a multi-plant investment decision. The multi-plant investment decision depends on the impact of transaction frequencies on transport costs, multi-product scale economies and tariffs. These factors explain why most foreign plants are smaller than home market plants and concentrate on fewer products. It was also argued that internal administrative organisation was an important variable in the multi-plant investment decision. Both the information gained in the sales branch and the flow and assessment of that information at head office were crucial to multi-plant investment decisions.

The model outlined above is a tentative first step towards a dynamic model of mode choice. Detailed quantitative testing on the size of multi-plants and the range of products produced in the host economy remains to be studied. Also the differences across industries, across host countries and across British, European and American parent MNEs awaits detailed study. More importantly, the internal administrative arrangements within branches and between branches and head office is an outstanding item on the research agenda. But it is these sorts of questions which business historians are best suited to answering. By tackling these issues, the business historian can make a major contribution to both the history and theory of the international firm.

Notes

1. M. Casson, *Alternative to the Multinational Enterprise* (London, 1979); P. Buckley and M. Casson, *The Future of the Multinational Enterprise* (London, 1976); S. Magee, 'Multinational Corporation, the Industry Technology Cycles and Development', *Journal of World Trade Law* (July/August 1977), pp. 297–321; J.C. McManus, 'The Costs of Alternative Economic Organisations', 8 (1975), pp. 335–50; A.M. Rugman, 'Internalization as a General Theory of Foreign Direct Investment', *Weltwirtschaftliches Archiv*, 116 (1980), pp. 365–79; A.M. Rugman, *Inside the Multinationals: The Economics of Internal Markets* (London, 1981).
2. This approach falls within the appropriability model which emphasises the ability of firms to capture the pecuniary value to society of firm-created public good

knowledge. See S. Magee, 'Technology and the Appropriability Theory of the Multinational Corporation' in J. Bhagwati (ed.), *The New International Economic Order* (Cambridge, Mass., 1976), pp. 317–40.

3. A.K. Calvet, 'A Synthesis of Foreign Direct Investment Theories of the Multinational Firm', *Journal of International Business Studies*, 12 (1981), pp. 43–57.

4. T. Horst, 'Firm and Industry Determinants of the Decision to Invest Abroad: An Empirical Study', *Review of Economics and Statistics*, 54 (1972), pp. 258–66.

5. J. Dunning, *International Production and the Multinational Enterprise* (London, 1981), p. 34.

6. R. Coase, 'The Nature of the Firm', *Economica* 4 (1937), p. 395.

7. A.K. Calvet, op. cit., p. 56; S. Nicholas, 'Towards a Dynamic Model of the Form of International Involvement' (unpublished mimeo, 1983), pp. 1–2.

8. G.B. Richardson, 'The Organisation of Industry', *Economic Journal*, 82 (1972), pp. 883–96.

9. O.E. Williamson, 'The Modern Corporation: Origins, Evolution and Attributes', *Journal of Economic Literature*, XX (1981), p. 1544.

10. M. Wilkins, *The Emergence of Multinational Enterprise* (Cambridge, Mass., 1970), pp. 207–13; M. Wilkins, *The Maturing of Multinational Enterprise* (Cambridge, Mass., 1979), pp. 417–22, 432–7.

11. S. Nicholas, 'British Multinational Investment Before 1939', *Journal of European Economic History* 11 (1982), pp. 620–1.

12. P. Buckley and B. Roberts, *European Direct Investment in the U.S.A. Before World War I* (London, 1982), pp. 44, 67, 87, 91–2.

13. J. Johansen and J.-E. Vahlne, 'The Internationalisation Process of the Firm: A Model of Knowledge Development and Increasing Foreign Market Commitments', *Journal of International Business Studies*, 8 (1977), pp. 23–32.

14. D. Hutchinson and S. Nicholas, 'Theory in Business History: New Approaches to Institutional Change' (unpublished mimeo, 1983).

15. R.E. Caves, 'International Corporations: the Industrial Economics of Foreign Investment', *Economica*, 28 (1971), p. 178.

16. For the pre-1939 period, 12 per cent of all British MNEs were in food; 10 per cent in textiles and 13 per cent in other low-technology consumer goods. See Nicholas, 'British Multinational Investment', p. 613.

17. These British firms seem to have similar characteristics to certain low-technology Japanese MNEs which have been analysed as 'deviant' MNEs by T. Ozawa, 'International Investment and Industrial Structure: New Theoretical Implications from the Japanese Experience', *Oxford Economic Papers* 31 (1979), pp. 72–92. The treatment of British low-technology MNEs within the transaction cost-appropriability model as non-deviant firms and thus as non-deviant forms of overseas involvement follows M. Casson, 'Transaction Costs and the Theory of the Multinational Enterprise' in A.M. Rugman (ed.), *New Theories of the Multinational Enterprise* (London, 1982), pp. 24–43.

18. O.E. Williamson, *Markets and Hierarchies: Analysis and Antitrust Implications* (New York, 1975); O.E. Williamson, 'Transaction-Cost Economics: The Governance of Contractual Relations', *Journal of Law and Economics* 22 (1979), pp. 238–45; B. Klein, R. Crawford and A. Alchean, 'Vertical Integration, Appropriable Rents and the Competitive Contracting Process', *Journal of Law and Economics*, 21 (1978), pp. 297–326.

19. P. Buckley and M. Casson, 'The Optimal Timing of a Foreign Investment', *Economic Journal*, 91 (1981), pp. 75–86.

20. B. Klein et al. 'Vertical Integration', pp. 298–302; B. Klein, 'Transaction Cost Determinants of "Unfair" Contractual Arrangements', *American Economic Review*, 70 (1980), pp. 356–7; B. Klein and K. Zeffler, 'The Role of Market Forces in Assuring Contractual Performances', *Journal of Political Economy* 89 (1981), pp. 615–7; O.E. Williamson, 'Transaction-Cost Economics', p. 234.

21. M.C. Jensen and W.H. Meckling, 'Theory of the Firm: Managerial Behaviour, Agency Costs and Ownership Structure', *Journal of Financial Economics*, 3 (1976), pp. 305–11; S. Ross, 'The Economic Theory of Agency: The Principal's Problem', *American Economic Review* 63 (1973), pp. 134–49.
22. O.E. Williamson, 'Transaction-Cost Economics', pp. 238–45; B. Klein, 'Transaction Cost Determinants', pp. 358–9.
23. S. Nicholas, 'Agency Contracts, Institutional Modes, and the Transition to Foreign Direct Investment by British Manufacturing Multinationals Before 1935', *Journal of Economic History*, 43 (1983), pp. 675–86.
24. Ibid., p. 684.
25. This contrasts with the argument that familiarisation applies to the market in general and not to each specific mode. See Buckley and Casson, 'Optimal Timing', p. 81. In our case, knowledge depends on both the time in the market and the type of mode.
26. Williamson, *Markets and Hierarchies*, p. 29.
27. Ibid.
28. A.D. Chandler, *The Visible Hand* (Cambridge, Mass., 1977), pp. 385–6.
29. Williamson, *Markets and Hierarchies*, pp. 29–30.
30. L. Hannah, *The Rise of the Corporate Economy* (London, 1971), pp. 97–8.
31. D. Barron, 'The Development and Organisation of Rowntree Mackintosh Ltd.' (LSE Seminar on the Problems in Industrial Administration, 449, 1975), Business History Unit Archives, p. 2.
32. Hannah, *Corporate Economy*, pp. 87–96, 98–100.
33. Nicholas, 'British Multinational Investment', p. 621.
34. Y. Aharoni, *The Foreign Investment Decision Process* (Boston, 1966), Chapters 4, 5.
35. F.M. Scherer, *The Economics of Multi-Plant Operations* (Cambridge, Mass., 1975), p. 24.
36. Ibid., pp. 54–5.
37. T. Horst, 'The Theory of the Multinational Firm: Optimal Behaviour Under Different Tariff and Tax Rules', *Journal of Political Economy*, 79 (1971), pp. 1059–72; T. Horst, 'Firm and Industry Determinants of the Decision to Invest Abroad: An Empirical Study', *Review of Economics and Statistics*, 54 (1972), pp. 258–66; T. Horst, 'The Simple Analytics of Multinational Firm Behaviour' in M.B. Connolly and A.K. Swobada (eds), *International Trade and Money* (London, 1973), pp. 72–84.
38. Nicholas, 'British Multinational Investment', pp. 616–17.
39. Horst, 'Simple Analytics', pp. 72–84; B. Swedenborg, *The Multinational Operations of Swedish Firms* (Stockholm, 1979).
40. Nicholas, 'British Multinational Investment', p. 616.
41. Aharoni, *Foreign Investment Decision Process*, p. 123.
42. Y. Doz, 'Strategic Management in Multinational Companies', *Sloan Management Review*, 22 (1980), pp. 27–45; Y. Doz and C.K. Prahalad, 'Headquarters Influence and Strategic Control on MNCs', *Sloan Management Review*, 22 (1981), pp. 15–29.
43. M. Wilkins and F. Hill, *American Business Abroad: Ford on Six Continents* (Detroit, 1964), Chapter 8.

5 Defining a Firm: History and Theory

Mira Wilkins

Introduction

As a business historian, I thought I knew what a firm was. If I started with the records of a company, I could see its growth and boundaries. Business history records defined for me an emerging operating entity, which had relationships with many otherwise independent firms. On occasion, when I studied the history of American business in its international dimensions, I puzzled over the limits of the firm. Most of the time, it seemed clear to me that I began with a US-headquartered company and could see it spreading its operations across borders—seeking new markets and new sources of supply and accordingly making foreign investments. I viewed the evolution of the multinational enterprise (MNE) as part of a process, whereby a domestic firm expanded into foreign investments. Theory helped in defining the advantages held by those enterprises that moved internationally, explaining why a firm in electrical equipment did and one in furniture did not invest in other countries. Recently, however, my research on foreign investment in the United States has plunged me into thinking about different theoretical considerations and into facing an immense and confusing secondary literature. Suddenly, I had a new problem, which was how to define the 'firm'.

The Problem

First, the theoretical issues. I have become interested in the transaction-cost and the market-hierarchy approach to business history.[1] This stimulating approach of Oliver Williamson has excited the attention of Alfred Chandler and others.[2] The theoretical questions posed are: When does a firm extend itself, and when does this extension stop? Why does one firm integrate vertically and another sell to agents or buy from independent suppliers?[3] What shapes the growth of and particularly the direction of the growth of a firm? When is the firm more efficient than the market? As I studied the history of multinational enterprise and considered such issues, obviously I had to define the limits of the firm. I had to decide what a firm is.

Second, the secondary literature issues. The more research I did on European investment in the United States, the more I faced works by economists on capital flows that ignored the firm, put it into a peripheral role, or took it for granted. Since I wanted to understand European investment in the United States and sought to do so in terms of what I already knew about the growth of multinational enterprise, I found that I was in trouble. Thus, I was back to the question of deciding what a firm is.[4]

Definition
I have no problem with a definition of the firm as a producer of goods and services, or as an allocator of resources.[5] Likewise, the firm as a nexus of implicit or explicit contracts or contracting relationships[6] seems legitimate. A domestic firm operates within one nation; a multinational firm extends over national borders to operate (to do more than export) under more than one national sovereign. The definitions of the firm by economists and historians are not confined to any single legal form. A firm can be a proprietorship, partnership, company, corporation, branch, 'enterprise', or a commonly controlled or administered cluster of any or all of the above. My difficulties related to the boundaries of the firm, the limits of what constitutes a firm, and particularly a multinational firm.[7]

Ownership and Control: The General Issues
As every business historian knows, the 'typical' pre-1850s firm combined ownership and control. The firm was one with its founder, owner, and manager. As business enterprise developed in the late nineteenth and twentieth centuries, there came to be a separation of ownership and control. Owners delegated to managers. An adminstrative organisation emerged. Overtime, relatively more people came to participate in administration, selling, research and development, and other such activities than in production *per se*.[8] There came to be not only top management, but middle management. The firm—in modern terms—has to be defined as separate from its owners.[9]

As a firm expanded over borders, over distance, there came very early to be a need for specialisation, delegation, and thus the separation of ownership and management. Indeed, unlike the typical domestic firm, already in the giant trading companies of the seventeenth century, the normal pattern was for the owners (shareholders) to remain in England, Holland or Sweden, and men were stationed overseas representing the owners.

Distance almost by definition meant delegation, since the individual owner could not be in two places at once.[10] In multinational enterprise, there came to be hierarchy not only in administrative, but in ownership delegation. The modern multinational 'enterprise' is in fact usually a cluster of owned firms (subsidiaries or affiliates) set up in foreign lands. In dealing with American multinational enterprise, I had had few problems. The firm was the owner; it controlled its overseas operations. Ownership and control was joined within the firm. I bypassed entirely the top ownership tier—that of the shareholders in the enterprise.

When I started to consider nineteenth and early-twentieth century European multinational enterprise, I needed to ask, when was ownership distinct from the firm and when was it one with the firm? What emerged was that 'owners' (individuals or firms) could be portfolio or direct investors or both, depending on *intention* and, more important, on the size of the investment relative to other investors in the same venture. If they were portfolio investors, ownership was separate from the firm. If they were 'direct' investors, it was one with the firm. Thus, individual owners had investments at home and abroad; some investments were large enough to exercise control or influence; these were direct investments. Likewise, firms had portfolio (purely financial) holdings *and* direct investments.[11] Domestic concepts of ownership and control were replicated internationally.

Ownership and Control: The Family
This brought me back to the family firm. The giant international trading companies of the seventeenth century were in a sense anomalies. Some (the Hudson's Bay Company, for example) persisted and changed their character. Modern MNEs, companies connected by rapid transmission of information between and among the associated companies in a grouping, are quite distinct from the early chartered companies.[12] Accordingly, as we look at the history of multinational enterprise, we must ask: did the family firm, which clearly was so important in European enterprise, extend itself abroad, and if so, how? By definition, a family firm joins ownership and control. In the late nineteenth and early twentieth century as the modern MNE began to take form, internationally brothers, sons, and relatives served to extend the family firm internationally—in trade, banking, *and* manufacturing.

The family was the binder, the 'cement' of an enterprise. Trust between members of the family linked separate businesses into one and lowered internal transaction costs. Families in trade shared confidences. The Lazard brothers, for example, in trade and banking set up distinct houses, but they acted in concert. Eberhard Faber, who made pencils in the United States from 1861, was in the same industry as his father had been, and his brothers were, in Germany. George Merck in the United States in the late nineteenth and early twentieth century established a manufacturing facility in the United States essentially separate from E. Merck in Germany, but the two businesses pooled profits, technology, product information, and marketing knowledge. Family loyalty unified these enterprises, making the actual legal, commercial, and financial structures (that varied from case to case) less relevant to our definition of the firm than the mode of carrying on business (the *implicit* internal contracts). We have to ask, were these family affairs a 'firm' or more than one? We have a cluster, at times a very loose cluster, but certainly a unity of behaviour. What are the boundaries of a firm?

As I tried to define the MNE in the context of the family, it seemed legitimate to see ownership and management as joined across borders through the extended family and appropriate to call these multinational enterprises. Only after the divorce between ownership and management has occurred does the firm become equated with the *operating* entity separate from the ownership tier.[13] Thus, the family that sent its sons and brothers around the world acted as a firm, providing an implicit unity of management—and we can, I believe, talk legitimately of the Lazard house, or the Speyers, Rothschilds, Fabers, Mercks or Barbours as firms, to cite some pre-World War I examples. The scale of business and the ties between the houses in different nations varied substantially; there was delegation; but in each case the association was real. The implicit internal contracts were present.

Now, I want to add a complication. The Coats family in Scotland was active in J. & P. Coats Ltd which had thread factories in many parts of the world, including the United States. No scholar would deny J. & P. Coats Ltd the designation of multinational enterprise. Individual members of the Coats family also controlled (or had controlling interests in) mining and timber companies in the United States. Was the Coats 'family' a firm? Could a family, as one of my colleagues (Jean-François Hennart) suggested, act as a modern-day conglomerate, allocating financial resources? How do we define the firm? We are back to the issues of separating ownership and control. Owners can be involved in various investments (linked only by financial planning); unlike the family that plans its financial interests, the modern-day conglomerate sets up a structure for coordination (however small the central office may be); ownership of the conglomerate (the unifier) is distinct from the institutional entity, which in turn has its network of owned and coordinated units that *are* part of the firm. In the case of the Coats family's multitude of investment projects, no institutional unity separate from the individual family members emerged to coalesce the mining and sewing thread investments. In short, to understand the firm, we have to see it as sometimes one with the family or individual investor

83

(the owner), but the unity of action must have some semblance of a separate 'operating' life. It did in the cases of the Faber and Merck families in Germany and the United States, and the Barbour family in Northern Ireland and the United States. It did not in the case of the Coats family in sewing thread and mining. Thus, we can see each of the personal Coats investments in the United States as a separate interest and define J. & P. Coats Ltd's investments in thread mills and marketing as that of *the* multinational firm.

Ownership and Control: Other International Investments
In the late nineteenth century, European capital flowed into US railroads. Investments were made by both individuals and non-railroad firms. The railroads were incorporated in the United States, had operating managements in the United States, and ownership was in the main divorced from management. To be sure, at times owners (domestic or foreign) had interests large enough to exercise control. When they could do so on a regular basis, there was a clear direct investment (the Erlangers in the Alabama Southern, for example). Normally, the firm (the railroad) and the ownership (foreign shareholders) were distinct.

Lord Strathcona had, for instance, giant investments in the Great Northern Railroad and in the Anglo-Persian Oil Company. As in an individual investor, nothing in his role *per se* united the American railroad with the British oil company. Thus, Lord Strathcona (like the Coats family in mining and sewing thread) did not act as a firm, much less a multinational one. Strathcona is, however, a foreign investor *in firms*. As an investor in the Great Northern Railroad (albeit a large one), he was separate and distinct from the Great Northern, which was the 'firm'.

The Free-standing Firm
My next problem involved the 'free-standing firm', incorporated in the United Kingdom, with a small head office there, but which did business in the United States.[14] S.J. Nicholas labelled such enterprises as 'little more than a brass nameplate someplace in the City'.[15] Were these 'multinational' firms? This form was not confined to business in the United States. The US Federal Trade Commission published a formidable list of British-organised or -controlled companies whose properties in 1914 were located outside the United Kingdom, United States, and Canada.[16] Students of British and continental European multinational enterprise must understand these ventures.[17] I am only going to discuss those that did business in the United States, since these are the ones I know something about, but the ideas I am presenting here

should have broader applications.

Typically, especially in the years 1865–1900, a promoter (American or British) would discover an 'opportunity' in the United States, a mine, a cattle ranch, or manufacturing plant. The promoter would establish a company incorporated in the United Kingdom to raise money in that country to buy the properties. The 'vendors' would be paid in cash raised in the United Kingdom and in the stock of the new British company. The sellers would sometimes be retained to manage the new venture; sometimes new management was installed. A board of directors was established in Britain, with a roster of important names (members of parliament, members of the nobility). Often on the board of directors there would be someone who knew something about mining, cattle raising, breweries, etc. The promoter of a brewery company, for example, would select important brewers in Britain to investigate the US facilities and sit on the board. This would reassure prospective investors. Sometimes (but not always) there was an American 'board' of management, or if a US subsidiary existed, even a US board of directors. The pinnacle board of directors was in Great Britain.[18]

After the initial flotation, the firm maintained a UK address; the British board of directors met (sometimes often: in one case, bi-weekly; sometimes seldom); a company secretary was appointed to monitor what was happening. In short, a home office in the United Kingdom existed, however minimal its functions. While the British home office did not market the output of the US mines, cattle ranches, flour mills, or breweries, it did intervene to varying degrees in financial and other decision-making. I asked whether I should treat such companies as multinational firms. They were not existing UK domestic businesses that extended themselves, nor were they family firms that became international. None the less, they were firms. They were the means by which capital was mobilised, *managed*, exported, and allocated. They had an ongoing institutionalised relationship with the capital that was transferred and provided a means of avoiding sending abroad 'disembodied' capital; by the latter, I mean exported capital not encased in any ongoing institutional 'hierarchy'. These firms are not the same as the capital flow from individuals or from firms into American railroads, where the railroad was distinct from its owners and where the capital input was not linked with any continuing operating relationship that extended beyond intermittent attempts to safeguard the investment.[19] These free-standing firms did cross borders; they did have ownership and the potential for control.

As theory pushed me to ask why a multinational firm is successful, I gained insights into why these free-standing multinational firms (at

85

least in the United States) were notoriously unsuccessful: They did not grow out of the needs of existing enterprises to become multinational. They did not build on existing UK operating entities that had knowledge, experience, technology, and goodwill; thus, they did not benefit from the economies of international management.

Their rationale for existence in the United Kingdom was to tap British capital markets. That was their 'advantage'. While some of the American mines may have gained from UK expertise, while some of the US cattle ranches certainly imported British quality cattle into the United States, while some of these firms had very knowledgeable part-time directors, in most instances (at least as far as the American case was concerned), the presence of a British suprastructure brought only additional cost. These free-standing firms were separate from their promoters (that was their origin, but not the rationale for their sustained existence)[20] and separate from their stockholders. I view them as a form of foreign direct investment (a type of MNE) that in the US setting often floundered because the firm was unable to capture the very advantages (experience, technology, goodwill) that provide the basis for effective and efficient multinational enterprise.

In this paper, I have been cautious to confine my generalised findings on the free-standing firm to the US case; yet, as noted, this type of firm was not simply an Anglo-American phenomenon. Did it function better in South Africa, Australia, India, Argentina, Persia? Was it identical in those contexts? More study is required. In less-developed countries, the extension of a known corporate and administrative structure to a locale where political uncertainty was high may well have provided benefits to offset the costs of such a form, whereas for the United States the introduction of a British legal corporate entity was usually redundant, that is, unnecessary for securing property rights and inadequate in and of itself for securing effective control. There is also evidence that in at least some of the non-US cases the British 'home office' rose to the opportunity, developed or acquired the needed expertise, bought the technology (and 'internalised' it within the firm), set up research and development establishments, and came to acquire an administrative organisation that was far more than one or a handful of individuals occupying an 'office.' In these cases, the firm succeeded, benefiting from the economies of international management.[21]

Why the Large Number of Free-standing Firms?

Why in Britain did all these free-standing firms exist while relatively fewer evolutions similar to those of the US multinational enterprise took place? Firstly, in the late nineteenth century, when this form began to proliferate, Britain was a major capital exporter. Available capital was an important British advantage. These firms captured, that is, institutionalised, the capital export process in a manner not unlike the other institutional forms that contemporaneously served that function (those typically associated with Lombard Street).

My second insight was similar. When I studied American business abroad, I found it emerged in the context of its special environment. The United States was the world's largest domestic market. Enterprises gained experience at home with business over distance. This was then reflected abroad. But what of Britain? In the late nineteenth century firms merged;[22] firms grew domestically; yet the experience in the domestic market with multi-plant interactions over long distance was, because of the geographical facts of life, less than that of US business. Perhaps the ubiquitous free-standing firms in international investment that appeared in Great Britain were an outcome of conditions at home. In the American case, firms were familiar with extending themselves domestically and they went over borders in a comparable fashion; in the British case, there was not the same experience with domestic extension and so the crossing over borders 'within an existing firm' was less of a natural process.

In passing, I might note the other side of the coin: as I have studied foreign business within the United States, I have been impressed with how many established multiplant operations and how rapidly. This was true of 'free-standing' companies (with their numerous breweries) as well as of the more typical British MNEs (English Sewing Cotton's American Thread Company, for instance, had from origin many plants in the United States). When I studied US business abroad, it was always, initially anyway, one plant per country; multiplant establishments in individual nations abroad came later in the sequence. The point is one with my discussion. American business was familiar with a large-scale market; markets in foreign countries were, relatively speaking, segmented. Foreign businesses in the United States knew (were prepared to cope with) a relatively limited domestic market and the geographical dimensions of the American market meant the requirement for many branches and several plants.

The Firm and its Special Relationships

A number of European companies developed in the United States special relationships that are hard to classify. Thus, for example, the Rothschilds sent August Belmont to the United States in 1837; he replaced two bankrupt former 'agents'. Belmont was not a member of the Rothschild family. Initially (but only initially), he appears to have been paid a salary. Yet he came to be 'the Rothschilds' in the United States and after his death in 1890 his son continued as the Rothschilds'

American representative. Was Belmont part of the firm? August Belmont & Co. had regular correspondence with N.M. Rothschild & Sons, London, and represented their interests. Yet the literature talks of no Rothschild house in the United States. How do we make the distinction?

Let us take the case of Pears' soap in America before World War I. The British soap company (before it was acquired by Lever Brothers) had for many years exported to the United States; it had an independent agent acting on its behalf. The agent proved extremely effective; Pears' soap was brilliantly advertised in the United States. The success of the agent seems to have militated against this company's integrating forward into direct investment in selling in the United States, although it seems to have owned a warehouse.

When I started to look at the market-hierarchy approach, I faced a problem. Belmont and Pears' agent would not have been part of 'hierarchy'—part of the Rothschild house or the Pears' firm—but the connections could hardly be described as arm's-length or market ones. Soon, however, I discovered that the market-hierarchy literature did not simply deal with the dichotomy between firm and market, but that Oliver Williamson had in 1979 specified an intermediate mode, which I found extremely helpful in looking at the nature of a firm in its foreign (as well as domestic) expansion.[23] I would like to argue that there are three *discrete* modes. The first mode is the firm that has limits, although they may be difficult to define. The second is the contract, by which I mean a whole range of special relationships that are not hierarchy, but are far from market. The third mode is the market, where there are arm's-length exchanges between parties to a transaction, that is, no special association can be identified between buyer and seller.[24]

What has long been evident is that firms as they expand internationally can simply export or purchase goods abroad; they can develop alliances or, alternatively, they can extend themselves, that is, make direct investments. We have long known that a firm often sells through an independent agent abroad, then in its largest markets replaces that agent with direct investment in marketing, and later makes further direct investments. The literature has discussed international licensing arrangements, managing agencies, management contracts. What theory has helped me to recognise is that most firms have all kinds of *regular, recurrent* involvements with 'outsiders' that are not part of the firm. This is true both domestically and internationally. I began to think about the nature of these close ties. There is the 'agent' who acts for the firm in specific capacities, who is not an employee. The Ford dealer uses the company name, has a recurring relationship, is dependent on the firm, but he is an 'independent dealer'. Many suppliers of giant enterprises rely for sales on their major (or only) customer; yet they are not part of that firm. Firms that are licensed to use a company's know-how, technology, patents, are often both distinct yet dependent. Division-of-market agreements between *otherwise independent entities* regularise connections without creating a firm.[25]

Hierarchical unity of administration (however loose) seems to define the firm.[26] This is what I see when I study business records. In the early years, the owner-manager are one; later there is dispersion of ownership and the divorce between ownership and control. The MNE owns firms abroad that are part and parcel of one business. The divorce occurs only at the top tier. A second mode must be the contract, which defines the rough edges of the firm, the special associations that most firms have that are not part of the firm, but are by no stretch of the imagination arm's-length. In this context, I am not using the word contract in legal terms of a written document. I see the contract as identifying a unique connection. Such a mode would cover the Rothschild dealings with August Belmont & Co. and those between Pears' and its agent. It encompasses franchising, licensing, long-term supply contracts, long-term leases, managing agency agreements, and cooperation within a cartel. None of these interactions involves an arm's-length relationship; all are recurrent; all reduce uncertainty by regularising arrangements; all lower transaction costs in this process; all imply a minimal control; none, in and of itself, requires ownership, although small minority ownership or financing frequently accompany 'contracts'.[27]

Some of these special interconnections that I have studied were over time transformed into internalisation (operations within the firm) and direct investment. Some direct investments have been abandoned for contract. The contract is an alternative to the firm. The market is not the only choice. In short, the contract defines the interactions of two or more otherwise independent firms.

This excursus helps in clarifying some of the dynamics of multinational enterprise. It aids in explaining the limits of a multinational firm as it expands over borders; there are alternatives; are they more or less efficient than internalisation? It helps to define activities that I never understood. For example, when I studied American business abroad, I found that American Sugar Refining Company had minority interests in Cuban sugar plantations, which were enough to keep the firm informed, to exercise some influence, but there was no evidence that control was imposed, nor that these plantations were managed by the sugar refining company. It would seem hard to call these plantation companies part of the sugar refining firm. The second mode, the 'contract', would seem appropriate. Likewise, when Rothschild interests acquired one-quarter of the stock of Anaconda, America's largest copper mine, and took over its European marketing, is it equally erroneous to call Anaconda part of the Rothschild multinational enterprise? In a sense it was, just as the sugar plantations were part of American Sugar Refining. In the case of Anaconda, the interest was sizeable, and operating responsibility (at least in European sales) was assumed. Business interests as distinct from purely financial considerations were at stake. Yet the records seem to indicate that Americans handled management and production decisions.[28] And what of Rio Tinto in Spain, to use a non-American example? Charles Harvey's history describes Rio Tinto as a firm.[29] Yet in this case the Rothschilds were large owners, concerned with the copper business, and represented on the management board. Should Rio Tinto be seen as part of the Rothschild firm?

When one deals with multinational enterprise, one often views firms within firms. There are, for example, separate business histories of Shell in the United States, Ford in England, Firestone in Liberia, and Sears, Roebuck in Mexico.[30] A multinational firm is a cluster, an administrative ordering, a hierarchy imposed in terms of decision-making. There is nothing in the definition of a firm that precludes delegation, or of the quasi-independence of affiliates. Accordingly, to understand the extent to which we can call Anaconda or Rio Tinto part of the Rothschild firm, we would have to examine the French and British Rothschild internal records. How did the Rothschilds as a firm see themselves in relation to Anaconda or Rio Tinto? Similar questions arise when we try to define the firm when considering, for instance, the connection between Burmah Oil and the Anglo-Persian Oil Company. R.W. Ferrier, the historian of Anglo-Persian Oil Company, would probably argue that APOC is the firm (and his history shows a unity of action). Yet T.A.B. Corley, a student of Burmah Oil, suggests—at least in the early years—the importance of the parent.[31]

Theory pushes us to try to define the MNE and its special relationships with outsiders. At the edge of the firm, the boundaries are at times hard to set. When does the firm expand by itself abroad? When does it join with others in its international business? What are its special links with others? Are they rooted in distinct transactions, such as marketing Anaconda's copper, or more intricate ones, such as those involving numerous types of joint venture, technology transfer, or agency interactions? Defining the firm becomes more difficult as we move to the perimeters of the firm and look at the firm's associations with other ones that are neither part of the MNE nor totally separate.

As we deal with the 'ragged edge of the firm', as we consider the intermediate mode, the contract, we obtain, I would like to suggest, a better sense of how a firm grows and its choices. Thus, we can take the case of the Dunlop tyre company in the United States. Its initial entry into the US market was export; its next stage was licensing; then apparently direct investment; it next sold its property rights to outsiders (and retained no interest). When it tried to resume its own corporate activity, when it saw the market potential, it sought once again to extend the firm.[32] The firm itself and its relationships with outsiders change over time.

Looking at the 'edges' of the firm helps us understand the connections between the MNE and the cartel. When does a firm absorb its rival? When does it divide world markets with an associated company, a competitor, a potential competitor? The concept of contract as a second mode helps answer those questions. Internalisation involves cost. As a firm expands, its internal transaction costs (its organisation costs) rise. Thus, the firm does not expand without limits. Yet, at least in a world that does not rigorously enforce anti-trust restrictions, the firm is not faced solely with the alternative of meeting competition. Returns on asset-specific investments can be increased through market divisions.[33] The cartel, 'the contract', regularises and stabilises relationships, eliminates uncertainty, and for the firm that finds the cost of extension of management too high a division-of-market agreement can simplify the task of internal management by imposing exogenous limits—that is, a firm's management need not worry about a competitor from abroad at home nor about expending resources to penetrate a market allocated to another firm.[34] The firm creates, through its accord, a high barrier to entry into its own market. Long-term supply contracts that at various periods of history have characterised purchases of raw materials and have substituted for backward integration are similarly amenable to this kind of analysis.[35]

In my study of foreign investment in the United States, as I consider direct investors I find many that fit comfortably into a model of multinational enterprise that views the firm expanding internationally (from a home base) with units producing goods and services. At the same time, I have pushed myself to define the limits of the expansion and the nature of the firm.

Conclusion

In conclusion, this paper has had three goals. First, I wanted to present some of the definitional problems I have faced in my studies of foreign investment in the United States. Secondly, I have sought to show how a theory pressed me to think about the limits of the firm—about hierarchy, contract, and market—and how this has served to clarify hitherto confusing data. And thirdly, I have shared with you some of the results I have reached in deciphering what is and what is not a multinational firm and, in the process, introduced my finding that there is a need to look at not only the firm itself, but the many special relationships that the firm enters into while doing business at home and abroad. I do not find a continuum between firm and market.[36] There is an institutional entity we can call a firm. It is conditioned by its home environment that affects how it operates abroad; likewise, circumstances in the host country shape its behaviour. This is true whether its foreign business is in the form of hierarchy, contract, or market. In 'contract', we see the limits of the firm. In this paper, I have not considered the easy cases of European multinational enterprise, for example, Courtaulds, Nestlé or Unilever.[37] Fundamentally, these can be analysed in the same manner I have considered the history of US multinational enterprise.[38] In this presentation, the difficult cases stimulated my interest and attention,[39] but in dealing with these, I find new light is cast on the timing, the contracts, and the degree of integration of the more familiar multinational corporations.[40] Clearly, many transactions of individual firms are neither intra-firm nor market ones. These are on the 'ragged edge' of the firm. The firm itself has to be, and can be, defined in administrative terms.

Notes

1. Although I treat them as one approach, clearly they can be considered as distinct and separate.
2. See O.E. Williamson, 'The Modern Corporation: Origins, Evolution, Attributes', *Journal of Economic Literature*, 19 (December 1981), pp. 1537–68; O.E. Williamson, 'Transaction Cost Economics: The Governance of Contractual Relations,' *Journal of Law and Economics*, 20 (October 1979), pp. 233–61; *Markets and Hierarchies* (New York, 1979); and O.E. Williamson, *Corporate Control and Business Behavior* (Englewood Cliffs, NJ, 1970). See also, O.E. Williamson, 'Microanalytic Business History' and A.D. Chandler, 'Evolution of the Large Industrial Corporation: An Evolution of the Transaction-Cost Approach', both in J. Atack (ed.), *Business and Economic History*, 2nd ser., vol XI (1982), pp. 106–34.
3. S. Nicholas, 'Agency Contracts, Institutional Modes, and the Transition to Foreign Direct Investment by British Manufacturing Multinationals before 1939', *Journal of Economic History*, 43 (September 1983), pp. 675–86, has an interesting discussion of firm and agency relationships, looking at transaction costs.
4. This had not been a matter of concern to me when I began to look at European business abroad, see, for example, M. Wilkins 'Multinational Enterprise', in H. Daems and H. van der Wee, *The Rise of Managerial Capitalism* (Louvain, 1974), pp. 213–35, and M. Wilkins, 'Modern European Economic History and the Multinationals', *Journal of European Economic History*, 6 (Winter 1977), pp. 575–95. The concern arose from my careful and full reading of the literature. Everything on European multinational enterprise did not fit neatly with what I knew about American business abroad.
5. Such standard definitions appear in introductory economics textbooks, for example, R.G. Lipsey and P. O. Steiner, *Economics*, 6th edn (New York, 1981).
6. A. Alchian and H. Demsetz, 'Production, Information Costs and Economic Organization', *American Economic Review*, 62 (December 1972), pp. 777–95.

7. I have benefited particularly and immensely from the theoretical work of economists especially R. Vernon, O.E. Williamson, R.E. Caves, K. Arrow, M. Casson, J. Dunning, C. Kindleberger, J.-F. Hennart and many others, some of whom are specifically cited in the footnotes of this article. To this list, I should add the useful N. Hood and S. Young, *The Economics of Multinational Enterprise* (London, 1979). I have gained rich insights from the research of historians too numerous to mention, but particularly A.D. Chandler.

8. This point is made explicitly in A.D. Chandler, 'Global Enterprises: Economic and National Characteristics', unpublished paper (1982). Chandler has made the point elsewhere as well.

9. M. Casson, 'Introduction' in M. Casson (ed.), *The Growth of International Business* (London, 1983), p. 21, makes the valid point that separation of ownership and control and the growth of modern management must be linked.

10. In some of the early trading operations, however, the merchant owned the ship and travelled on it to carry out transactions—so even with distance, ownership and control for a time were united. See J.G.B. Hutchins, *American Maritime Industries and Public Policy 1789–1914* (Cambridge, Mass 1941), p. 241.

11. R. Gilpin, *U.S. Power and the Multinational Corporation* (New York, 1975), p. 11, made the point that British investments in the nineteenth century were by individuals, banks, and through bond markets; American ones in the twentieth century were by corporations. The distinction is too simple. Corporations in the nineteenth century made foreign investments, both portfolio and direct investments.

12. See A.D. Chandler, *The Visible Hand* (Cambridge, Mass., 1977) on the importance of economies of speed to modern business organisation.

13. A.A. Berle and G.C. Means, *The Modern Corporation and Private Property* (New York, 1968).

14. T.C. Coram, 'The Role of British Capital in the Development of the United States c.1600–1914', unpublished Master's thesis (University of Southampton, 1967), called them 'syndicates'. J. Stopford, 'The Origins of British-based Multinational Manufacturing Enterprises', *Business History Review*, 48 (Autumn 1974), pp. 303–45, saw them as "expatriate" firms, a special type of portfolio investment.

15. S.J. Nicholas, 'British Multinational Investment Before 1939', *Journal of European Economic History*, 11 (Winter 1982), p. 606. He tells me that this designation was suggested to him by Leslie Hannah.

16. US Federal Trade Commission, *Report on Cooperation in American Export Trade* (Washington, 1916), II, pp. 537–74. Other sources for such firms are Burdett's *Official Stock Exchange Intelligence* and the Stock Exchange Year Books. G.H. Nash, *The Life of Herbert Hoover 1874–1914* (New York, 1983) shows the proliferation of 'free-standing' British companies world-wide that were linked through 'service sector' multinationals—e.g. a mining engineering firm.

17. Historians of French, German, Dutch, and possibly Swiss multinational enterprise need to look at this very same phenomenon—companies incorporated in France, Germany, Holland, Switzerland that carried on business in a single country abroad. A very interesting discussion of free-standing firms in the United Kingdom is in E.T. Powell, *The Mechanism of the City* (London, 1910), pp. 144–5.

18. On 'double' boards of directors, see C. Wilson, 'The Multinational in Historical Perspective', in K. Nakagawa (ed.), *Strategy and Structure of Big Business* (Tokyo, n.d. [1976?]), p. 269, and Powell, *The Mechanism of the City*, p. 145.

19. When there were railroad bond defaults, protective committees of shareholders (and bondholders) were established; they were shortlived and did not constitute ongoing relationships.

20. Thus I do not like to call these 'syndicate' investments.

21. A good example of this is provided in R.W. Ferrier, *The History of the British Petroleum Company* (Cambridge, 1982). In this context, we also need more study of

the managing agent and the mining-engineering firm as multinational enterprises, providing initially at least economies of international management to the free-standing firm.

22. See L. Hannah, 'Visible and Invisible Hands in Great Britain', in A.D. Chandler and H. Daems, *Managerial Hierarchies* (Cambridge, Mass, 1980), and other splendid works of Leslie Hannah, conveniently cited in *Managerial Hierarchies*, p. 72.

23. Williamson, 'Transaction Cost Economics'. When my article was virtually completed, I read G.B. Richardson, 'The Organization of Industry', *Economic Journal* 82 (September 1972), pp. 883–96, and discovered that over a decade ago, Richardson had been troubled by similar problems—that is the oversimplification involved in the dichotomy between the firm and market.

24. I have discussed these ideas at length with Jean-François Hennart. Likewise, much of my discussion is along the same lines suggested in Stephen Nicholas's paper in this volume. I wrote this before I had read his contribution. Richardson in 'Organization of Industry', p. 890, talks of direction (or consolidation), cooperation, and market, which is similar to what I refer to as hierarchy, contract, and market.

25. Geoffrey Jones's forthcoming case study (in *Business History Review*) of the history of the Gramophone Co. provides a splendid illustration of the special relationships between this British company and an American one.

26. I am using here—as before—the word 'hierarchy' as one with the concept of associations that exist within a firm. Within the firm there are people who report to others—that is, a hierarchy. My colleague Jean-François Hennart takes exception to this unified usage, and so, I suspect, would Mark Casson (see his 'Introduction' to Casson (ed.), *Growth of International Business*). Nonetheless, I am at present still convinced of the legitimacy of the usage.

27. Richardson, 'The Organization of Industry', specified four different types of inter-firm cooperation; while his categories differ from mine, he was arguing the identical point. His four were (1) backward vertical associations, long-term contracts and minority shareholdings; (2) subcontracting; (3) backward vertical associations that involve a retailer with its regular suppliers, but without formal contract; and (4) arrangements to pool or transfer technology.

28. My forthcoming study of foreign investment in the United States will give details and documentation.

29. C.E. Harvey, *The Rio Tinto Company* (Penzance, Cornwall, 1981).

30. K. Beaton, *Enterprise in Oil: A History of Shell in the United States* (New York, 1957); there are two unpublished histories of Ford in England, one by Norman St. John Stevas (1954) and one by C. Fawcett (1961); W.C. Taylor, *Firestone in Liberia* (Washington, DC, 1956); R. Wood and V. Keyser, *Sears Roebuck de México, S.A.* (Washington, DC, 1953).

31. T.A.B. Corley, 'Strategic Factors in the Growth of Multinational Enterprise: the Burmah Oil Company, 1886–1928', in Casson, *The Growth of International Business*, pp. 214–35.

32. Geoffrey Jones has been very helpful on Dunlop history. See G. Jones, 'The Growth and Performance of British Multinational Firms before 1939: The Case of Dunlop', *Economic History Review*, 2nd ser., 37 (Feb. 1984), pp. 35–53.

33. 'Asset-specificity' involves the degree of specialisation of physical or human assets. The term is Williamson's (see O.E. Williamson, 'The Modern Corporation'.). As John H. Dunning and many other students of multinational enterprise have long accepted, the firm must have some advantage in its move abroad. Dunning calls this advantage 'ownership specific advantage'. See, for example, J.H. Dunning, 'International Business in a Changing World Environment', *Banca Nazionale de Lavoro Quarterly Review* (December 1982), 351–2.

34. A superb discussion of various kinds of market division agreements is in W.J.

Reader, *Imperial Chemical Industries* (London; 1970). The problem with a cartel, however, is that it often pays for individual participants to cheat; thus, the cartel may not create the needed stability.

35. Jean-François Hennart has work in progress on this. See also D.J. Teece, 'Technological and Organizational Factors in the Theory of Multinational Enterprise', in Casson, *The Growth of International Business*, pp, 56–7, 60–61.

36. Richardson, 'Organization of Industry', p. 887, suggests the notion of continuum, but then backs away from this suggestion, p. 896.

37. Three excellent studies of multinational enterprise provide data on these particular firms. D.C. Coleman, *Courtaulds* (Oxford, 1969, 1982), II and III; J. Heer, *World Events, 1866–1966, The First Hundred Years of Nestlé* (Rivac, Switzerland, 1966); and C. Wilson, *Unilever*, 3 vols. (New York, 1968).

38. See M. Wilkins, *The Emergence of Multinational Enterprise: American Business Abroad from the Colonial Era to 1914* (Cambridge, Mass, 1970) and M. Wilkins, *The Maturing of Multinational Enterprise: American Business Abroad from 1914 to 1970* (Cambridge, Mass, 1974).

39. Thus, the companies considered by Stopford, 'The Origins' and L. Franko, *The European Multinationals* (Stamford, Conn., 1976) have not captured my attention in this paper, although I devote substantial attention to them in my forthcoming book on foreign investment in the United States.

40. For example, the timing of Samuel Courtauld & Co.'s entry into US business, Nestlé's relations with Borden, and Lever's association with Lamont, Corliss, all of which I will deal with in my forthcoming book.

6 The Performance of British Multinational Enterprise, 1890–1945[1]

Geoffrey Jones

Introduction

This essay attempts to correct a curious bias in the growing literature on the historical origins of British-based multinational enterprise. Despite the many aspects of contemporary multinational activity explored by economists, business historians have chosen to focus their attention rather narrowly on the chronology and dimensions of British multinational growth, and explanations of that growth.[2] In contrast, the issue of what happened to British foreign direct investments after they were made has hardly been discussed. This omission badly distorts our historical understanding of British multinationals, and there are many theoretical debates, especially concerning the allocative efficiency of multinationals, which would benefit from empirical data on performance.

It is hard to find such data. There are formidable methodological problems in measuring performance. One obvious measurement is the revenue earned by a parent company from its overseas subsidiary. However, the opportunities for the alteration of prices of intra-company transactions are such that published profits of subsidiaries bear little relationship to the true value to the investing company. Archivally-based company research can produce more reliable evidence on the subject, although this paper will suggest that the interpretation of this evidence is a difficult matter.

This paper focuses on three British manufacturing companies—Dunlop, Courtaulds and Cadbury Brothers—which possessed extensive multinational investments before 1945. These firms were chosen because, apart from the obvious matter of data availability, they represent to a certain extent a cross-section of British multinationals of the period. They manufactured products in three different industries, and between them invested in the principal areas of British manufacturing multinational activity—the United States, Western Europe and the British dominions.

Dunlop grew from a small firm established in 1889 to become the eighth largest British company, measured in terms of estimated market value of capital, in 1930. The firm was the largest tyre and rubber goods manufacturer in Britain in the inter-war years. Dunlop established manufacturing subsidiaries in France and Germany (1892), the United States (1893), Japan (1909), Canada (1927), Australia (1928), South Africa and Ireland (1935), and India (1936). Courtaulds evolved from a small domestic manufacturer of silk in the nineteenth century to become the dominant British manufacturer of rayon or artificial silk and the fourth largest British company in 1930. The firm established factories in the United States (1911), Canada and India (1925), Spain and Denmark (1926), Italy and France (1927) and Germany (1928). Cadbury Brothers also developed from a long-established nineteenth-century drinking chocolate manufacturer into Britain's largest chocolate and confectionery firm. In 1919 the firm merged with J.S. Fry & Son to form a holding company, the British Cocoa and Chocolate Company Ltd, which was the twenty-fourth largest British company in 1930. The firm established factories in Canada (1920), Australia (1922), New Zealand (1930), Ireland (1933) and South Africa (1937).[3]

Successes and Failures of British Multinational Investment

These three companies indicate that the most striking feature of British multinational performance before 1945 was its diversity. At one end of the spectrum there were the divestments and expropriations. Dunlop sold its American factory in 1898, and made a completely fresh investment after the First World War. During the Second World War the firm had its German, French and Japanese subsidiaries expropriated. Courtaulds was even more unlucky. By 1943 it remained in possession of only its small factory in Canada. The firm's Danish, Spanish and Indian factories were liquidated during the 1930s; the German, French and Italian factories fell into enemy hands; while the American subsidiary, the American Viscose Company, was forcibly sold in order to secure wartime lend lease from the United States. There were many other examples of divestment and expropriation, though there are no systematic data for the pre-1945 period, or indeed, the contemporary period. The subsidiary of the British firm of Marconi dominated the American wireless industry until 1919, when the investment was sold. During the 1920s, several British motor manufacturers established foreign factories, but subsequently liquidated the investments. Examples include Rolls Royce in the United States and William Morris in France. The 1930s brought many divestments, especially in Continental Europe. The armaments firm Vickers, for example, abandoned most of its foreign subsidiaries in this period. Overall, it seems likely that many early British multinational ventures were abandoned for one reason or another.

At the other extreme, there were brilliant success stories. Courtaulds in the United States is the classic example. In 1910 Courtaulds, which possessed the patent rights for artificial silk in Britain, acquired a similar monopoly in America and established a factory. Tariffs guaranteed the American Viscose Company's (AVC) large profits. By 1914 the gross return on subscribed capital exceeded 150 per cent. By 1920 AVC contributed 38 per cent of Courtaulds' gross cash income, and by 1930, 50 per cent. There were similar success stories in other sectors. In 1899 the Chairman of J. & P. Coats, a Scottish sewing-thread manufacturer which was the largest British manufacturing firm of that time, observed that 'by far the largest part of the company's profits were ... derived from shares in foreign manufacturing companies, and not from mills in the United Kingdom'.[5] J. & P. Coats made extensive foreign direct investments in the late nineteenth century. The firm practically monopolised the cotton-thread industries in Tsarist Russia and several other countries, and shared with the American subsidiary of English Sewing Cotton (with which it had trade agreements) most of the United States market. The rewards were evidently high.

It is difficult to make generalisations about the performance of British multinationals without very detailed archival research on individual firms. The interpretation of profit and revenue data in published company accounts presents many problems. There are serious data limitations in British company balance sheets, especially before 1929,[6] and even the accounting data 'behind' the balance sheets is difficult to use. Concepts of profit and rate of return varied widely and inter-firm comparisons can be misleading. Profit figures were naturally adjusted for tax-planning purposes. Courtaulds' French subsidiary declared a net trading loss of 81.4 million francs to the French fiscal authorities for the period 1927–37, but actually made a trading profit of 82.5 million francs. The transformation was achieved by charging very high depreciation rates which, as the firm's accountants observed in June 1937, led to 'considerable over-evaluation of true depreciation'.[7] The limited development of management accounting meant that most British multinationals before 1945 possessed only a crude knowledge of their costs and other internal financial information. The devaluations of currencies and exchange controls of the 1930s made calculations of costs, revenues and profits in international companies particularly complex. Imperfect managerial knowledge helps to explain many features of multinational behaviour in this period, but it does render measuring performance difficult.

However, if British firms before 1945 were often vague about their financial results, there is evidence that many were seriously concerned about the performance of overseas subsidiaries. Board minutes and other qualitative internal evidence at Cadbury, Courtaulds and Dunlop suggest that these firms considered the performance of many of their foreign subsidiaries inadequate, both in terms of revenue repatriated to the parent company and reinvested earnings (which provide a basis for future profits). When rates of return on capital invested were calculated they were often lower than those the firm earned in the United Kingdom, or even negative. None of Courtaulds' other multinational investments, for example, matched the success of AVC. The small continental European plants were continual money-losers. The Danish subsidiary had to be liquidated in 1933 with a net capital loss of £132,000. The Spanish company made constant losses in the 1930s, even before the Spanish Civil War, and finally had to be liquidated in 1943 with a loss of over 60 per cent of the original capital investment of £60,000. Courtaulds' French subsidiary was not the loss-maker portrayed to the French taxman, but the firm's management were very dissatisfied that gross profit earned by the subsidiary between 1927 and 1936 was only 3.4 per cent of capital investment.[8] Even AVC ran into difficulties during the 1930s when—in common with many American industrial companies in that depressed decade—profits declined, and in 1938 the subsidiary actually made a loss. ~~230443~~

The investments by Cadbury in Australia and Canada were long-term loss-makers. By 1930 Cadbury had earned no return from its £700,000 investment in Australia, and the subsidiary had made trading losses of £140,000 over the period. Between 1930 and 1933 further trading losses of £45,000 were accumulated, together with exchange losses of £250,000. In May 1933 the capital of the company was written down by £200,000. The firm was kept going by loans from its parent. By 1936, Cadbury were owed £533,000. Although the surviving data on the Canadian subsidiary is not so specific, there were also large losses for practically the whole inter-war period. In contrast, the performance of the Cadbury joint venture in New Zealand in the 1930s was quite different. The company experienced rising turnover and made profits of nearly £200,000 between 1930 and 1941, helping to balance the large losses in Australia and Canada.[9]

Data on the performance of the pre-1914 direct investments of Dunlop is scanty. The performance of American Dunlop before it was sold in 1898 is unknown. However, it is clear that the board of directors in London was deeply dissatisfied with the French and German subsidiaries, in which the British company had only minority shareholdings. Both the French and German companies remained confined to cycle-tyre production, and failed to follow the British company into the motor-tyre business. Their poor performance led Dunlop to buy out the local shareholders in France in 1909 and Germany in 1910 and make an attempt to improve the range and quality of these firms' products, but it proved a long task. In the five years between the acquisition of the French subsidiary by the British parent in 1909 and the outbreak of war, the firm accumulated trading losses of over £200,000.

In the inter-war years, Dunlop's largest investment was in the United States. By 1930 Dunlop had invested nearly £4 million (in loans and equity) in the American subsidiary. It was also the firm's most unsuccessful investment. The factory at Buffalo started production in 1923, at a time of growing excess capacity in the American tyre industry, and made almost constant losses until 1939. By 1936 Dunlop America had accumulated losses of over £4 million (14 per cent of the parent firm's estimated market value in 1930).

During the 1930s calculations made at Dunlop on the profitability of its overseas subsidiaries suggested that they detracted from, rather than added to, the overall profitability of the group. A calculation in 1936 estimated that £6.5 million, or 53 per cent of the total issued share capital of the Dunlop Rubber Company, was invested in 'unproductive' (defined as non-revenue-earning) foreign subsidiaries. This included £3.1 million in the American company, £500,000 in Canada, £620,000 in Australia, £450,000 in Germany, and £1.8 million in overseas plantations rendered unremunerative by the falling world rubber prices. An estimate was also made of the rate of return on capital invested in some of the foreign subsidiaries. In 1936 the United States and Canada yielded negative rates of return. Dunlop's French and German companies yielded small returns of 3.9 per cent and 4.6 per cent respectively, although exchange controls rendered it impossible to repatriate any profits from Germany. The Japanese company earned 9.2 per cent, but it was also subject to exchange controls. The new South African company delivered a handsome 12.6 per cent during its first year of operation. These returns on capital employed compared badly with those earned in Dunlop's home investments. In the early 1930s the return on capital employed at the Fort Dunlop tyre division in Birmingham was estimated at over 35 per cent.[10] However, the earnings of the foreign subsidiaries in the 1930s compare more favourably to Merret and Sykes's calculation of the achieved returns in real terms on share investments in the United Kingdom, which are estimated at 15.1 per cent for 1919–29 and 3.6 per cent for 1929–39.[11]

There does not exist a sufficient number of case studies to enable one to ascertain whether the poor revenue-earning performance of many of the Courtaulds, Cadbury and Dunlop subsidiaries was characteristic of

British multinational performance before 1945. The available evidence points to a very mixed performance. A recent study of the performance of the four large British clearing banks which established branches on the continent of Europe between 1919 and 1939 revealed that these investments also made considerable losses over long periods.[12] The foreign subsidiaries of the same parent often produced different results. The well-researched case of Lever Brothers, the soap manufacturer, illustrates this point. Before 1914 Lever had highly profitable factories in Belgium and Canada, and a heavy loss-maker in Australia. The American subsidiary was between the two extremes before the First World War, making small profits for most of the period except for losses in 1903 and 1912.[13] It would be quite misleading, however, to offer firm generalisations from such limited anecdotal evidence.

This evidence on performance, although interesting, is not generally surprising. Both theory and empirical evidence on contemporary multinationals has pointed to multinational investment as a risky strategy with considerable information costs. Average profits of new foreign subsidiaries might be expected to be low and one might also anticipate a high failure rate. There are, however, two surprising features in the three case studies. First, the immediate success of certain subsidiaries, notably the American Viscose Company, is noteworthy. Secondly, the long-term nature of the poor performance of certain subsidiaries, such as Dunlop in the United States and Cadbury in Australia, is surprising. While it would be anticipated that profit rates would be related to the age of a subsidiary, these subsidiaries were earning negative rates of return for nearly two decades.

The issue of success or failure is complicated, however, by a number of factors. The gains to a firm from a multinational investment, for example, are not limited to revenue repatriated to the parent company. There are, for example, potential 'feedback' gains from foreign subsidiaries, in such matters as technology, management structure, or marketing methods. The case studies indicate that a variety of gains of this nature were secured. An exchange of cost data between Dunlop's British factories and the new American factory in the early 1920s led to a drive for efficiency at the British factory.[14] Courtaulds' joint venture in Cologne with the German firm VGF pioneered a number of important technical advances in the 1930s, which were later transferred to the British company.[15] Courtaulds also benefited from its large shareholding in the Italian company Snia Viscosa. The Italian firm made considerable advances in staple fibre technology which were transferred to Courtaulds.[16]

It may be doubted whether similar gains were secured by many British manufacturing multinationals. Technological feedback is most likely to arise from investments in 'knowledge' productive industries in technologically advanced countries, yet many British multinationals before 1945 were in the consumer goods sector. The technology flows between Cadbury and its overseas subsidiaries in the inter-war years were all from the parent to the subsidiaries. This argument, however, cannot be pushed too far, as a very significant roll-call of British multinationals—such as Dunlop, Marconi and even Courtaulds—were not in the consumer goods sector. It does seem clear that, for whatever reason, licensing rather than foreign direct investment was a far more important source of technological gain to British companies before 1945. There are major examples in practically all industrial sectors. Imperial Chemical Industries gained considerably from its patent-sharing agreement with DuPont and IG Farben.[17] English Electric had a valuable licensing agreement with the American Westinghouse Corporation.[18] Metal Box was transformed during the 1930s through licensing a new technology from Continental Can of the United States.[19]

A further gain to a firm from foreign direct investment could arise from the procurement of raw materials at prices below those which would otherwise have to be paid. Many British manufacturing companies made supply-oriented investments abroad before 1914. Dunlop purchased rubber estates in Ceylon and Malaya after 1909. By 1917 Dunlop owned about 60 000 acres of rubber-growing land, all in the Malay Peninsular except for 2000 acres in Ceylon. Cadbury purchased two small estates in Trinidad in 1897 for growing cocoa beans. The most famous example before 1914, however, was Lever Brothers. In the first few years of the twentieth century land for copra production was acquired in the Solomons, and by 1913 over 30 000 acres were in cultivation. On a much larger scale, in 1911 Lever Brothers acquired large quantities of land in the Belgian Congo.[20]

The results of these investments were mixed. The Trinidad estates of Cadbury served a useful quality control function, but the vast majority of the firm's requirements were met by direct buying from independent producers in West Africa.[21] Lever's raw material ventures nearly ruined the firm after the First World War.[22] Dunlop's plantations were valuable before 1914 when the world market price for rubber was rising sharply, but a burden in 1919–23 and again in the 1930s when world prices fell.

A second area of difficulty in addressing the matter of success or failure concerns the need to take into account the effects of a firm's not undertaking foreign direct investment. The problem of estimating the alternative position has bedevilled attempts to measure the impact of multinationals. The Reddaway Report, which investigated the performance of selected British multinationals between 1955 and 1964, was widely criticised for its underlying assumption that all foreign investment was required to maintain markets, and that the export displacement effect was zero.[33] Although many British foreign direct investments do fit this category, there is no empirical evidence to suggest what proportion do so.

It is clear that many British multinational investments before 1945 were made because the companies faced the loss of markets through tariff or other barriers.[24] The foreign investments of Cadbury fit this model exactly. Before 1914 Cadbury had a profitable export trade, equivalent to 40 per cent of the value of the firm's domestic chocolate sales. The export trade was largely located in the so-called 'White' dominions. The decision to manufacture in Australia, Canada, New Zealand and Ireland was the direct result of the imposition of tariffs, while the decision to build a factory in South Africa was taken against the background of rumours about tariff increases as 'an insurance against the possibility of export being at a prohibitive cost'.[25]

However, many of the foreign investment decisions of Dunlop and Courtaulds were not due to tariffs. In the inter-war years in particular investment decisions were taken against the background of the oligopolistic interaction between large international firms. There are many examples where the most important influence on a firm's policies was the behaviour, or anticipated behaviour, of its competitors. Courtaulds' decision to manufacture in France was taken because of fears that the British government's decision to impose duties on imported artificial silk in 1925 would prompt their French competitors to jump the tariff barrier and manufacture in Britain. The French subsidiary, as Courtaulds' Chairman later put it, was intended 'not ... as a money-making venture, but rather as a piece of artillery in the enemy's country ... it was considered essential to have interests abroad in case foreign yarns became a nuisance in England'.[26] Similarly, Dunlop's loss-making French company was supported as a part of a strategy to combat the firm's French rival Michelin. How is success to be measured in these cases? Dunlop's determination to re-establish itself as a manufacturer in the United States during and after the First World War stemmed from a desire to overcome a major problem faced by the firm in British and third-country markets. The automobile makers of the world were dominated by American manufacturers such as Ford and General Motors. These companies almost invariably gave their first equipment tyre business to American tyre companies. Dunlop hoped that if it had an American manufacturing subsidiary this would encourage the American car-makers to fit Dunlop tyres on their exported cars. This would have given the company a reasonable chance of securing the replacement business when the original tyres ran out. A further reason for making or retaining foreign investments was prestige considerations. Although foreign investment policies are often rationalised by arguing that managements were aiming to secure long-term expected cash flows rather than short-term current profits, considerations about the importance of not losing corporate face seem to have carried great weight with boards of directors. This raises further problems for estimating 'alternative positions'.

An additional complication is that the 'alternative position' to export is not simply foreign direct investment. Both licensing and participation in some kind of international restrictive agreement were viable alternatives which British companies adopted before 1945.

Factors Influencing Performance
The factors which influenced the performance of British multinational investments before 1945 naturally varied according to each particular case. This section suggests three general areas of explanation.

The first factor was acts of God, or at least of inconsiderate men. Both World Wars saw the liquidation of British direct investments in continental Europe, although British losses were not as devastating as those of German multinationals. £55 million of British capital invested in Russian industry and banking was wiped out by the Bolshevik Revolution. Most of this sum was portfolio lending, but J. & P. Coats, Vickers and the Shell group were among the companies with direct investments that suffered heavy losses. The Second World War brought a much more dramatic fall in British overseas assets, including foreign direct investment.[27] Again, the Depression ruined markets for many products in continental Europe and the United States in the 1930s, while exchange controls in Germany and Japan prevented British parents from benefiting from profitable subsidiaries. The collapse of primary product prices in the inter-war years, with a trough between 1929 and 1932, inevitably caused difficult market conditions for Cadbury and other British firms in Australia and Canada. The joint-venture foreign subsidiaries which Vickers had established before 1914 in Japan, Italy, Canada and Spain were overwhelmed by a combination of excess capacity in the armaments industry in the 1920s and the rise of nationalism. Vickers' investments were sold or liquidated in all four countries, after years of earning unsatisfactory returns.[28] Firms with established investments had no short-term freedom to manoeuvre from loss-making situations in depressed markets or totalitarian countries, although a well-managed company could be expected to insure against risk through prudent action and diversification.

A second area of explanation focuses on market dominance and entry barriers. British multinational firms before 1939 required a very large 'advantage' for their products over local competitors to survive and prosper. Without such an advantage, or when the advantage was eroded by domestic competitors, early British multinationals faltered. The most successful of the investments surveyed in this paper, Courtaulds' AVC, had no domestic competition for its first nine years, and was largely protected from outside competition by high tariffs. Dunlop's French and German subsidiaries were established in the early 1890s when the British firm was in possession of a strong technological lead. They floundered as Michelin in France and the Continental Company in Germany developed. Dunlop America in the inter-war years was never able to take a significant market share against the American rubber companies with their well-established links with American car manufacturers. Cadbury in Australia in the 1920s could not make progress against the leading local firm of MacRobertsons, any more than Lever Brothers succeeded against Australian soap manufacturers in the 1900s. In contrast, the Cadbury venture in New Zealand in the 1930s, which was a fifty-fifty venture with a local confectionery manufacturer and which faced little competition, earned good returns.

A number of factors may have made early British multinationals particularly vulnerable to competition. First, many British multinationals seem to have been handicapped by unsatisfactory management structures. The slower development of managerial hierarchies in British firms compared to their American counterparts has been well documented.[29] Arguably, the unsophisticated management structures of many British firms had a particularly unfortunate impact on their foreign activities. Multinational business is typically more difficult to conduct than domestic business, as it requires a considerable extension of managerial control. Managers are also required to deal with a higher degree of uncertainty in foreign business and therefore greater skills are required. Deficient management structures meant that British firms were often not equipped to sustain and develop subsidiaries in foreign countries in the face of tough competition. Dunlop, for example, possessed an extremely *ad hoc* management structure dominated by the founding du Cros family. A more professional management was not installed until the early 1920s after an ill-considered scheme for re-entering the American market had nearly wrecked the company.[30] Again, although Cadbury had effectively taken over Fry in 1919, there was no merger between the two firms' organisations. Fry managed the Canadian subsidiary, and Cadbury ran the Australian subsidiary in the 1920s. Courtaulds' system of managing its foreign subsidiaries was also very *ad hoc*, and it was not until 1928 that a standing subcommittee of the board of directors was constituted to oversee foreign investments. British multinationals in the extractive sector, such as oil companies, would also appear to have been slow to develop appropriate management structures in the opening decades of the twentieth century.[31] Significantly, J. & P. Coats, one of the more constantly successful British multinationals, was one of the few British companies in the early 1900s that developed an efficient bureaucratic structure supported by efficient costing systems.[32] British manufacturing companies may have been as prolific as American ones in establishing factories in foreign countries before 1939, but they clearly lagged in developing appropriate multinational company structures.

Secondly, the kind of products manufactured by British multinationals may have made them vulnerable to competition. It is possible that British products such as Cadbury's chocolates or Dunlop tyres were easier for indigenous manufacturers to emulate than, say, American branded consumer goods such as Quaker Oats, or the research-intensive products offered by German chemical and engineering multinationals.

Thirdly, British multinationals may have suffered, at least in comparison with American firms, from a lack of competitive vigour. The willingness of British firms to establish foreign factories was not matched by a willingness to develop new international marketing skills. British firms were prone to emphasise the 'quality' of their products at the expense of price competitiveness in foreign markets. As a result the mass market often went by default to others. Again, many British firms had a preference for the negotiated business environment rather than the rough and tumble of the market. Often, especially in the inter-war years, the fortunes of a foreign subsidiary of a British company were preserved by the conclusion of a cartel or other restraint-of-trade agreement with competitors. The presence or absence of cartel agreements has been isolated as a major reason in explaining the regional differences in ICI's profitability.[33] It seems generally true that British firms prospered where market-sharing agreements were in existence and had difficulties where they were not. Dunlop America, for example, was unable to restrain the competition of its four large American rivals. Participation in cartels had its dangers. Both the French and the German subsidiaries of Courtaulds joined tight cartel agreements before they had established significant market shares, thereby trapping themselves with turnovers barely able to cover overheads. It was in order to avoid such a situation that Cadbury vetoed its local management's schemes to join a manufacturers' cartel in Australia in the early 1920s, although during the 1930s—and after market share if not profitability had risen—the firm did enter such schemes.[34]

If further research sustains the accusation of lack of competitive vigour, one line of explanation might be found in the home market of British companies. The British legal system was permissive of trade associations and agreements. The relatively small size of the British market compared to the American was also important. The American market was enormous and diverse, permitting American companies to try out propositions at home and learn the skills of management over a distance. The United States was also a country of cultural heterogeneity. American companies were obliged in their home market to come to terms with peoples of different tastes and standards. The comparative homogeneity of British society may have handicapped British firms when they did business abroad.[35]

A fourth factor which influenced the performance of British multinational investments was the appropriateness, or otherwise, of the strategy pursued by the company. Firms sometimes underwent a costly learning process. Dunlop's experience before 1920 was a classic example. The company opted to minimise capital commitments, and therefore expanded overseas by using a series of licensing agreements or by taking minority shareholdings. Minority shareholdings were taken in the French and German companies, while licensing agreements were concluded with companies in Canada (in 1894) and Australia (in 1899). The only wholly-owned subsidiary, in the United States, was sold in 1898, together with Dunlop's right to trade in the United States in tyres 'for use on cycles and other vehicles'.[36] The transformation in the market for tyres in the 1900s created severe problems for this strategy. The tyre business was transformed by the development of the motor car. Dunlop started manufacturing car tyres in Britain in 1900, but its power to influence the Dunlop companies elsewhere in the world to follow suit was strictly limited. As mentioned earlier, the French and German shareholders had eventually to be bought out. The Australian Dunlop Company, though it lacked the resources to make motor tyres, resisted the offer of the British company to lend technical assistance or to acquire a shareholding. Meanwhile, the 1898 agreement prevented Dunlop from exporting to the largest tyre market in the world and the centre of the car industry.

Other early British multinationals experienced hiccups with their initial foreign investment strategies. These were often caused by minority shareholdings or joint ventures. The Cadbury subsidiary in Australia included a minority shareholding by the small British confectionery firm of Pascalls. Problems were caused in the 1920s by the two sides' reluctance to share recipes, even though they were producing in the same factory. Vickers seems to have experienced very similar problems to Dunlop in exerting any managerial influence over foreign subsidiaries in which it had only a partial shareholding.[37] Sometimes it was the implementation of strategies which occasioned problems. Both Courtaulds and Cadbury appointed former selling agents to run several of their manufacturing subsidiaries, almost invariably with poor results. There is some evidence that British enterprises despatched poor-quality staff to foreign subsidiaries. Certain managements were visibly out of sympathy with their environments. Courtaulds in India in the 1930s was managed by a man who greatly disliked the growing nationalist movement. It was perhaps appropriate that the firm's reputation in India was ruined when he began marketing rayon saris which were so slippery that they were impossible to wear.

British managements appear to have faced particularly high knowledge disadvantages in continental Europe, or at least they have been prone to take particularly poor decisions in the region. Apparently sensible British companies, often successful in the dominions, took quite bizarre decisions once in France and Italy. During the inter-war years, for example, one of the British clearing banks that established a Continental branch network appointed as its Paris manager a man who loathed the French and who refused to communicate with them. Barclays Bank set up a branch in Rome in 1925 after its Chairman became convinced that the Bank could capture the Pope's bank account, and maintained the branch in the increasingly forlorn expectation of holy money until 1950.[38]

The poor performance of certain British firms on the Continent is not surprising, once one forgets the red herring of Britain's geographical proximity to the Continent. Ties of language, law and culture were much closer between Britain and the dominions than between Britain and the Continent. Indeed, British firms often considered factories in the dominions as an extension of their domestic operations rather than a 'foreign' investment. Unfamiliar environments imposed extra costs, and increased the risks of failure. The difficulties of the Continental subsidiaries of British multinationals such as Metal Box and Bowater since 1945 indicates the long-term persistence of such cultural factors.[39] Arguably, too, however, given their alleged lack of dynamism, British multinationals needed 'softer' markets—such as the dominions where they were often given a free hand under international cartel agreements—in order to prosper.

The degree of control exercised by the British parent over local subsidiaries often caused problems. Most firms before 1945 feared the consequences of allowing local managements autonomy. Lever Brothers, for example, was a mediocre performer in the American market before 1914 until it learned the art of delegation. The appointment of an American, Francis Countway, to run the subsidiary was soon followed by a surge in profitability. Again, Courtaulds' American subsidiary was kept under close scrutiny in the inter-war years by frequent visits by a British-based managing director. This policy contributed to the subsidiary's growing conservatism in the 1930s, and to the suspicion in which it was held in the United States which helped to lead to its virtual sequestration in 1941.[40] The subsidiaries of other British multinationals, such as Rolls-Royce in America, seem to have suffered to a similar degree from tight managerial control from Britain.[41] The management of Cadbury in the inter-war years was inclined towards encouraging local management autonomy, but the British parent was always torn between the pursuit of this desirable theoretical goal and the wish to intervene to prevent undesirable policies being followed.

Conclusion

This paper has argued that the returns from British multinational investment before 1945 were very diverse. The three company case studies included the highly successful American subsidiary of Courtaulds, but also many foreign subsidiaries which demonstrated low or negative returns over long periods. Despite the considerable methodological complexities in interpreting this evidence, it does seem to confirm that multinational investment was a risky strategy which often went wrong. Unfortunately it is impossible, given the current state of research, to establish whether British multinationals were more or less successful than those of other countries. An internationally comparative study of multinational performance before 1945 should be high on any agenda for future research. There is already sufficient evidence, however, to stress that British firms were not alone in experiencing multinational failures. Pre-World War I American firms such as George Westinghouse and Diamond Match had dismal international careers, as did Coca Cola before the Second World War.

A number of factors had a significant impact on British multinational performance before 1945. Apart from purely exogenous factors, the size and durability of the 'advantage' held by a firm in a market seemed crucial. The foreign subsidiaries of British firms were often very vulnerable to competition. Inappropriate business strategies and lack of competitive vigour were among the handicaps of British companies operating abroad. British firms were willing to make foreign direct investments but slow to devise appropriate multinational structures. Arguably this remained the case until the 1970s, when more genuinely multinational organisations developed, and rates of return from British direct investments edged upwards. Certainly, the few business historians who have gone beyond the Second World War have indicated that certain British multinationals continued to perform rather poorly, often for similar reasons as before 1945. The foreign subsidiaries of Courtaulds, for example, earned few returns during the 1950s and 1960s. The attempt to re-establish the firm in the United States, after the loss of the American Viscose Company, proved a painful and unprofitable struggle.[42] As before, however, the picture was a mixed one. Bowaters, the paper and newsprint manufacturer, made an enormous success of its North American subsidiaries in the 1950s, but its direct investments in continental Europe were visible failures.[43]

The arguments and data presented in this paper have implications for a number of empirical and theoretical debates concerning multinationals. An implicit assumption in much of the literature that multinational growth is a sign of 'dynamism' needs qualification. Dynamism needs to be evaluated in both the decision to invest abroad at all, and the success or lack of success of the venture. By the second criterion British firms before 1945 may well score badly. This empirical research also raises the matter of the social rate of return to the British economy of multinational activity before 1945. The Macmillan Committee in 1931 compared British foreign direct investment favourably with portfolio investment in 'foreign government and municipal loans, which absorb our available foreign balance while doing little for our industry and commerce'.[44] No evidence was put forward to support this assertion, and as the Committee did not have access to confidential business records it is unlikely that it possessed a full picture of the benefits of British multinational investment. Research in business archives provides one means of discovering what the United Kingdom gained—or conceivably lost—by being the home economy to so many multinationals before 1945.

Notes

1. This revised paper owes a great deal to the comments made on the original version by Mira Wilkins during the Florence Conference. I would also like to thank Malcolm Falkus, Leslie Hannah and Francesca Sanna-Randaccio, and the members of a seminar at the University of Reading in May 1984, for helpful suggestions and criticisms.
2. For a cross-section of recent work, see S. Nicholas, 'The Motivation and Direction of U.K. Direct Investment 1870–1939', *Journal of European Economic History* (1982), pp. 605–30; P. Buckley and B. Roberts, *European Direct Investment in the USA before World War I* (London, 1982); M. Casson (ed.), *The Growth of International Business* (London, 1983) and G. Jones, 'The Expansion of British Multinational Manufacturing', in T. Inoue and A. Okochi (eds), *Overseas Business Activities: Proceedings of the Ninth Fuji Conference* (Tokyo, 1984), pp. 125–53.
3. Information on the three companies has been drawn from the confidential archives

of the three firms, hereafter referred to as Cad(bury) A(rchives), C(ourtaulds) A(rchives), and D(unlop) A(rchives). Courtaulds is the only firm to possess a scholarly business history: D.C. Coleman, *Courtaulds: An Economic and Social History*, 3 vol. (Oxford, 1969, 1980). Cadbury and Dunlop now have case studies of aspects of their pre-1945 multinational careers: see G. Jones, 'Multinational Chocolate: Cadbury Overseas 1918-1939', *Business History* (1984), pp. 59-79; G. Jones, 'The Growth and Performance of British Multinational Firms before 1939: The case of Dunlop', *Economic History Review* (1984), pp. 35-53. The dates given for subsidiaries refer to the dates when the factories began operations.

4. D.C. Coleman, op. cit., vol. 2.
5. H. Macrosty, *The Trust Movement in British Industry* (London, 1907), p. 128.
6. S. Marriner, 'Company Financial Statements as Source Material for Business History', *Business History* (1980), pp. 203-35; J.R. Edwards and K.W. Webb, 'The Influence of Company Law on Corporate Reporting Procedures, 1865-1929', *Business History* (1982), pp. 259-79.
7. Notes on Profits and Dividends, 26 June 1937, FDC 17, C.A.
8. Les Files de Calais, S.A., Summary of Profit and Loss Accounts, FDC 20, C.A.
9. Data from Cad. A., especially papers prepared for the Joint Board. For a more extensive discussion of the multinational investments of Cadbury, see G. Jones, 'Multinational Chocolate: Cadbury Overseas 1918-1939'.
10. G. Jones, 'The Growth and Performance of British Multinational Firms before 1939: The Case of Dunlop'.
11. A.J. Merrett and A. Sykes, *The Finance and Analysis of Capital Projects*, 2nd edn, (London, 1973), pp. 55-6. The achieved returns in real terms on share investments is defined as the discounted returns achieved on an investment of a lump sum in shares, where the net cash flow comprises the net of tax dividends, and the capital sum realised at the end of the period examined. It should be stressed that the figures quoted, which are after payment of tax at standard rate, are only given for very crude comparative purposes.
12. G. Jones, 'Lombard Street on the Riviera: The British Clearing Banks and Europe 1900-1960', *Business History*, (1982), pp. 186-210.
13. C. Wilson, *Unilever*, vol. 1 (London, 1954). D.K. Fieldhouse, *Unilever Overseas* (London, 1978), p. 566, found diversity in performance to be a conspicuous feature of Unilever's multinational investments. Data on the performance of Lever's American subsidiary from Mira Wilkins.
14. Board Paper 2850, 5 December 1935, D.A.
15. Report by J.P. Koppel, 1947, GCC 74, C.A.
16. D.C. Coleman, op cit, vol. 2, p. 379.
17. W.J. Reader, *Imperial Chemical Industries*, vol. 2 (Oxford, 1975), *passim*.
18. L. Hannah, *The Rise of the Corporate Economy*, 2nd edn (London, 1983), p. 117.
19. W.J. Reader, *Metal Box: A History* (London, 1976).
20. D.K. Fieldhouse, op. cit.; C. Wilson, op. cit.
21. I.A. Williams, *The Firm of Cadbury 1831-1931* (London, 1931), pp. 146-51.
22. C. Wilson, op. cit.
23. W.B. Reddaway, *Effects of United Kingdom Direct Investment Overseas*: Interim Report (1967), Final Report (1968).
24. A.D. Chandler, 'The Growth of the Transnational Industrial Firm in the United States and the United Kingdom', *Economic History Review* (1980), p. 401.
25. Cadbury Board Minutes, 18 December 1935, Cad.A.
26. Foreign Relations Committee, 13 November 1935, C.A.
27. C.H. Feinstein, *National Income, Expenditure and Output of the United Kingdom 1855-1965* (Cambridge, 1972), p110. A comprehensive survey of British industrial investments in Tsarist Russia is in G. Jones and G. Gerenstain (eds), PV 01', *Foreign Capital in Russia* (English edition, New York, 1983).
28. R.P.T. Davenport-Hines, 'The British Armaments Industry during Disarmament

1918–36' (PhD thesis, University of Cambridge, 1979), pp. 293–312.
29. L. Hannah, 'Visible and Invisible Hands in Great Britain', in A.D. Chandler and H. Daems, (eds), *Managerial Hierarchies* (Cambridge, Mass., 1980), pp. 52–8.
30. G. Jones, 'The Growth and Performance of British Multinational Firms before 1939: The Case of Dunlop'.
31. G. Jones, *The State and the Emergence of the British Oil Industry*, (London, 1981) pp. 21, 57–8; R.W. Ferrier, *The History of the British Petroleum Company*, (Cambridge, 1982), especially Chapter 8.
32. P.L. Payne, 'The Emergence of the Large-scale Company in Great Britain, 1870–1914', *Economic History Review*, (1967), pp. 529–30.
33. W.J. Reader, *ICI*, vol. 2, pp. 229–30.
34. Minute Book File No. 417, 19 March 1926, Cad.A.
35. I owe the suggestions in this paragraph to Mira Wilkins.
36. Evidence of Harvey du Cros to Dunlop Investigation, 1922, vol. 18, D.A.
37. R.P.T. Davenport-Hines, op. cit., p. 304.
38. G. Jones, 'Lombard Street on the Riviera'.
39. W.J. Reader, 'The Corporation and the Culture: Opportunity or Trap', paper presented at the Florence Conference, examined the post-war performance of Metal Box and Bowater subsidiaries on the Continent, and put forward a strong case on the importance of 'culture' for multinational performance.
40. D.C. Coleman, op. cit., vol. 2.
41. I. Lloyd, *Rolls-Royce* (London, 1978), pp. 80–1.
42. D.C. Coleman, op. cit.
43. W.J. Reader, *Bowater: A History*, (Cambridge, 1981). Among other studies of British companies with substantial multinational investments which include discussions on the post-1945 period are: D.K. Fieldhouse, *Unilever Overseas*; W.J. Reader, *ICI*, vol. 2 (Oxford, 1975); and W.J. Reader, *Metal Box: A History*.
44. (Macmillan) Committee on Finance and Industry, *Report* (Cmd. 3897) p. 165.

7 German Multinational Enterprise before 1914: Some Case Studies

Peter Hertner

After 20 years of growing interest and research in the field of multinational enterprise (MNE), the business historian does not suffer from a shortage of definitions of what constitutes the structure and the behaviour of the firms concerned. If he had to evaluate, in a very pragmatic way, the theories that best fit his sources on the historical development of direct investment, he would probably start with what Dunning calls the 'monopolistic competitive theories' presented by Hymer, Kindleberger and Caves.[1] If he then considered more recent contributions, he would quickly become aware that they try to combine the results of international trade theory, location theory, theories of the firm, and theories of imperfect competition.[2]

From the historian's point of view there can be no doubt that the internalisation paradigm, first presented by R.H. Coase[3] and further developed by O.E. Williamson in the framework of a 'new institutional economics' approach,[4] gives important insight particularly for empirical research. It is more than evident that industry has been organised in quite different ways as one follows the line of historical evolution from medieval craft to modern trusts, cartels, and giant corporations. Nevertheless, the historian's conceptual framework can only profit from those seemingly obvious statements which are at the origin of the internalisation process, namely that economic 'co-ordination can be effected in three ways: by *direction*, by *co-operation*, or through *market transactions*'.[5] On the other hand, the historian would find it somewhat difficult to accept the flat statement by A.M. Rugman that 'internalization is the modern theory of the multinational enterprise'.[6] He would rather take sides with M. Casson who accepts internalisation 'as a key element in the theory of the multinational enterprise' but stresses at the same time that

> Internalization is in fact a general theory of why firms exist, and without additional assumptions it is almost tautological. To make the theory operational, it is necessary to specify assumptions about

transactions costs for particular products and for trade between particular locations.[7]

It has been accepted that the multinational type of internalisation takes place when (a) there is a strong incentive to control raw material resources via backward integration; (b) research-and-development-intensive industries want to exploit their knowledge advantage; and (c) tariffs, international tax differentials and foreign exchange controls favour transfer pricing. Casson, however, pleads for an extension to cases where buyer uncertainty can be reduced by internalisation, the MNE thus guaranteeing quality control by international marketing through its established brand names.[8] Without any doubt this attempt to extend the practical validity of the internalisation concept to the specific needs of consumer industries can, as will be shown later, be most useful to historical research.

Empirical investigations into the long-term development of MNEs will, however, inevitably have to start with the causes that motivate individual firms to go abroad, switching eventually from exporting to licensing or to direct investment. Particularly for these initial phases one can agree with Dunning that 'the internalisation paradigm may be more helpful in explaining degrees of multinationality than discrete acts of foreign investment.'[9] The business historian might therefore choose Dunning's eclectic approach which, taking into account R. Vernon's stage concept of the 'product cycle', stresses the essential relationship between trade and international production and sees the engagement in foreign production by a firm as dependent on its 'comparative ownership advantages *vis-à-vis* host country firms and the comparative location endowments of home and foreign countries'. If these ownership advantages are obtained and if the advantages of location speak in favour of direct investment then there must be, as a third condition, 'the possibility of internalising the firm's activities and thus substituting in part functions of the market.'[10]

There remains the problem, already mentioned in the introduction to this volume, of how a MNE should be defined. Should it be the 'broad definition' adopted by Dunning that MNEs are 'firms that engage in foreign direct investment',[11] or should the MNE be seen, following R.E. Caves, as 'an enterprise that controls and manages production establishments—plants—located in at least two countries'?[12] Should we, in the end, agree with L.G. Franko who considers that 'the word "multinational" ... only denotes the existence of manufacturing operations, owned to significant extent by the parent firm, in numerous countries'?[13] In any case, it will be quite a difficult task to find a definition based on purely structural aspects (equity quotas, number of

114

foreign subsidiaries) which at the same time satisfies the needs of a majority of economists and business historians.[14] The growing importance assumed by the internalisation concept in recent studies seems, however, to facilitate the problems of historical analysis of the MNE which is now being considered as 'any firm which owns outputs of goods *or services* originating in more than one country'.[15] Since this definition presupposes only a minimal threshold level of multinationality and includes firms which merely operate foreign sales subsidiaries,[16] it seems to be ideally suited to historical research concentrating on the origins and early phase of development of the MNE and, in fact, it has already been accepted by business historians.[17]

We still lack a comprehensive study of German MNE before World War I,[18] and in this chapter only a few cases of German multinational investment can be presented. Nevertheless, an attempt will be made to respond to some of the questions put forward in the introduction to this volume, notably: the transfer of technology via direct investment as an example of a typical 'ownership advantage'; the effects of visible and invisible trade barriers—'location-specific advantages'—on multinational investment; the influence of the size of the firm on multinational investment; some effects of the MNE on the economy of the host countries.

Finally, to a greater degree than has been done so far in empirical studies which cover only the contemporary period, it will be shown how advantages—firm-specific or country-specific—can change over time,[19] thus demonstrating that the process of internalisation can either continue its course, or in certain circumstances, owing to internal or external causes, revert. We should in any case agree with Thomas Horst who wrote over a decade ago '... if we are ever to unravel the complexity of the foreign investment process, a systematic study of the dynamic behaviour of firms must be undertaken'.[20]

Multinational Activity in the Consumer Goods Sector: Merck and Kathreiner's

The pharmaceutical firm of E. Merck grew out of an apothecary shop founded in 1654 in Darmstadt, then a small residential town south of Frankfurt. It started to produce pharmaceuticals on a larger scale in the 1820s. In 1900 it employed 800 workers, 50 chemists, pharmacists, engineers and doctors and an administrative staff of 150. By 1913, employment had risen to 1629 workers, while the scientific and administrative staff numbered 440. At that time, the firm specialised 'in alkaloids and organo-therapeutical compounds'.[21] Measured in employment figures, Merck was the largest of the 'purely' pharmaceutical companies existing in Germany before 1914, followed by Schering of Berlin which in 1913 employed 935 workers and an administrative staff of about 300. Some of these firms were incorporated by that time, but Merck remained a partnership owned by the same family since 1668.[22] In addition to these relatively small firms many of the large chemical companies, among them especially Bayer and Hoechst, dedicated part of their activities to the manufacture of pharmaceuticals. This renders the delimitation of the market particularly complicated since it meant a high degree of potential competition due to the technical capacity and the financial power of these very large chemical firms. Bayer's total turnover in 1913, for instance, was about six times as high as Merck's, and Hoechst employed in 1913 more than five times as many workers and staff—10 360 to be exact—as Merck.[23]

The Darmstadt firm was an extremely active exporter. In 1900–1 only 23 per cent of its sales went to Germany, 49 per cent to other European countries and 28 per cent to the rest of the world. Germany's share in Merck's sales gradually rose, and by 1912 had reached 33 per cent, while Europe took 43 per cent and the rest of the world 24 per cent.[24] The most important foreign markets in 1900–1 were Russia (17.6 per cent of total sales), followed by Latin America (11.4 per cent) and New York which evidently served the US market (11 per cent). Then came Britain (5.5 per cent), Austria-Hungry (5.3 per cent), Spain and Portugal (5.1 per cent), and Italy (4 per cent). These proportions did not change dramatically until 1912. The growth in importance of the German market was accompanied by a shrinking quota of exports to Russia (12 per cent in 1912) and to the United States and Canada (7.5 per cent in 1912).

This latter trend was probably caused by an internal factor. George Merck, a member of the Darmstadt family, had emigrated to the US, where in 1887 he founded a sales affiliate in New York. A contract concluded in 1890 between George Merck and the Merck firm of Darmstadt shows that the former received $200 000 which constituted his entire participation in a partnership he was establishing together with a certain Theodor Weicker of New York, probably another German emigrant. In 1894 the Darmstadt firm gave another $50 000 and, in return, George Merck had to deliver his entire profit share to the parent company.[25] In 1899 the firm of Merck & Co was founded, and started production of pharmaceuticals in Rahway, NY. When in 1917 it was taken into custody under the Trading with the Enemy Act, its capital amounted to $1 million. During the last years before the War it had built up an integrated production which no longer depended exclusively on the imports of German intermediates.[26] The relatively high American import duties on pharmaceuticals, and the fast growth as well as the dimension of the American market must have been the principal reasons for this direct investment in manufacturing.[27] A further motive might have been supplied by the particular structure of American demand where the ordinary drugstores selling pharmaceuticals were not supervised by scientifically trained pharmacists which meant that preference was given to ready-made and packed drugs.[28] The diminishing exports of Merck to the United States were thus probably a consequence of direct investment by the same firm.

If we follow Merck through particular foreign markets, Italy and France might serve as good examples of attempts to increase gradually the degree of internalisation. The Italian market was never a principal one for Merck, but it grew slowly from 1899–1900, when its share in total sales amounted to 3 per cent, until 1912, when it reached 4.3 per cent. Merck had established a number of small sale agencies all over the peninsula (in Genoa, Florence, Rome, Livorno, Naples, Palermo and Catania) whilst Milan was the main bridgehead for the conquest of the Italian market. Around 1900—the exact date could not be determined—the Milan agency was enlarged by the addition of a depot, and from then on the Italian customers were increasingly being served from there. Whereas in 1900–1, 87 per cent of Merck's exports to Italy were delivered directly by the Darmstadt factory, in 1913 this proportion had diminished to a mere 34 per cent.[29] Clients increasingly preferred being served from the Milan depot because it released them from the nuisance of getting their orders through the complicated formalities of the Italian customs service.[30] Discussions took place on bottling and packing in the Milan depot the products for which there was greatest demand, thereby economising on freight and customs duties. This was finally realised in 1910, and Milan served as example for a corresponding initiative in London in the following year. The entire size of the Milan affiliate remained rather limited. The deposit and its packing and bottling department employed only eight persons; all machines came from Germany; the commercial staff of the agency consisted of seven 'gentlemen', three of them Germans who occupied the leading positions.[31]

In France, where the same problems of passing goods through customs existed, a depot had already been set up in Paris in 1902.[32] A limited joint venture with a Paris firm (Bousquet) was started. Merck authorised its French partner to use its brand names for certain so-called 'specialities' which were then bottled and packed in France, a measure certainly provoked by the French prohibition against the import of pharmaceuticals in tablet or capsule form.[33] Moreover, the French patent law of 1844 did not allow the patenting of any type of medicine. This certainly did not favour the growth of a vigorous national industry and, as a result, according to contemporary sources, shortly before the outbreak of World War I 90 per cent of the fine chemicals needed for French pharmaceutical production came from Germany or passed through French affiliates of German industry.[34]

The problem of establishing a direct manufacturing investment in France was pondered over and over again by Merck, especially as the joint venture with Bousquet did not prosper as planned. Furthermore, the existing tariff was, if one is to believe the Merck officials, continuously changed whenever a new French 'infant' pharmaceutical competitor entered the scene.[35] Finally, in 1910, a small chemical factory at Montereau near Paris was bought and, after considerable investment exceeding all previous calculations, production of some pharmaceutical chemicals, such as glycerophosphate and theobromine, started two years later. The initial difficulties were immense, and in the spring of 1913 Merck almost decided to give up the Montereau plant. Up to that point 574 000 marks had been invested and over the same period a total loss of 128 000 marks had accumulated, including depreciation. Nevertheless, prestige considerations encouraged Merck to keep the Montereau factory open, although the outbreak of World War I prevented its capacity to survive being clearly demonstrated. When the works were seized by the French authorities in 1914, their value was calculated at 671 000 marks (839 000 francs).[36]

The already mentioned structure of Merck's exports reflects fairly well the overall export figures of the German pharmaceutical industry, which in 1913 held a dominant 30.3 per cent share of world exports, followed by Britain (21.3 per cent), the USA (13 per cent) and France (11.9 per cent). 21.4 per cent of these German exports went to Russia, 13.7 per cent to Austria-Hungary, 11.3 per cent to Britain, 10.7 per cent to the USA, 4.8 per cent to Italy, and 3.4 per cent to France.[37] Russia, the principal export market, was a notoriously high-tariff country, and Merck considered direct investment there as almost inevitable in the long run. However, the German firm preferred to establish only a bottling and packing department at its Moscow agency in 1906,[38] and when war broke out, it had not yet started manufacturing. Schering of Berlin, one of its major competitors, did, on the other hand, take this step and established in 1905 a pharmaceutical factory in Moscow which imported the chemical raw materials and intermediates from Germany. In addition, a charcoal plant using the immense resources of Russian timber was built at Wydriza in the Mogilev province.[39]

Another typical example of a producer of a consumer good is the case of Kathreiner's Malzkaffee-Fabriken, founded in 1892 in order to produce malt coffee, a substitute made from barley with odorous substances added to give it at least a certain coffee flavour.[40] It was a typical low-income product but, with the help of intensive publicity, the firm tried to persuade the public that its malt coffee, being free of caffeine, was also an extremely 'healthy' product and not only a second-best solution. Special emphasis was laid on the diffusion of the brand name and, particularly in the US, marketing efforts were directed at German immigrants.[41]

Up to 1914, the company had built seven factories in Germany. Sales increased from 17 718 quintals in 1891–2 to 57 812 quintals in 1901–2 and to 496 582 in 1913–14, doubtless pushed up after 1910 by the rapid rise in the price of coffee. In 1914 the firm was established in nine different foreign countries. It had given licences to a French, a Swiss, and a US firm, whereas it had undertaken direct investment in manufacturing companies in Austria-Hungary, Sweden, Russia, and, in 1912, in Spain after a sevenfold increase there in customs duties on malt coffee. The tariff situation in Argentina, where sales developed in a very satisfactory way, suggested a similar move but this was then prevented by the outbreak of the First World War. The Belgian and Dutch markets were supplied by a Rotterdam sales affiliate, and in Italy a sales depot was established in 1893 in Milan. One year later, a manufacturing company was created together with Italian partners in Genoa but it had to be closed down very soon afterwards because of internal differences with the Italian co-entrepreneurs and because of a newly established tax on production. There was probably also a misapprehension as to the taste of the Italian consumer who seemingly preferred if not 'real' coffee, at least the substitutes made from chicory with their stronger flavour. Kathreiner's Italian sales showed, in any case, a very slow development between 1900 and 1914.

Both cases of consumer goods producers examined here illustrate in detail the process and different modes of internalisation. Moreover, the Italian experience of Kathreiner's suggests that it was not a one-way process. In certain circumstances plans had to be rapidly revised, which meant that the dynamics were not limited to expansion only. Finally, the example of Merck shows that it was not necessarily the large oligopolistic firm which went for direct investment.[42] Particularly in the early phases of development of a specific market, ownership advantages were to be found also with smaller companies and could, if the market subsequently became more differentiated, as was certainly the case with the pharmaceutical industry, eventually be maintained.

Multinationalisation and the Transfer of Technology: Bosch and Mannesmann

In the middle of 1914, the Stuttgart firm of Robert Bosch employed 4 726 workers and staff. Its production consisted almost entirely of magneto ignitions for automobiles and, to a much lesser degree, for aeroplanes. Shortly before the war a diversification into other electrical equipment for the car industry, such as starters and headlights, was undertaken. In the first half of 1914 Bosch had agencies and factories in 25 countries and 88 per cent of its production was exported.[43] The firm had grown out of a small mechanical and electrotechnical workshop founded by Robert Bosch in Stuttgart in 1886. Its growth gained in momentum when Bosch started to produce magneto ignitions for automobiles in 1898. In 1901 his firm employed a work-force of 45, but thereafter it expanded very rapidly in parallel with the rapid growth of the car industry, to 506 employees in 1906 and to more than 4000 in 1914.[44] Bosch, a self-made man who never gave up control of his company during his lifetime, founded in 1899 the 'Automatic Magneto Electric Ignition Company Ltd', which was made responsible for sales in France and Belgium and later changed its name to Compagnie des Magnétos Simms-Bosch. His British partner Frederic R. Simms represented the Stuttgart firm in Britain[45] but sold his share in the French affiliate to Bosch in 1906.[46] The fact that in 1908 the French firm changed its name to Société des Magnétos Bosch reflected the new ownership situation. In 1907 it started to produce magneto ignitions for trucks since subsidies given by the French state to producers of these vehicles depended on the condition that all parts had to be French made.[47] The French automobile industry, the most important in pre-1914 Europe, was an extremely important customer, and it seems that Bosch had 'un quasi monopole sur le marché français' with annual sales that amounted to 10 million francs just before the outbreak of the war.[48] In Britain Bosch separated from Simms in 1907 and founded a new affiliate in London called The Bosch Magneto Company Ltd.[49] When it was required that racing cars and all their components had to be made in Britain if they wanted to participate in certain events, production, which seems, however, to have been largely assembly, was started in London. During the first half of 1914 Bosch satisfied approximately 85 to 95 per cent of British demand for magnetos and spark plugs.[50]

When the collaboration with Simms, who was also a general agent for the US came to an end in 1906, Bosch immediately founded an American affiliate in New York.[51] Soon agencies in Chicago (1908), San Francisco (1909), and Detroit (1910) followed.[52] The US market was of the greatest importance but exports suffered from the cost of freight and especially from a tariff which in the case of magnetos amounted to not less than 45 per cent of their value.[53] There were certainly enough ownership advantages due to the firm's technology to induce Bosch to start direct investment in manufacturing. Consequently, in 1910 construction of a magneto factory was undertaken in Springfield, Massachussets.

Production started in 1912. Two years later, the plant employed 2000 workers and staff and was considered a 'model factory' by American observers.[54] The US Alien Property Custodian who seized the American Bosch properties in 1918 gave an impressive report on the company's achievements.[55]

The Bosch Magneto Co. was a tremendously powerful organization. Its combined capital and surplus exceeded $6,500,000. It owned and operated a modern factory at Springfield, Mass., with branches at Detroit, Chicago, and San Francisco. Its main office and sales department was in New York City, but it had agencies and supply depots in over one hundred American cities. Its product had obtained first place in the minds of the American purchasing public and was indeed regarded as the standard with which all other similar products were compared.

In 1912 Bosch acquired 45 per cent of the equity capital of the Eisemann Magneto Company, an American affiliate of its principal German competitor. In the same year, there followed the purchase of the Boonton Rubber Manufacturing Company of Boonton, NY, 'the largest producer of molded insulation, a product which was essential to the magneto industry. Again, in May 1914, it acquired outright, at a price of $750,000 in cash, the plant, business and goodwill of ... the Rushmore Dynamo Works at Plainfield, N.J. ... This factory was shortly thereafter shut down and dismantled.'[56] This latter fact speaks for itself and indicates clearly an oligopolistic market structure; as a matter of fact, according to the Alien Property Custodian, Bosch and Eisemann together produced 'at least half' of all the magnetos sold in the USA before war broke out in Europe.[57]

Turning now to Mannesmann, the company showed great technological originality, but for almost two decades its growth was much more hesitant and never led to a dominant position in its sector. Based on the highly original invention, patented in 1886, for producing seamless rolled tubes, the firm seemed to become a MNE right from the outset.[58] In practice however, in addition to the original plant owned by the two inventors Reinhard and Max Mannesmann, between 1887 and 1889 three other companies were created, each of them formally independent: one at Bous near Saarbrücken, one at Komotau in the then Austro-Hungarian Bohemia and one in Britain, where the Siemens family had an interest and took a licence for a plant which was to be installed at Llandore. The German and Austrian works were amalgamated in 1890 as the Deutsch-Österreichische Mannesmannröhren-Werke, with a capital of 35 million marks and under the financial guidance of the Deutsche Bank, the two inventor brothers receiving half of the new shares for bringing in their patents. Since the tube rolling process was at the beginning scarcely ripe for continuous production, the first years of the new firm were overshadowed by considerable technical and, consequently, financial difficulties. The two Mannesmann brothers left the firm quite soon and sold out their shares in 1900, the Deutsche Bank becoming the uncontested 'entrepreneur' and financier of the company. No dividend could be distributed until 1906; by then several rationalisation measures and the generally favourable economic climate guaranteed solid further growth.

Around the turn of the century the process of multinationalisation was resumed. In 1899 the Landore Mannesmann Tube Company, which otherwise would have had to be closed down and which was completely independent from the German firm, was taken over. This move into direct investment was motivated by the attempt to get control of the British market for seamless tubes. Moreover, being based in Britain, Landore was able to profit from Empire preferences which were increasingly built up by the dominions.[59] As a 'national' firm Landore became also one of the main suppliers of boiler pipes for the British navy. In 1913 the construction of a second and larger rolling mill at Newport near Cardiff was decided, its future production intended as a replacement for imports from the German parent firm, notably large-diameter tubes so far not produced in Britain. The Newport works had not yet gone into operation when the war broke out.[60]

In 1906, when, as we have seen, the Mannesmann firm started to distribute its profits, the establishment of a rolling mill in Italy was decided; up to that moment, the peninsula had been an export market of growing significance.[61] The investment was made not so much because of the Italian tariff, but in the hope that it could profit from State orders for the railways, the navy or for the new programme of municipal aqueducts in southern Italy. In practice, State orders went increasingly to national businesses even if its tenders were up to 5 per cent higher than the average tender from abroad. Accordingly a company was founded under Italian law and with an Italian metallurgical firm as a minority partner. The works were built at Dalmine near Bergamo where two electric furnaces were also installed in order to be able to produce the special type of steel needed for rolling seamless tubes. Production started in 1909 but the technical difficulties were considerable, and after two rather unsuccessful years the Italian partner withdrew its participation. A real improvement as far as output and profitability were concerned came only in 1912. Still, technically and financially the Società Tubi Mannesmann depended entirely on the parent company at Düsseldorf. As an example, the parent company waived its right to the licence fees fixed by contract in order to 'improve' the balance sheet of the Italian affiliate. Credit lines opened by Italian banks were used only at the end of 1913; up to that point all financial means were provided from Germany. When Italy entered the war in May 1915, the firm was seized. Nevertheless, Mannesmann succeeded in selling the Dalmine works in 1916 to a group of Italian banks, a transaction made with the agreement of the Italian government via neutral Switzerland.[62]

The most important foreign asset of Mannesmann remained, however, the Austrian affiliate, 'which reached about one third of the Mannesmann combine's total turnover in the last pre-war year' when all non-German subsidiaries accounted for 45 per cent of the overall volume.[63] The Komotau works certainly profited from high Austro-Hungarian tariffs and soon succeeded in attaining a share of 35 per cent in the tube cartel of the country.[64]

In brief, one could say that both firms, Bosch and Mannesmann, possessed strong ownership advantages through their patented technology. Foreign direct investment in manufacturing was, however, only induced when additional country-specific factors such as tariffs or non-tariff trade measures became effective in the particular foreign country. In the case of Bosch, its nearness to important customers such as the French and the American automobile industry certainly also played an important role.

Patent Legislation, Tariffs and Multinationalisation: the Case of the German Chemical Industry

The dominant position of the German chemical industry up to World War I is common knowledge among economic historians. If one excludes petroleum refining, which was particularly important in the US chemical sector, the German chemical industry retained a clear lead in world chemical production. Its exports 'accounted for an estimated 28 per cent of world exports in chemicals'.[65] The German superiority in the artificial dyestuffs sector was crushing. The total value produced by eight firms and their foreign subsidiaries in 1913 amounted to 75–80 per cent of world production, and some 85 per cent of German production was exported.[66] It is commonly accepted that the rapid rise of the German chemical industry which started in the 1860s was due to country-specific advantages like the German university system which favoured the training of chemists and chemical engineers. There were industry-specific advantages like the oligopolistic market structure and the access to fuel and raw materials. In some sectors enterprise-specific advantages shrank after 1900 and in the dyestuffs sector this resulted in the formation of two *Interessengemeinschaften*, the so-called Dreibund

(BASF, Bayer and AGFA), and Hoechst, which controlled Casella and Kalle on the other hand. The largest of these firms had gone abroad fairly early. In Russia, BASF, Bayer and Hoechst founded or participated in producing affiliates in 1877, 1883 and 1885 in response, as is generally asserted, to growing Russian protectionism after the tariff moves of 1877.[67] The smaller chemical firms (Cassella, Kalle, and AGFA) came to Russia in the following years. Especially in the dyestuffs sector, production by these affiliates comprised only the final stages; intermediate products on which the duties were much lower were imported from the parent firms; in this specific case they contributed up to 80 per cent of the value added.[68] Tariff problems, but even more the French patent law which required an immediate start of production in the country by patent holders, were responsible for the foundation by Hoechst in 1881 of the Compagnie Parisienne de Couleurs d'Aniline which started production of aniline dyes and pharmaceutical products at Creil (Oise) in 1884.[69] BASF had started a plant in 1878 at Neuville-sur-Saône near Lyon.[70] A change in British patent legislation occurred in 1907 which prescribed that a foreign patent, after its transfer to Britain, had to be exploited there or else it would be revoked. As a result Hoechst, representing also Cassella and Kalle, established a plant in Ellesmere Port near Liverpool and BASF, acting for the Dreibund, founded the Mersey Chemical Works not far from there and transferred nearly one-fifth of its patents to this new affiliate. In the following years Hoechst produced practically the whole volume of domestic production of indigo, amounting to about 50 per cent of domestic demand, at Ellesmere Port, whereas the BASF subsidiary concentrated on other aniline dyes. Patent transfers from Germany decreased, however, very soon after it became clear that British jurisdiction had, in practice watered down the enforcement of the 1907 Patent and Designs Act.[71] Looking to the situation of British producers, Haber is probably right when he states that apart from the virtual failure of the new patent legislation, another possible measure, 'a tariff, would not have helped the British producers because they lacked patents, know-how and, above all, research and enterprise'.[72]

The impact of patent legislation is also shown in the case of the United States where there was no legal obligation to use patents given by the US administration in the country itself. For this reason the BASF thought it useless to establish a factory there. It registered, however, up to 1914 about 1000 patents. Roughly the same number were registered by Bayer, which owned, however, a factory at Albany, NY and another company, the Synthetic Patents Company, Inc., which held all the Bayer patents registered in the US and gave licenses to the American Bayer Company; the latter was thus able to reduce its tax burden because gains from licenses paid lower taxes than gains from production.[73] All the other German dye makers had little in the way of manufacturing in the United States; they did have, however, very extensive commercial organisations.

A final illustration could be given by the Italian case where there was, up to the First World War, no artificial dyestuffs production at all; in 1913, Germany provided 77 per cent of Italian dyestuffs imports. By making concessions to agricultural imports from Italy, the German negotiators succeeded after 1878 in all tariff discussions in keeping dyestuffs and related chemical imports totally free of all duties. Consequently there was not one German chemical plant of any importance in Italy.[74]

The dominant position of the German chemical industry before 1914 was certainly due to patented technology and intangible know-how based on significant outlay on research and development. If at the same time foreign states were not willing to respect the simple registration of patents but demanded that they be actually implemented within the national frontiers, if they constructed tariff walls or if they fell back on non-tariff trade measures, then direct investment was the logical consequence if a specific market was to be conserved.

Technology and Finance: the German Electrical Industry

The last sector that will be considered here is electrotechnical production where German industry shared world-wide leadership with US trusts. According to one estimate, Germany in 1913 had a share of about 35 per cent of world production as compared to a United States share of 29 per cent,[75] whereas another estimate gives a figure of 31 per cent for Germany and 35 per cent for the United States.[76] There is agreement, however, that German industry dominated world exports of electrotechnical material with its share of 46 per cent, followed by the British with 22 per cent and their American competitors with 16 per cent.[77]

This is not the place to discuss the rise of the German electrotechnical industry as such.[79] I should only mention that Siemens & Halske started as early as 1847 and owed its success during the first three decades of its existence mainly to business in the telegraph and later in the slowly developing telephone sector. Its main competitor, the Allgemeine Elektricitäts-Gesellschaft (AEG), only started in 1883 as the German license-holder of Edison. During its first decade it depended, apart from its technical ties with the American Edison companies, quite heavily on the Deutsche Bank and Siemens itself, both of which took equity participations. The rise of the AEG took place in the high-voltage sector right from the beginning and still more so when it had finally gained complete independence from Edison and Siemens in 1894. Siemens, the older firm and more conservative in its outlook, fell back comparatively because it did not involve itself so much in the high-voltage business during the late 1880s and the early 1890s. However, at the turn of the century, it began to expand again in this sector too, when it had been transformed into a limited liability company and its liquidity problems had been solved. Like a considerable number of smaller companies, the third competitor, Schuckert, founded in 1873, could hardly survive the crisis of 1901 which hit the German economy particularly hard and above all its too rapidly growing electrical industry. In 1903 Schuckert merged its plant with Siemens which combined it with its own high-voltage activities in the new firm of Siemens-Schuckert, although Schuckert remained independent as a holding company detaining participation in a considerable number of domestic and foreign power, tram and lighting companies. In any case, after 1903 the German electrotechnical industry was characterised by a virtual duopoly of Siemens and AEG which dominated the market, leaving space however to a host of smaller so-called 'specialised' firms.

What interests us in this context is the international dimension of this sector, and there can be no doubt that it was important right from the beginning. It started at a very early stage in the case of Siemens, which, as a consequence of considerable orders from the Russian government for the construction and maintenance of a telegraph network, established a plant at St Petersburg as early as 1855, where parts sent from Berlin were assembled. The Russian business was directed on the spot by Carl Siemens, brother of Werner, the firm's founder, and it was another brother, William, who represented the Siemens interests in Britain from 1850 and directed the British Siemens subsidiary (founded in 1858), which started with the production of sea cables in 1863.[79] In order to settle disputes about responsibility and profit distribution which had arisen between the brothers, the whole firm was reorganised in 1867 under the roof of a common business (*Gesamtgeschäft*) with its seat at Berlin; it split up into two companies, Siemens & Halske in Berlin and Siemens Brothers in London; the Russian branch was assigned as an affiliate to Siemens & Halske.[80] One could talk, of course, at first sight of a multinational group, which had been formed with a centre in Berlin and direct investments in Britain and Russia. But if one looks more closely, one sees that at least in the British case William Siemens operated quite independently, relying financially on his brother Werner in Berlin on occasions. The whole family enterprise structurally was more similar to more traditional models, for instance to the business of Huguenot bankers and merchants in the Refuge operating contemporaneously in Geneva, Amsterdam and London, if not in Paris.[81] Even after the turn of the century 'the great principle of international family unity' characterised the different Siemens branches,[82] and this meant that when there were problems a member of the family was called in to manage the various foreign affiliates. Expansion abroad continued in the sense that in 1903, for instance, there were 30 so-called technical bureaux installed, eight of them in European countries.[83] Some of these started production, normally at first by assembling parts sent from the mother firm, as for instance in 1879 in Vienna and in 1903 in Bratislava, in the Hungarian part of the Habsburg Empire, where after the merger with Schuckert its plant was incorporated.

In some countries, as for instance France, where anti-German feelings after 1871 certainly did not favour sales and autonomous direct investment, joint ventures proved to be a viable solution. Thus in 1889 Siemens & Halske, Siemens Brothers (London) and the Société Alsacienne de Constructions Mécaniques (Mulhouse) founded a jointly-owned company which was supposed to produce high-voltage material in Belfort, just on the French side of the border. The Mulhouse firm which held a share of 37.5 per cent was to provide all the non-electrical mechanical equipment, and Siemens the electrical parts. In the longer run the Belfort company proved to be quite successful but Siemens had to withdraw from it in 1904 since the merger with Schuckert the year before had left Schuckert's French subsidiary, the Compagnie Générale d'Electricité de Creil, founded in 1897, practically at Siemens' disposal. Consequently, Siemens rented the Creil works from the Schuckert holding which formally was still independent. With the Société Alsacienne a jointly-owned cable factory at Belfort was nevertheless continued.[84]

In Russia production for low- and high-voltage material started in 1880–2. The reason must be seen not so much in the increasing Tsarist tariff duties as in the growing pressure from the Russian administration which insisted on domestic production for continuing State orders.[85] The AEG for its part resisted such pressures for quite a long time and tried to look after its Russian business through local agents. In 1898 it founded an affiliate for Russia which was simply a sales company based in Berlin and had to transfer its legal seat in 1902 to St Petersburg so as to avoid being thrown out of business. Only in 1905, after its merger with the Union Elektricitäts-Gesellschaft, previously controlled by General Electric, could the AEG get hold of the Union's electrotechnical factory at Riga.[86]

We could go on listing other examples of direct investment by the German electrotechnical industry, but looking at the motives we would find in most cases State intervention in the form of tariffs or non-tariff

127

trade measures, especially if the State was an important customer, as in the case of Russia. However, there must have been still other factors at stake if, for instance, in 1913, 87 per cent of all electrotechnical imports to Russia came from Germany,[87] if in the same year in the Italian case the quota of imports from Germany reached 70 per cent[88] and if the German electrotechnical industry succeeded in taking up regularly about half of Argentinian imports in this field between 1903 and 1913.[89] The reason must be found in the so-called *Unternehmergeschäft*, which meant that the large German trusts created their own market by founding local and regional power, tramway and lighting companies in those countries (for example Russia, Italy, Spain, Latin America) and for those customers (particularly local public authorities) which suffered from chronic lack of capital, and because these new companies were forced by statute to buy their electrotechnical material from their big industrial founders.[90] No doubt these operations were further steps in internalisation bound to reduce the risks of selling in a foreign market. On the other hand, the risk was created of accumulating a growing volume of equity capital and bonds in the portfolio of the electrotechnical producers and a dangerous reduction of their liquidity. The solution lay in founding financial holdings together with the great banks. These financial holding companies took over the shares and bonds of the newly created public utility companies, held them in their portfolio during the period of construction and initial development and sold most of their holdings to the general public as soon as they had 'matured' and yielded a profit, afterwards in general only retaining controlling minority holdings.[91] Each of the German producers possessed such an intermediate financial holding. AEG had the Bank für elektrische Unternehmunger, founded in 1895 in Zürich by itself and a number of German and Swiss and, to a minor extent, Italian and French banks. The same holds for Siemens with its Basel-based Schweizerische Gesellschaft für elektrische Industrie, created in 1896, and its Elektrische Licht- und Kraftanlagen AG, founded at Berlin in the same year. Schuckert and the minor electrotechnical producers possessed, of course, their own *Finanzierungsgesellschaften*. The fact that part of these financial holdings were based in Switzerland or Belgium (in the latter country, for instance, was the AEG-controlled SOFINA) arose mainly from the very liberal company law and stock exchange regulations of these countries. In part, it probably owed something to the participation of the influential Swiss and Belgian banks in these holdings.[92] One can further observe an increasing regional specialisation by the creation of national or regional subholdings controlled directly by the electrotechnical producer and its banks or by one of its financial holdings such as, for instance, the

Società per lo sviluppo delle imprese elettriche in Italia and the Deutsche Überseeische Elektricitäts-Gesellschaft, the one 'responsible' for Italy, the other for Argentina, Chile and Uruguay, both of them emanations of AEG.[93] As a result, in 1913 about 50 per cent of the capital of the Italian and about 40 per cent of the Russian companies producing electrical energy were controlled by German capital.[94]

Even if one can agree that the German *Elektrokonzerne* enjoyed substantial ownership advantages because of their superior quality of management, their advanced technology in electrotechnical mass production, their thorough marketing techniques and their after-sales service, the high-voltage material itself was by the mid-1890s technically 'mature' and in the medium term few observers expected radical innovations. For German industry this meant probably slowly shrinking advantages and growing competition on the world market, especially from its US rivals. It could, up to a certain degree, meet this challenge—particularly in countries where investment capital was relatively difficult to obtain—through the extraordinary process of internalisation described above, which was made possible by the advantage of easy access to factor markets, that is, in this case to international capital via its financial holdings and ultimately via its close ties to the German type of mixed banks.

When the First World War ended this access to the international capital markets and led to the loss of the major part of German direct investment, the high-voltage business of the type described above found itself in considerable difficulties. But—and the Italian example shows this quite well—the then technologically faster advancing low-voltage sector (above all the telephone installation business) survived much more easily and its exports performed comparatively better in the inter-war period.

Summing up, it must be emphasised that the examples and brief case studies offered in this chapter do not provide a comprehensive study of German MNE before 1914. What is needed in the future are studies that concentrate on the historical development of a specific German multinational as well as the type of synthetic overview that Mira Wilkins has done for US MNE. At the same time the point must be made that the astonishing vitality of the pre-1914 German economy and its rapid international expansion cannot be described in a convincing way without reference to the MNE, its concept and its gradual evolution.

Notes

1. S.H. Hymer, *The International Operations of National Firms: A Study of Direct Foreign Investment* (Cambridge, Mass., 1976); C.P. Kindleberger, *American Business Abroad. Six Lectures on Direct Investment* (London, 1969); R.E. Caves 'International Corporations: The Industrial Economics of Foreign Investment', *Economica* (1971), pp. 1–27.
2. B. Swedenborg, *The Multinational Operations of Swedish Firms. An Analysis of Determinants and Effects* (Stockholm, 1979), p. 39.
3. R.H. Coase, 'The Nature of the Firm', *Economica* (1937), pp. 386–405.
4. O.E. Williamson, *Markets and Hierarchies: Analysis and Anti-trust Implications* (New York, 1975), especially chapter 1; O.E. Williamson, 'The Modern Corporation: Origins, Evolution, Attributes', *Journal of Economic Literature* (1981), pp. 1537–68.
5. G.B. Richardson, 'The Organisation of Industry', *The Economic Journal* (1972), p. 890 (italics in original).
6. A.M. Rugman, 'Internalization and non-equity forms of international involvement' in A.M. Rugman (ed.), *New Theories of the Multinational Enterprise* (London, 1982), p. 11.
7. M. Casson, 'Transaction Costs and the Theory of the Multinational Enterprise' in A.M. Rugman (ed.), *New Theories of the Multinational Enterprise*, p. 24.
8. Ibid., p. 36.ff.
9. J.H. Dunning, 'Explaining the International Direct Investment Position of Countries: Towards a Dynamic or Developmental Approach', *Weltwirtschaftliches Archiv* (1981), p. 33.
10. J.H. Dunning, *International Production and the Multinational Enterprise* (London, 1981), p. 27.
11. Ibid., p. 3.
12. R.E. Caves, *Multinational Enterprise and Economic Analysis* (Cambridge, 1982), p. 1.
13. L. Franko, 'The Origins of Multinational Manufacturing by Continental European Firms', *Business History Review* (1974), p. 279, note 10.
14. Y. Aharoni, 'On the Definition of a Multinational Corporation' in A. Kapoor and P.D. Grub (eds), *The Multinational Enterprise in Transition* (Princeton, NJ, 1973), pp. 4ff; F. Grünärml, 'Kritische Anmerkungen zu einer merkmalspezifischen Typologie multinationaler Unternehmen', *Jahrbuch für Sozialwissenschaft* (1975), pp. 228–43.
15. M. Casson, op. cit., p. 36 (emphasis added).
16. Ibid.
17. See, for example, M. Wilkins, 'Modern European Economic History and the Multinationals', *Journal of European Economic History* (1977), pp. 575–95, particularly p. 578, note 11.
18. See, however, the various contributions mentioned in notes 28–30 of the introduction to this volume.
19. See, for instance, P.J. Buckley, 'New Theories of International Business: Some Unresolved Issues' in M. Casson (ed.), *The Growth of International Business* (London, 1983), pp. 34–50, particularly p. 42.
20. T. Horst, 'Firm and Industry Determinants of the Decision to Invest Abroad: An Empirical Study', *Review of Economics and Statistics* (1972), p. 265.
21. Cited in L.F. Haber, *The Chemical Industry 1900–1930. International Growth and Technological Change* (Oxford, 1971), p. 133; see also J.H. Merck, *Entwicklung und Stand der pharmazeutischen Grossindustrie Deutschlands* (Berlin, 1923), p. 12; W. Vershofen, *Wirtschaftsgeschichte der chemisch-pharmazeutischen Industrie*, vol. 3 (Aulendorf, Württ., 1958), p. 39ff.
22. L.F. Haber, op. cit., p. 133ff; J.H. Merck, op. cit., p. 14.
23. L.F. Haber, op. cit., p. 121, 131; Merck archives, Darmstadt, F3 Nr. 17.

24. Merck archives, F3 Nr. 5 and Nr. 16.
25. Ibid., H 1 Nr. 45/46.
26. T.R. Kabisch, *Deutsches Kapital in den USA. Von der Reichsgründung bis zur Sequestrierung (1917) und Freigabe* (Stuttgart, 1982), p. 234; 65th Congress. 3rd Session, Senate Documents, vol. 8 (Washington, D.C., 1919), p. 59 (hereafter referred to as *Alien Property Custodian Report*).
27. See T.R. Kabisch, op. cit.
28. R. Schmitt, 'Die pharmazeutische Industrie und ihre Stellung in der Weltwirtschaft' (unpublished thesis, Frankfurt am Main, 1932), p. 124.
29. Merck archives, F3 Nr. 5–17.
30. Ibid., F3 Nr. 9.
31. Ibid., F3 Nr. 14, H1 Nr. 9.
32. Ibid., F3, Nr. 5/6.
33. Ibid., F3 Nr. 6.
34. R. Schmitt, op cit, p. 123; E. Grandmougin, *L'essor des industries chimiques en France*, (Paris, 1917), p. 173ff.
35. Merck archives, F3 Nr. 6, 9.
36. Ibid., H1, Nr. 22, 23, 24, 25, 29; see also R. Poidevin, *Les relations économiques et financiéres entre la France et l'Allemagne de 1898 à 1914* (Paris, 1969), p. 740.
37. R. Schmitt, op cit, pp. 218, 164.
38. Merck archives, F3 Nr. 10.
39. H. Holländer, *Geschichte der Schering Aktiengesellschaft* (Berlin, 1955), p. 36ff.; Schering, or at least a member of the Schering family, participated in the New York firm of Schering & Glatz in the late 1870s and took in 1897 a short-lived participation in a borax mine in Chile, a typical raw-material venture (ibid., p. 15, 19).
40. For the following see above all *Denkschrift anlässlich des 25-jährigen Bestehens von Kathreiners Malzkaffee-Fabriken, 1892–1917* (München, 1917); H. Aust, *Organisation eines Markenartikel-Grossunternehmens der Nahrungs- und Genussmittelindustrie* (undated typewritten manuscript in the library of the Institut für Weltwirtschaft at Kiel, Germany), particularly p. 35ff., 167ff.
41. For an analogous strategy in the same market but with another type of coffee surrogate see the case of the Heinrich Franck firm of Ludwigsburg mentioned by T.R. Kabisch, op. cit., p. 280ff.
42. R.E. Caves, 'International Corporations' and T. Horst, 'The Multinational Corporation and Direct Investment. A comment' in P.B. Kenen (ed.), *International Trade and Finance. Frontiers for Research* (Cambridge, 1975), pp. 368–9 see the typical MNE as a large oligopolistic firm whereas B. Swedenborg, op. cit., pp. xiv, 153ff., looking at the historical development of Swedish multinationals, comes to the conclusion that 'large firms do not have a higher propensity to produce abroad than small firms do' (ibid., p. 188).
43. O. Debatin, *Sie haben mitgeholfen. Lebensbilder verdienter Mitarbeiter des Hauses Bosch* (Stuttgart, Robert Bosch GmbH, 1963), p. 37ff; *Fünfzig Jahre Bosch 1886–1936* (Stuttgart, 1936), pp. 27, 290.
44. O. Debatin, op. cit., p. 46; see also T. Heuss, *Robert Bosch: Leben und Leistung* (München, 1975; 1st edn Tübingen 1946); *75 Jahre Bosch 1886–1961. Ein geschichtlicher Rückblick* (Stuttgart, Robert Bosch GmbH, 1961).
45. *Der Bosch-Zünder. Eine Zeitschrift für alle Angehörigen der Robert-Bosch-AG und der Bosch-Metallwerk AG, Stuttgart und Feuerbach*, vol. 1, no. 4. (1919), p. 59.
46. Ibid., p. 60; O. Debatin, op. cit., p. 23.
47. O. Debatin, op. cit., p. 20.
48. R. Poidevin, op cit, p. 20.
49. *Fünfzig Jahre Bosch*, p. 25.
50. O. Debatin, *op cit*, p. 32ff.

51. *Der Bosch-Zünder*, p. 60; *75 Jahre Bosch*, p. 31, T Heuss, op. cit., p. 121.
52. *Der Bosch-Zünder*, p. 61ff; *75 Jahre Bosch*, p. 34.
53. O. Debatin, op. cit., p. 68ff.; T. Heuss, op. cit., p. 122; T.R. Kabisch, op. cit., p. 32.
54. O. Debatin, op. cit., p. 55ff.; T. Heuss, op. cit., p. 150ff.
55. *Alien Property Custodian Report*, p. 109.
56. Ibid.
57. Ibid., p. 108.
58. See especially *75 Jahre Mannesmann. Geschichte einer Erfindung und eines Unternehmens, 1890–1965* (Düsseldorf, Mannesmann Aktiengesellschaft, 1965), p. 27ff.; P. Hertner, 'Fallstudien zu deutschen multinationalen Unternehmen vor dem Ersten Weltkrieg' in N. Horn und J. Kocka, *Recht und Entwicklung der Grossunternehmen im 19. und im frühen 20. Jahrhundert* (Göttingen, 1979), pp. 388–419, particularly p. 400 ff; H. Pogge von Strandmann, *Unternehmenspolitik und Unternehmensführung. Der Dialog zwischen Aufsichtsrat und Vorstand bei Mannesmann 1900 bis 1919* (Düsseldorf, 1978); A. Teichova, 'The Mannesmann Concern in East Central Europe in the inter-war period' in A. Teichova and P.L. Cottrell, *International Business and Central Europe, 1918–1939* (Leicester, 1983), pp. 103–37, particularly pp. 103–6.
59. *75 Jahre Mannesmann*, p. 82; for the problem of Empire preferences see, for instance, F. Capie, *Depression and Protectionism: Britain between the Wars* (London, 1983), pp. 23, 42.
60. R. Bungeroth, *50 Jahre Mannesmannröhren 1884/1934* (Berlin, 1934), p. 135.
61. See P. Hertner, 'Fallstudien', p. 403ff; P. Hertner, 'Deutsches Kapital in Italien: Die "Società Tubi Mannesmann" in Dalmine bei Bergamo, 1906–1916', *Zeitschrift für Unternehmensgeschichte* (1977), pp. 183–204, (1978), pp. 54–76.
62. P. Hertner, 'Deutsches Kapital in Italien', p. 66ff.
63. A. Teichova, op. cit., p. 105.
64. Ibid.
65. L.F. Haber, op. cit., p. 108.
66. Ibid., p. 121.
67. P.A. Zimmermann, *Patentwesen in der Chemie* (Ludwigshafen am Rhein, 1965), p. 113; C. Schuster, *Vom Farbenhandel zur Farbenindustrie. Die erste Fusion der BASF* (Ludwigshafen am Rhein, 1973), p. 71ff; N. Kirchner, 'Die Bayer-Werke in Russland, 1883–1974. Ein deutscher Beitrag zur Industrialisierung Russlands', H. Lemberg *et al.*, *Osteuropa in Geschichte und Gegenwart. Festschrift für Günther Stökl zum 60. Geburtstag* (Köln 1977), pp. 153–70; *Dokumente aus Hoechst-Archiven*, 43 (Frankfurt am Main, 1970), p. 7, 11ff.
68. F. Redlich, *Die volkswirtschaftliche Bedeutung der deutschen Teerfarbenindustrie* (doctoral thesis, Berlin, 1914), p. 83; L.F. Haber, op. cit., p. 173; L.F. Haber, *The Chemical Industry during the Nineteenth Century* (Oxford, 1958), p. 142.
69. *Dokumente aus Hoechst-Archiven*, 44 (Frankfurt am Main, 1970), p. 7.
70. P.A. Zimmermann, op. cit., p. 113; *Die Badische Anilin- & Soda-Fabrik* (1921), p. 17; for these subsidiaries and others founded in France by Casella and AGFA see also R. Poidevin, op. cit., p. 29.
71. L.F. Haber, *The Chemical Industry 1900–1930*, p. 146ff.; P.A. Zimmermann, op. cit., p. 121ff; F. Redlich, op. cit., p. 81; *Dokumente aus Hoechst-Archiven*, 45 (Frankfurt/Main, 1971), p. 7ff, 14ff; it was for the same reasons that Schering, the above mentioned pharmaceutical firm, decided after 1908 to establish a manufacturing subsidiary near London which was to cover the markets of Britain and its Empire (H. Holländer, op. cit., p. 37).
72. L.F. Haber, *The Chemical Industry 1900–1930*, p. 148.
73. T.R. Kabisch, op. cit., p. 164ff., 225ff.
74. P. Hertner, 'Das Auslandskapital in der italienischen Wirtschaft, 1883–1914. Probleme seiner Quantifizierung und Auswertung' in H. Kellenbenz (ed.),

Weltwirtschaftliche und währungspolitische Probleme seit dem Ausgang des Mittelalters (Stuttgart, 1981), pp. 93–121, particularly p. 105.

75. P. Czada, *Die Berliner Elektroindustrie in der Weimarer Zeit* (Berlin, 1969), p. 48ff.
76. G. Jacob-Wendler, *Deutsche Elektroindustrie in Lateinamerika. Siemens und AEG (1890–1914)* (Stuttgart, 1982), p. 11.
77. Ibid.; P. Czada, op. cit., p. 48ff.; see also the statistical tables in the Siemens Museum, München, Firmenarchiv (hereafter referred to as Siemens archives), SAA 11/Lb 581 (Liedtke).
78. See, among others, G. Siemens, *Geschichte des Hauses Siemens*, 3 vols. (Munich, 1947/1952); '50 Jahre AEG' (printed manuscript, Berlin, Allgemeine Elektricitäts-gesellschaft, 1956); J. Kocka, 'Siemens und der aufhaltsame Aufstieg der AEG', *Tradition* (1972), pp. 125–42; G. Eibert, *Unternehmenspolitik Nürnberger Maschinenbauer (1835–1914)*, (Stuttgart, 1979), pp. 182–281, 311–404 (on Schuckert).
79. S. von Weiher and H. Goetzeler, *Weg und Wirken der Siemens-Werke im Fortschritt der Elektrotechnik 1847–1972, Tradition*, Beiheft 8, (1972), p. 15; J.D. Scott, *Siemens Brothers 1858–1958* (London, 1958), pp. 31, 52.
80. G. Siemens, op. cit., vol. 1 (Munich, 1947), p. 87.
81. See the monumental work by H. Lüthy, *La banque protestante en France de la révocation de l'édit de Nantes à la Révolution*, 2 vols. (Paris, 1959).
82. J.D. Scott, op. cit., p. 79.
83. G. Siemens, op. cit., vol. 2, p. 206.
84. Siemens archives, SAA 68/Li 177.
85. I. Mai, *Das deutsche Kapital in Russland 1850–1894* (Berlin, DDR, 1970), p. 99ff., 197; G.S. Holzer, 'The German electrical industry in Russia: from economic entrepreneurship to political activism, 1890–1918' (PhD thesis, University of Nebraska, 1970), pp. 29ff., 41; W. Kirchner, 'The Industrialization of Russia and the Siemens firm 1853–1890', *Jahrbücher für Geschichte Osteuropas*, new series, 22 (1974), pp. 321–57, particularly p. 330; S. von Weiher, 'Carl von Siemens 1829–1906. Ein deutscher Unternehmer in Russland und England', *Tradition* (1956), pp. 13–25, particularly p. 23.
86. *50 Jahre AEG*, 94ff., 132, 158; G.S. Holzer, op cit, p. 34, 41ff.; 83; J. Mai, 'Deutscher Kapitalexport nach Russland 1898–1907' in H. Lemke and B. Widera (eds), *Russisch-deutsche Beziehungen von der Kiever Rus' bis zur Oktoberrevolution* (Berlin, DDR, 1976), pp. 207ff.; V. Djakin, 'Zur Stellung des deutschen Kapitals in der Elektroindustrie Russlands', *Jahrbuch für Geschichte der UdSSR und der volksdemokratischen Länder Europas* (1966), p. 122ff.
87. V. Djakin, op. cit., p. 142ff.
88. P. Lanino, *La nuova Italia industriale*, vol. 2 (Rome, 1916), p. XXVIII.
89. G. Jacob-Wendler, op. cit., p. 69.
90. See the fundamental contribution by R. Liefmann, *Beteiligungs-und Finanzierungsgesellschaften. Eine Studie über den modernen Kapitalismus und das Effektenwesen* (Jena, 1913), in particular p. 103ff.
91. F. Fasolt, *Die sieben grössten deutschen Elektrizitätsgesellschaften. Ihre Entwicklung und Unternehmertätigkeit*, doctoral thesis, Heidelberg (Borna-Leipzig, 1904), p. 31ff.; M. Jürgens, *Finanzielle Trustgesellschaften*, doctoral thesis (Stuttgart, 1902), p. 117ff.
92. A. Strobel, 'Die Gründung des Züricher Elektrotrusts. Ein Beitrag zum Unternehmergeschäft der deutschen Elektroindustrie' in H. Hassinger (ed.), *Geschichte-Wirtschaft-Gesellschaft. Festschrift für Clemens Bauer zum 75. Geburtstag* (Berlin, 1974), pp. 303–32; H. Grossmann, *Die Finanzierungen der Bank für elektrische Unternehmungen in Zürich*, Staatswiss. Diss. Zürich (Zürich, 1918); K. Hafner, *Die schweizerischen Finanzierungsgesellschaften für elektrische Unternehmungen*, Jur. Diss. Fribourg (Genève, 1912), p. 32ff.; P Hertner, 'Banken und Kapitalbildung in

der Giolitti-Ara'; *Quellen und Forschungen aus italienischen Archiven und Bibliotheken* (1978), pp. 466–565, particularly p. 508ff.

93.   P. Hertner, *Banken und Kapitalbildung*, p. 526f.; G. Jacob-Wendler, op. cit., p. 71ff.
94.   P. Hertner, *Das Auslandskapital*, p. 104; V. Djakin, op. cit., p. 142f.

8 Swedish Multinational Growth before 1930

Ragnhild Lundström

Introduction

In comparison with the foreign direct investments of the United States and Great Britain, those emanating from Sweden are rather insignificant: in the early 1980s, Sweden accounted for a mere 2 per cent of the total world figure, compared with 48 per cent from the United States and 11 per cent from Britain.[1] However, Sweden ranks second after Switzerland in foreign direct investment per capita and fifth for such investments relative to gross national product. The percentage is very close to that for the United States, although of course 7-8 per cent of the United States' GNP is very much larger than the same percentage of Sweden's GNP.

From a national point of view, Sweden's foreign direct investment is certainly not insignificant and Swedish multinationals play an important role in the Swedish economy. In the early 1980s, almost 50 per cent of the Swedish industrial labour force was employed by Swedish multinationals, and they also accounted for nearly 60 per cent of total Swedish exports.[2] Manufacturing industry clearly dominates the Swedish foreign direct investment scene—accounting for 75 per cent—with a high concentration in the engineering sector. This is quite different from the pattern of American and British investment.[3]

As much as 80 per cent of Swedish foreign direct investment originates in firms that were already multinational by the middle of the 1920s.[4] Consequently, when analysing Swedish multinationals, it is important to go back in time to the period when these firms entered the international scene.

The aim of this paper is to examine the early period of Swedish multinational growth before 1930. In so doing I shall stress both the preconditions and the direct reasons for their starting production abroad. I shall also examine the relevance of some of the better known theories of multinational enterprise to the history of early Swedish multinationals.

The paper is based mainly on company biographies and the scattered statistics that are to be found. A multinational is defined here as a firm that controls manufacturing subsidiaries, or production units, in at least *two* countries other than Sweden.[5] Companies with only sales subsidiaries in foreign countries will not be included.

Wicander

In view of the fact that Sweden was late to industrialise, Swedish companies started investing abroad surprisingly early. Tables 8.1 and 8.2 indicate the geographical spread of certain Swedish multinational investments in 1910 and 1922. It should be emphasised that both tables depict only a selection of companies, and they include only those firms that had invested in production in at least two countries besides Sweden. There were many more companies that had only invested in one foreign country at this time, and hundreds which had invested in sales subsidiaries. All the firms on these lists had sales subsidiaries in several other countries: SKF, for example, had 22 sales subsidiaries in 20 countries in 1922, besides the production subsidiaries listed here.

The first Swedish firm to start manufacturing abroad was a cork company.[6] In 1868, August Wicander entered the cork business by accident. He had traded his farm in the middle of Sweden for a piece of real estate in Stockholm. When inspecting his new property, he found that a shed in his back yard, which had contained the small cork-carving shop of the former proprietor, was still full of cork and tools. Wicander decided to continue the cork-carving shop, at least for the time being. At this time cork was both cut and carved by hand, and Wicander had some ten workers on his payroll. However, Wicander had learned about a machine for carving cork which had been exhibited some years earlier. He managed to find the inventor and buy the machine from him. As the first cork-carving machine in the world, it had been patented already in 1847 by a Swedish *mecanicus* who had not been able to sell one single machine before the patent elapsed. Soon after, Wicander bought more machinery from a small engineering workshop which had made improvements to the original machine and which also constructed machines for cutting the cork strips and for stamping the brewer's brand on the cork. Wicander's was the first bottle-cork firm in the world to mechanise its production.

Wicander produced a better, more even product, and its reputation spread. Wicander received a huge order from one of the largest breweries in the Nordic countries, situated in Helsinki and with exports to St Petersburg, an order which far exceeded the production capacity of Wicander's factory. Wicander's second bottle-cork factory started manufacturing in Finland in 1871. Wicander's decision to invest abroad, instead of exporting, was logical. The two alternatives were

TABLE 8.1 Some Swedish Multinationals in 1910 (number of production subsidiaries)

Firm	Product	Norway Denmark and Finland	Russia	United Kingdom	Germany	France	Rest of Europe	USA	South America
AGA	beacons	1						1	
ASEA	electrical machinery	1		1					
Bolinder	mech. eng. saw frames	1		1					
De Lavals Ångturbin	steam turbines	1							
L.M. Ericsson	telephone equipment		1	1		1		1	1
Lux	gas lamps gas light equipment	1	1			1	3	1	1
Separator	cream separators				1		1	1	
Jönköping & Vulcan	matches		1	1					
SAT	telephone operation		1			1	1		
Sv. Konservfabr.	preserves + methods	3							
Wicander	cork linoleum	3	3		1		2		

Sources: H. Runblem, *Svenska företag: Latinamesika* (Uppsala, 1971); K. Key-Åberg, *Svenska Aktiebolag och enskilda banker* (Stockholm, 1910–23); and various company biographies. It is sometimes difficult to separate manufacturing subsidiaries from sales subsidiaries, especially in the case of AGA.

TABLE 8.2   Some Swedish Multinationsl in 1922 (number of production subsidiaries)

Firm	Product	Norway Denmark and Finland	Russia	United Kingdom	Germany	France	Rest of Europe	USA	South America	Rest of World
AGA	beacons railway signals	3		1	2		3	1	4	
ASEA	electrical machinery	1	1	1						
Baltic	dairy equipment			1				1		
C.E. Johansson	precision gauges			1				1		
Electrolux (incl. former Lux)	domestic electrical equipment			1					1	1
ESAB	electric welding			1			1			
Jungner (Nife)	alkaline accumulators (batteries)	1		1						

L.M. Ericsson	telephone equipment & operation		1		1	4	2
Pump-Separator	dairy equipment			2			
Separator/ Alfa Laval	cream separators dairy equipment		1	1		1	2
SKF	ball/roller bearings		1	1	1		1
Sv. Konservfabr.	preserves & methods	1	1		1		
Swedish Match	matches	*	*	*		*	*
Wicander	cork linoleum	2	1	1		3	1

*In most cases there was more than one manufacturing company. However, the purchase of many of these was still being kept secret in the early 1920s, and formal ownership held by proxies. See L. Hassbing, *The International Development of the Swedish Match Company 1917–1924* (Stockholm 1979).

Sources: see Table 8.1.

either production in Sweden and exports during the eight or nine months of the year at most that boats in those days could travel between Sweden and Finland, or production in Finland with deliveries to customers all the year round and with a large prospective market in Russia because of the favourable tariff treatment for Finnish products. Moreover, the establishment of a factory in Finland was not capital-intensive, as the overall scale of business was small. Nor were there problems about training new workers, at least at the beginning, since Wicander persuaded some of his Swedish workers to go along.

The reasons for Wicander's decision to start manufacturing in Berlin in 1883 were rather different. Considering the generally depressed economic conditions in all countries at that time, Wicander's investments in Germany seem to reflect the optimistic view of a successful entrepreneur. Wicander was by then the second largest buyer of cork in the world.[7]

In the meantime, Wicander had undertaken some horizontal integration by buying out his largest competitor in Stockholm and several bottle-cork manufacturers in other Swedish cities. The purchase of other firms and the establishment of the Berlin factory were made possible by ploughing back profits. When in 1885 Wicander wanted to start manufacturing in Russia, however, he had to resort to external financing as well.[8] The reason for wanting to build a factory in Russia lay in the overtures that had been made to introduce a tariff barrier between Finland and Russia. When this was later enacted, in 1888, Wicander's new factory was ready to start manufacturing within the Russian borders. In 1891, the company went into shipping. When in that same year August Wicander died, his sons continued the business.

At the end of the 1890s, when world economic conditions improved, there was a new spurt of expansion for Wicander. In Denmark, the firm started a new factory and acquired an old one. In 1897 they went into the linoleum business where they could use cork waste from their own factories. A linoleum factory was erected in Libau, the first such factory within Russian borders. The only existing linoleum factory in Sweden was purchased. They also acquired their largest competitor in the cork business in Russia and they integrated backwards by buying up some agencies for cork in Portugal and Algiers.

The reason why Wicander has been dealt with at such length is that it is an illustration of what it took to become a multinational in the pre-1914 period. It is also an interesting example of the forms of international production. Wicander's factories were separate private companies at the start, but in 1889 the holdings in Sweden were amalgamated to form a joint-stock company and some brewery owners became shareholders, whilst the Wicander family held the majority of

140

shares. Until 1904, the companies outside Sweden were kept as separate entities under the ownership of the Wicander family. Then, with the assistance of the Stockholms Handelsbank, they were taken over by the Swedish joint-stock company, the capital of which was raised. The members of the Wicander family received new shares in exchange for their foreign holdings.

AB Separator

The second Swedish company that started production abroad on any large scale was probably AB Separator. Some ten years after Wicander, this small company appeared on the international market.[9] Today, with its name changed to Alfa Laval, it is the largest producer of dairy and barn equipment in the world.

In 1879, production of a cream separator, constructed and patented by Dr Gustaf de Laval, was started in a small way in an engineering workshop. De Laval claimed that his separator was an improvement in comparison with existing ones, since it operated 'continuously'. Certainly the firm soon managed to develop a good export market. In the second half of the 1880s, Swedish sales accounted for 15 per cent and German sales for 30 per cent of Separator's receipts, while the United States accounted for 10 per cent and Australia and New Zealand for 12 per cent respectively.

In 1889 the Separator company acquired the Alfa patent from a German engineer. This was to be the key to the great success of the company. The separators manufactured by this principle were superb and during the 1890s Separator became world market leader.

Sales were originally made through exports from Sweden. In the United States, because of the high tariffs on finished products, separator parts were exported and assembled and finished by American dealers. In 1883 de Laval interested some American financiers in founding a sales company, in which de Laval held only a minority shareholding. This arrangement did not work very successfully, and in 1890 Separator purchased all the shares. The move to manufacturing in the United States sounds like Swedish location policy of the 1980s. The now Swedish de Laval company in America was approached by representatives of Poughkeepsie in New York State who offered the company an industrial site free of charge provided the company engaged 200 workers within five years. The city's savings bank offered a favourable loan of $10 000. The stipulation was fulfilled well in advance of time, and by the end of the decade the company employed around 1,000 workers.

The American company proved a veritable gold mine. Around 1910, 75 per cent of the profits of the Swedish parent company emanated from its American subsidiary. In the American dairy states it had about 70 per cent of the separator market, and overall it had around 50 per cent of the entire American market. Apart from the American company, no other foreign manufacturing subsidiary was founded or acquired while the patent lasted, with the single exception of a small engineering business manufacturing dairy equipment in Vienna, purchased in 1897, which was intended to function also as a sales company for separators with an eye on the Hungarian market.

At the turn of the century, Separator was the largest and probably the most successful company in Sweden. From the 1890s it had rationalised production: new machine-tools were introduced, and the workers turned into machine operators. From the very start of production in the US there had been a mutual give and take between the Swedish parent company and its subsidiary. In such technical matters as construction, testing and quality, the parent company was usually the giver, at least until the 1920s. In contrast, the matters that had to do with production methods and organisation of work, the flow of information often went in the opposite direction as American methods were more advanced.

In 1903 the Alfa patent elapsed and competing separator companies mushroomed. Around 1905, there were more than 50 competing brands in Germany, of which no less than ten originated in Sweden. Separator countered the growing competition in various ways. Sales subsidiaries were founded in several countries where before it had been served by agents.

Separator also acquired some of the competing companies, including one in Denmark which was considered as the most dangerous. The Danish firm's production was immediately discontinued. It also, though reluctantly, bought a German company manufacturing dairy equipment, a company that had for many years been its sales agent in Germany. The reason for this seems to have been the plans of the company to start its own manufacture of separators.

Almost from the day of its incorporation as a limited company, the Separator company had a salaried manager. The company can probably be described as run by the management, although the manager at times had to walk a tightrope, particularly when around the turn of the century, the company's shares were subject to speculation, and the majority of ownership changed. The president of Stockholms Diskontobank was on the board of directors, and the bank helped in issuing debentures, and also in some long-term lending at the beginning of the 1900s around the time when the Alfa patent elapsed. The bank apparently also helped in financing the takeover of the German company. The purchase of the Danish company was financed by a loan from the American company. Share capital was raised almost fivefold in 1910. Thus, when competition increased in the first decade of the 1900s, Separator was large enough, and had, or could acquire, the financial means to offset that competition.

Ericsson and SAT

There are two telephone companies on the list of Swedish multinationals in 1910 given in Table 8.1. In that year, these two companies were already cooperating and in 1918 they merged.[10] L.M. Ericsson was originally a company manufacturing telephones and telephone equipment, while Stockholms Allmänna Telefon AB (SAT) started as a telephone operating company and later began manufacturing telephones. L.M. Ericsson was founded in 1876 as an engineering workshop for repair work by a mechanic of the same name.[11] At about this time began the import of a small number of Bell telephones, many of which had to be sent to him for repair. Lars Magnus Ericsson started experimenting to improve the Bell-Blake telephone, and in 1878 began producing his own telephones. The Stockholm market was closed to him since the Bell Telephone Co., which had begun a service there, naturally took its telephones from its own factories. However, when other telephone operating companies were founded in smaller cities, they usually placed their orders with L.M. Ericsson. So at first did the Swedish Telegraph Office, which opened a second line in Stockholm, and Stockholms Allmäna Telefon AB, founded in 1883, which started the third line in Stockholm.

Both the State-owned telegraph office and SAT eventually started their own production of telephones, and the importance of the Swedish market decreased for L.M. Ericsson. He continuously worked on improving 'his' telephone, and in the 1880s constructed the one-piece telephone, with receiver and microphone in the same unit, which is now used all over the world, whereas the Bell Telephone Co. for a long time stuck to their two-piece apparatus. In the 1890s, when world economic conditions improved, the L.M. Ericsson company gained a large export market and by 1900 the Swedish market accounted for only 5 per cent of their sales. The largest market was in Great Britain, where 50 per cent of Ericsson's production was sold. The National Telephone Co. in Britain bought all its telephones from L.M. Ericsson and was Ericsson's largest single customer. The two companies in 1903 jointly established a British company for the manufacture of telephone equipment, each company holding 50 per cent of the shares, with an understanding that L.M. Ericsson was to buy out National Telephone in 1911. When in 1904 production began in England, Ericsson's exports to Britain subsequently decreased and later ceased altogether.

Overly confident because of his success elsewhere, Ericsson ventured into the United States. In 1904, the company's sales subsidiary in the United States was turned into a production subsidiary. However, Ericsson was not successful in Bell's home country, and production was discontinued in 1920. The firm also invested in Russia in the middle of the 1890s. When competition from the other telephone producing companies grew harder in Sweden, Lars Magnus Ericsson had plans for moving his entire production, including workers, to Russia, but when other export markets picked up, he settled for the founding of a manufacturing unit in St Petersburg in 1897.

In 1900 Stockholms Allmäna Telefon AB (SAT) decided to go international. The company, founded by an engineer and graduate of Stockholm Institute of Technology, H. Cedergren, had had no difficulty in competing with the Bell Telephone Co. However, it was confined to the Stockholm area with no possibilities of further quick expansion.

When the concessions for telephone operation in Moscow, St Petersburg and Warsaw, previously held by the Bell Telephone Co., were opened for competition, a syndicate was formed consisting of SAT, Stockholms Enskilda Bank, a Danish and a French bank and a German banking house with the aim of entering the competition. The cooperation of the Danish bank was politically useful because of the close connection that existed by marriage between the Danish and Russian courts. The syndicate's tenders for Moscow and Warsaw were accepted, and concessions for 17 years obtained. Two new telephone operating companies were founded, Svensk-Dansk-Ryska Telefon AB for Russia and AB H. Cedergren for Poland, SAT receiving the majority of shares. SAT was now transformed into a holding company.

Large telephone operating concessions like those for Moscow and Warsaw required sizeable amounts of long-term capital because of the considerable time lag between construction and income received. Svensk-Dansk-Ryska Telefon AB obtained a large loan against debentures in France with the Stockholms Enskilda Bank as intermediary and negotiating party. A few years later, concerning a concession in Mexico, a similar procedure was adopted by SAT and Marcus Wallenberg Senior of Stockholms Enskilda Bank in cooperation with L.M. Ericsson. The Ericsson company received 60 per cent of the shares in the new Mexican Telephone Co. Ericsson.

By that time, the fight between the Ericsson company and SAT had been settled. Realising that its own production capacity would not suffice, should the concessions in Russia be obtained, SAT had made arrangements with L.M. Ericsson already before the syndicate submitted its tenders.

Although after 1904 SAT and L.M. Ericsson were linked through the ownership of each other's shares, the two firms remained independent until their merger in 1918. Ericsson's tender for telephones and equipment to the State-owned French monopoly PTT was accepted in 1908, provided the products were produced in France. Some years later Ericsson acquired an Austro-Hungarian company with a product mix similar to that of their own. The financing, both of the building of the new factory in France and the purchase of the company in Vienna, was made possible with the help of Ericsson's old bank connection, Stockholms Handelsbank.

What were the preconditions and the reasons for the internationalisation of the Swedish telephone companies? As for preconditions, they are much easier to pinpoint for Ericsson than for SAT. Ericsson was marketing an excellent product, their one-piece table telephones. Ericsson also worked continuously on improvements to their products. The reasons why Ericsson decided to start production abroad are not very obvious. Only the French manufacturing subsidiary was founded because of government regulations in the host country. In Great Britain there was no need to take such factors into consideration. Despite its name, the National Telephone Co. was just an ordinary company, competing in the market with several others. It would appear that Ericsson decided to start manufacturing in England because production facilities were offered them. In the Russian case there were no direct government regulations regarding telephone equipment that prompted the decision to start manufacture in 1897, but the Russian government was known to favour domestic production, and this factor might well have influenced Ericsson's decision.

For SAT as a telephone operating company, the preconditions for going abroad were of a quite different character. SAT must have possessed considerable organisational skills. However, the most important factor for telephone concessions was financial strength, either held by the concessionaire itself or in connection with financial institutes. Such connections had been obtained by SAT at the time of its entering the world telephone market.

Seeking Larger Markets
The development of the companies described above also reflects the general development of the Swedish economy and industry. The period which witnessed the first phase of Swedish multinational growth—1870 to 1910—was also the period of the industrialisation of Sweden.

The year 1868, when Wicander started his small cork business, was the last year of great famines in Sweden's history. Sweden was not yet a united national market, especially in wintertime when the Gulf of Bothnia was icebound. Industrialisation had begun only slowly; there

145

were only a few local railways; the banks that existed were small and most of them local.

Like many early American entrepreneurs, Swedes with products and ideas for starting a business of their own left their home country to do so abroad.[12] Markets were larger and capital more accessible in other countries.

In Sweden, Alfred Nobel and his brothers are the most striking examples of this trend. Immediately after having founded a small nitroglycerine company in Sweden in 1864, Alfred Nobel left the country in search of capital for expansion. Subsequently, although much slower than he had envisaged after having invented dynamite, Nobel found financiers and established local companies in Germany, the United States, France, Italy, Spain, Switzerland and Scotland. It was not until competition between the various companies began in the 1880s that these firms were merged into two trusts. Certainly these trusts were multinationals, although not Swedish multinationals. Meanwhile Alfred Nobel's brothers developed a small empire of their own in Russia. Starting with an engineering business, they later founded a petroleum company on large oil concessions in Baku.

The development of both the Separator company and the telephone company of L.M. Ericsson is typical of the growing engineering industry in Sweden. The engineering workshops, jacks of all trades, were first mechanised, and later started specialising. In the process of specialising, they soon discovered that the Swedish market, at least in the short-term, was too small. Most of their production was exported. If it was deemed necessary, for example, because of protective tariffs in other countries, they invested in production units in other countries.

The early foreign investors did not need that much capital because the barriers to entry were low. Nevertheless the importance of the banks grew gradually. There emerged a group of larger banks with both a more national and a more international outlook than that of the local banks. (Sweden was a capital-importing economy until the First World War, and it was these larger banks that negotiated State and city loans on the international financial market, thereby gaining knowledge and contacts.) For Swedish companies wanting to invest abroad, bank connections became increasingly important. Banks served as advisers, sometimes as financiers themselves, sometimes as intermediaries for capital from other sources, both foreign and domestic.

Swedish Match
Such contracts with financial intitutions for the furtherance of growth on the international market were carried to their utmost in the Swedish match industry during the 1920s. Through a combination of

entrepreneurship of an unusual ingenuity for Sweden, and the financial backing of Sweden's two largest banks, Skandinaviska Banken and Svenska Handelsbanken (and particularly of the former in later years) the Swedish match industry almost conquered the world market. These events have been described in four books, and one pending, all translated into English, by a group of economic historians at Uppsala University.[13] It is only necessary, therefore, to say a few words here.

Iva Kreuger managed to merge a small group of Swedish match factories, already united in Förenade Svenska Tändsticksfabriker (in one part of which his family already held a controlling interest), with a larger group of match factories, united in Jönköping & Vulcan. As a result, Kreuger secured control of the entire Swedish match industry. At the time of the merger, Jönköping & Vulcan had already made direct investments in a splint factory in Russia, in order to secure raw materials, and in an 'assembly' plant in England, in order to bypass the Australian tariff regulations which gave preference to imports from Britain.

Kreuger continued the internationalisation of the Swedish match industry, which already before 1914 accounted for 25 per cent of world exports and 8 per cent of world production. Kreuger began by acquiring controlling interests in established match manufacturing companies, and later, from his position of strength, by obtaining match monopolies in no less than 15 countries in exchange for large State loans. From this position Kreuger negotiated price and trade agreements with the other large match companies in the world, the foremost of which were the British Bryant & May and the American Diamond Match Co.

Kreuger's empire was large and complicated, embracing holding companies such as Kreuger & Toll, banks and numerous other companies including some outside the match industry. At its height the group included 144 match manufacturing companies in 33 countries. Cash flowed between its various parts in a way similar to that nowadays practised in most large multinationals, but Kreuger's methods were perhaps not always in line with what would today be regarded as sound business principles. Kreuger himself did not fare so well when the Depression began. He committed suicide in 1932. Swedish Match, however, survived. The firm was reconstructed and Swedish Match was left with the controlling interest in 70 factories in 31 countries. Immediately before the Second World War, it had approximately 60 per cent of world exports and around 20 per cent of world production.

Such a combination of entrepreneurship and capital was not unusual on the international scene of the 1920s, the most well-known example being the founding and growth of ITT by the combined forces of Sosthenes Behn, the National City Bank and the Morgan group.[14]

There are similarities between this and SAT in Russia and L.M. Ericsson in Mexico, although ITT at its start did not include any telephone operating or producing firms. Even Kreuger might have fared better had he not chosen matches, an industry where barriers to entry were still low in many countries. Swedish Match was reconstructed in cooperation with Swedish banks. It was due to these banks that Swedish Match and L.M. Ericsson, in which Kreuger had acquired the majority interest, remained Swedish-owned multi-nationals.

SKF

None of the other Swedish companies which expanded their multinational operations in the early 1920s appeared quite as spectacular to contemporaries as Swedish Match, although some were equally or perhaps more successful. This last point applies particularly to SKF, the Swedish ball and roller bearings company, which had been founded in 1907, and within ten years had production subsidiaries in Britain, the United States, France and Russia.[15]

At its inception, SKF had literally no market in Sweden. Swedish customers were highly suspicious of the new ball bearings and preferred the old type, made in Germany. However, British and French customers preferred those made in Sweden, perhaps for political reasons, while in the United States 'made in Sweden' came to represent quality bearings. In 1910 SKF started production in Britain, its largest market, giving as reasons the need for proximity to customers and the use of the inch system. It also made plans for eventually starting manufacturing in France and the United States, once an opportunity arose. The opportunities came with the outbreak of the First World War. American demand for SKF ball bearings increased rapidly. In 1915 SKF started manufacturing in America, with most of the sales of its subsidiary going to war production. In 1917 it began producing in France after a request from the French government.

The inventor of SKF's spherical, self-regulating ball bearings had started experimenting when still an engineer at a well-established textile manufacturing company in Gothenburg. The company had supported him and it also financed the start of production of the new type of bearings. Due to the rapid growth of demand from abroad, with resulting enlargements of production facilities, new share capital had to be raised frequently, in 1911 no less than three times, and the group behind the textile company guaranteed the issues. When production was to be started in the United States, SKF had to turn to the American capital market as well. Marcus Wallenberg Senior of Stockholms Enskilda Bank served as an intermediary and did so also two years later when SKF had to resort to the French capital market when starting production in France.

Developments during the 1920s

The list of Swedish multinationals in the early 1920s might have been longer had it not been for the Russian Revolution of 1917. During the pre-war period, and especially after 1910, Russia appeared to be the most promising market for Swedish industry, especially for the young Swedish engineering industry. Swedish exports to Russia soared and numerous Swedish companies founded Russian subsidiaries. The Nobel family had an interest in many of the larger companies. The great success of the Nobels, of Wicander, and of L.M. Ericsson and SAT encouraged both large and small Swedish companies to start their international careers on the Russian market. Unfortunately for many, their international careers also ended there.

A number of companies also ceased being multinationals during the 1920s. This included C.E. Johansson, the company founded on the invention of precision gauges. C.E. Johansson's invention was probably the single most important one for the development and growth of the engineering industry in any country. SKF relied on it for its precision machinery. During the First World War the Johansson gauges had been indispensible for the American war production, for production of interchangeable parts in large series (as in weapons production) and had been exported from Sweden to the United States in the American diplomatic courier mail. The American federal authorities also helped to facilitate the formal arrangements for Johansson to start a manufacturing subsidiary in the United States.[16] A company was also founded in Great Britain. In 1923, the American company including patents was sold to Henry Ford. Precision gauges were indispensable for the conveyer belt production introduced by Ford in the automobile industry. Why did C.E. Johansson's Swedish company cease being a multinational at this time? Either Swedish financiers did not realise the full potential of the product, or Ford appreciated it to such a degree that it was more remunerative for Johansson to sell out to Ford. Johansson later worked in a senior position in the Dearborn factory until 1938.

Swedish Multinational Experience and the Theories of Foreign Direct Investment

It can be seen that the development of early Swedish multinationals does show certain distinct characteristics which seem to fit rather well with some of the theories or models of foreign direct investment. The theories of Hymer and Caves, for instance, which suggest a unique asset or differentiated product on the part of the foreign investor appear to be applicable to Swedish developments.[17]

Most of the Swedish companies that had invested in production abroad before 1930 were found in the new engineering industry. Many of them had been founded on the basis of either original inventions or improvements of existing inventions. Besides those already mentioned, these included AGA, with Dalén's invention of automatic lighthouses using acetylene gas, for Electrolux with Wennergren's improvement of the vacuum cleaner and later its Platen-Munter refrigeration system, for the Jungner company, with its alkaline accumulators, and for ASEA, with the Wenstrom three-phase system for transmission of electricity.

Most of Swedish foreign direct investments were market-oriented. Only a few firms, such as Wicander and Jönköping & Vulcan, made investments in order to secure raw materials abroad. The home market was limited for the new Swedish engineering companies, and for some was almost non-existent. A large part of their production, therefore, had to be exported. Growing economies of scale, above all because of improvements in the production of interchangeable parts, in most cases made exports from Sweden preferable to manufacturing abroad. As a result some companies even discovered that they had gone abroad with production too quickly. ASEA was one example. By 1900 the firm had invested in a manufacturing subsidiary in Britain, and purchased interests in companies in Denmark, Finland and Norway. Between 1904 and 1907 it disposed of its interests in the Scandinavian firms.

In many cases the 'uniqueness' of the assets of the young Swedish engineering firms is open to question. Research and experimentation was carried out along the same lines in many countries at about the same time. Similar patents were applied for in different countries by different inventors, sometimes literally simultaneously. Since several of the Swedish companies started manufacturing in other countries so early in their careers, they had not had the time to acquire any deeper knowledge of production which was particularly valuable to transfer across borders.

SKF is an example of this phenonemon. There were several much larger and more experienced ball bearing companies in Germany and the United States, some of which also became multinational. At the start SKF bought both machinery and steel from abroad. It improved on its products and its production methods as it expanded internationally. As a latecomer it geared its marketing into niches which the older and larger companies had not filled. What kind of asset does this experience imply? The firm did not have any home market to practice on, since the German ball bearings producers dominated the Swedish market. Knowledge of marketing, therefore, could not have been its 'unique' asset, at least not at the beginning. SKF apparently possessed entrepreneurial foresight. But was it unique, different, more advantageous as compared with the foreign and indigenous producers with which SKF had to compete in most markets? In the years before 1914, SKF benefited from being owned by a neutral country. With the outbreak of the war, however, not even that was an asset. France demanded domestic production and Britain demanded that all 'balls', part of which had hitherto been imported from Sweden, be produced at the subsidiary in England. Later SKF undoubtedly benefited during the war when German companies were unable to export and had difficulties with their subsidiaries in enemy countries. The success of SKF cannot be seen apart from the historical developments of the time.

In several ways, the growth of Swedish firms and their evolution into multinationals differs from that of American firms as described by A.D. Chandler.[18] Swedish companies started production abroad early. Few had had the time, or the opportunity, to develop into national firms before becoming multinational. They eventually did, in several cases thanks to their success on the international market, and began integrating both vertically and horizontally at home during their internationalisation process. This development has continued until today. Many of these early multinationals are the only existing, or by far the largest, domestic companies in their particular field within Sweden.

There are also more general objections to the asset type of theories of foreign direct investments. All such theories assume that a foreign-owned firm is at a disadvantage relative to existing or potential domestic producers, the cost of which has to be counterbalanced by an ownership advantage such as differentiated product, or marketing or organisational skill. Historians require this approach to be modified, the disadvantage graded in some respect. It is hard to see the psychological disadvantage of a firm in the German-speaking part of Switzerland investing in Germany, or of a firm in the French-speaking part investing in a company in France. Or of an American company investing in Canada, or a Norwegian in Sweden. And how are British and French investments in former colonies, or British investments in the dominions, to be considered? The disadvantage or cost in many such cases must be rather minimal, and the advantage to balance them accordingly smaller.

Moreover, the disadvantage for a company, the foreign investments of which take the form of purchases of already existing companies in other countries, needs to be assessed from case to case. In 1928 Wicander sold its entire cork business to a Spanish firm, thus becoming part of a Spanish multinational, but rebought it only four years later, again becoming a Swedish multinational. There were no changes in the meantime, either in management or methods because of the change in onwership. There are, of course, numerous such examples. In many cases advantages are also acquired by purchases of existing firms abroad.

As for Sweden, the period of its early multinational growth was a time when over a million Swedes, or one-third of Sweden's population, emigrated. It was also a period when it was the custom for technicians, people who wanted to become foremen, students at the universities and technical institutes, to spend several years abroad, working or studying. It seems plausible that, under such circumstances, starting a business abroad was not considered to be so difficult.

Another objection to the disadvantage postulate and the ensuing theories of foreign direct investment is that it is hard to see why *producing* abroad would be more difficult than *selling* abroad. If cultural differences exist, and of course they do although to a varying degree and dependent on the parent and 'subsidiary' countries in question, such differences appear to be greatest in the field of marketing and selling. Therefore, one would have expected that multinationalisation would have been carried out along the lines of marketing, namely by forming conglomerates. As regards the early Swedish multi-nationals, this was not the case. To a certain degree, however, it is applicable to the later development and growth of some Swedish multi-nationals, for example, Separator (Alfa Laval) which diversified into milking machines and other barn equipment, and Electrolux which diversified into other durable consumer goods, both being able to use existing sales organisations.

Even should the postulate be adequate in all cases, the 'advantage' theories appear somewhat truistic. In essence, what they say is that 'for a firm to be successful on the international scene, it has to be successful'.[19]

From the point of view of the Swedish experience there is less objection to the group of theories that focus on the growth of firms. Several of these theories can be applied also to the development of Swedish multinationals. This goes for the theory of internalisation of transactions costs, where multinationalisation is seen as one form of growth, and also for the more dynamic models that outline a framework of conditions for the continuous growth process of firms.[20]

As for the 'internalisation theories' in relation to early Swedish multinationals, they are rather convincing for explaining the foundation of sales subsidiaries in foreign countries. However, when it comes to explaining foreign direct investments, they are less helpful as, in this respect, they are counter factual. Foreign direct investments were made by several Swedish companies in several countries before an actual market for their products had developed there. Of course, the eventual success of Swedish firms in such markets proves that their internalising of prospective transaction costs was profitable, which again appears rather truistic. It does not say much more than Swedish firms started manufacturing in other countries for institutional reasons, such as tariffs—sometimes in combination with high transport costs—and government regulations, and in so doing they were successful. One stresses the invisible, the other the visible hand.

What then would I, as an economic historian, want to add to the general theories of growth of firms in order to explain Swedish foreign direct investments? Naturally, a historical dimension, and in particular for this period the importance of nationalism needs to be stressed. The direct reasons why Swedish companies started production in other countries instead of exporting there are mostly to be found in the host economies. The period dealt with in this paper is the period of the reintroduction of protective tariffs in most industrialising countries, of growing nationalism, and of war. Many of the Swedish engineering companies that made foreign direct investments had public authorities as their customers. This goes for AGA's beacons and lighthouse equipment, the Lux company's lighting equipment for harbours and railway stations, ASEA's generators and turbines (which were often sold to publicly-owned waterpower enterprises), and, later, pharmaceutical companies. Even today, most public authorities give preference to domestic products when buying for public consumption and public investments. Therefore the general growth of the public sector in most countries has no doubt contributed to an increased degree of multinational production.

The development of the Swedish engineering firms in a sense illustrates Vernon's product cycle in reverse.[21] The most important markets were located outside Sweden. The potential large markets were Great Britain, Russia, France, the United States and Latin America.[22] When production had become more standardised, and the industrialisation of Sweden had proceeded, the home market increased.

Why under such circumstances did there ever develop anything like a Swedish multinational? Until the end of the nineteenth century, international business meant portfolio investments, or entrepreneurs moving to other countries when starting a business there, or separate firms being established abroad. Towards the turn of the century, there had developed a national capital and investment market. Through cross-investments, strong ties were developed between industry and the banks.[23] At the same time, nationalism grew in Sweden as well as in the rest of Europe. It grew among Swedish businessmen and bankers alike. The aggressive, State-supported export policy of German industry and the trade policy of Germany was one reason, and the failure of the Scandinavist movement another.[24] The prestige, not only of Swedish industrialists, but also of investors, bankers and politicians came to be linked to the success of Swedish firms. If production abroad was necessary for the growth of these firms, such production was started. Surprisingly many of these early Swedish multinationals were successful. Again, however, part of that can be ascribed to the fact that Sweden was neutral and stayed out of the First World War. In several instances it was also thanks to the action of Swedish banks, not only that Swedish firms became multinational, but also that Swedish multinationals remained Swedish.[25]

All this is doubtless an oversimplification of a long and complicated process with many cross-influences. Nevertheless, I will venture the conclusion that, judging from the Swedish experiences, multinationals were the result of nationalism. Foreign direct investment has been the predominant form of their growth for almost 100 years. Gradually, however, new forms of multinational enterprise have developed. Multinationals have become entities by themselves, leading their own lives. Although once originating within a specific country the multinationals have over time contributed to, and called for, a greater internationalisation of both business and capital. Therefore, in a much longer historical perspective, one might eventually find reason to say that foreign direct investment was the form, or stage, of international business during nationalism.

Notes

1. Statens offentliga utredningar (State official investigations, hereafter referred to as SOU) 1983:17, p. 56.
2. SOU 1982:27, p. 52.
3. A 1982 survey of Swedish foreign direct investments showed that 37 per cent were within the mechanical engineering industry, 15 per cent in the electrical engineering industry, 14 per cent in the ferrous and non-ferrous metal industry, 11 per cent in transport equipment (SOU 1982:27, p. 74).
4. Ibid., tables on p. 294ff.
5. The reason for choosing two countries is rather arbitrary. By so doing firms that started production in Russia but never got any further during this period are eliminated. Two countries indicates a certain element of success.
6. The account of Wicander and its business is based on C.A. Wicander, *Wicanders, Industriidkare och affärsmän under tre generationer*, volumes 1–3, (Stockholm, 1950, 1951, 1952), and *Forshaga 1896–1946* (Göteborg, 1946).
7. The direct reason why Wicander started production in Germany was a disagreement with its dealers over deliveries of corks of inferior quality, which they had disposed of on the large German market. Wicander now decided they might as well start a factory there and manufacture superior corks with inferior corks as a complementary product.
8. Wicander was given funds by a private banker in Stockholm, Louis Fraenckel, who

was later to become head of one of the larger Swedish banks, the Stockholms Handelsbank.

9. This account of Separator is based on the following books: *Separator AB 1883–1908* (Stockholm, 1908); T. Althin, *Gustaf de Laval 1845–1913* (Stockholm, 1943); T. Gårdlund and M. Fritz, *Ett världsföretag växer ram. Alfa Laval 100 år* vols. 1 and 2 (Stockholm, 1983); and K. Wohlert, *Framväxten av svenska multinationella företag. En fallstudie mot bakgrund av direktinvesteringsteorier, Alfa Laval och separatorindustrin 1876–1914* (Uppsala, 1981).

10. The history of these firms has been published in three volumes, A. Attman, J. Kuuse and U. Olsson, *L.M. Ericsson 100 år* (Stockholm, 1976). It is on the first volume, *Pionjärtid, kamp om koncessioner och kris 1876–1932*, that this account is based. Reference is also made to O. Gasslander, *Bank och industriellt genombrott. Stockholms Enskilda Bank kring sekelskiftet 1900* (Stockholm, 1956).

11. Lars Magnus Ericsson, who had no formal schooling above elementary level, had worked as a repairman with the State-operated telegraph service. He had spent three years abroad on a state scholarship in electrotechnical studies, part of which were carried out as an apprentice at Siemens & Halske in Berlin, one of the leading companies in that field in Europe.

12. M. Wilkins, *The Emergence of Multinational Enterprise: American Business Abroad from the Colonial Era to 1914* (Cambridge, Mass., 1970), p. 17ff.

13. The four books available are: L. Hassbring, *The International Development of the Swedish Match Company 1917–1924*; H. Lindgren, *Corporate Growth. The Swedish Match Industry in its Global Setting* (Stockholm, 1979), from which the figures in the paper are taken; H. Modig, *Swedish Match Interests in British India during the Interwar Years* (Stockholm, 1979); U. Wikander, *Kreuger's Match Monopolies, 1925–1930. Case Studies in Market Control through Public Monopolies* (Stockholm, 1980).

14. A. Attman, J. Kuuse, U. Olsson, op. cit., vol. 1, p. 323f.

15. B. Steckzén, *Svenska Kullagerfabriken 1907–1957* (Göteborg, 1957), has information on SKF.

16. S. Lundström, 'Mått och steg i blockadpolitiken mot Sverige 1917–1918' in *Och somt föll vid vägen. Till Karl-Gustaf Hildebrand* (mimeo, Ekonomisk-historiska seminariet, Uppsala, 1961), pp. 95–104.

17. R.E. Caves, 'International Corporations: The Industrial Economics of Foreign Investment', *Economica* (1971), pp. 1–27.

18. A. Chandler, *The Visible Hand* (Cambridge, Mass. 1977).

19. SOU 1983:17, p. 72.

20. For example, O.E. Williamson, *Market and Hierarchies: Analysis and Antitrust Implications*, (New York, 1975); E.T. Penrose, *The Theory of the Growth of the Firm* (Oxford, 1959).

21. R. Vernon, 'International Investment and International Trade in the Product Cycle', *Quarterly Journal of Economics* (1966), pp. 190–207.

22. Except for the very early period when transport even between the Scandinavian countries was inadequate, Swedish foreign direct investments did not go to these countries in the first place. It is true that sales subsidiaries were often founded there early in the internationalisation of Swedish firms. However, with the growing economies of scale, it was not economic to start manufacturing there. Despite its high protective tariffs, Germany was seldom the first choice of a Swedish engineering firm wanting to expand its markets. The output of the Swedish engineering industry was too similar to that of the German.

23. Usually one group of shareholders centred around one of the larger banks and also around the corporate customers of that bank.

24. S. Lundstrom, 'Östersjöhandeln och linjesjöfarten på Nordamerika 1905–1920' (unpublished thesis, University of Uppsala, 1962), p. 46.

25. This refers, for example, to ASEA, which the German AEG wanted to acquire in the beginning of the century, and which General Electric wanted to acquire at the end of the 1920s, and to L.M. Ericsson, which ITT wanted to incorporate in the early 1930s. For ASEA see J. Glete, *ASEA under 100 år 1883-1983. En studie i ett storföretags organisatoriska och ekonomiska utveckling* (Våsterås 1983).

9 The Growth of Multinational Activities in the French Motor Industry, 1890–1979

Patrick Fridenson

Historical knowledge of multinational corporations, though improving rapidly, still remains uneven.[1] The motor industry has had many important works devoted to it, from the pioneering research of Mira Wilkins to the recent synthesis by George Maxcy, which have given us a global picture of the process of multinationalisation,[2] yet the foreign operations of the French motor companies remain less well known. A study of their development will enable us to draw out the similarities with and differences from their European and American counterparts, and to assess the growing impact of foreign business activities on men, products and companies.

The Period before 1919: Importance of Exports and the Limits of Multinationalisation

The earliest move abroad in the transport industry was made by France. In 1880 a company financed by both French and German capital, and with a French managing director, was founded in Germany to produce the French industrialist Amédée Bollée's steam-powered vehicles. By 1883 it had failed.[3] When the internal combustion engine became dominant, however, French car makers were slower than some of their foreign competitors to venture into multinational enterprise. The most rapid of all was the German Daimler company, which in 1899 founded an Austrian subsidiary, Austro-Daimler, which began manufacturing in 1902. This was the first multinational motor company.[4] The boldest was the Fiat motor company in Italy. It created manufacturing branches in Austria (1907), the United States (1909), and Russia (1912) to produce small, but growing, numbers of its more expensive models.[5]

In contrast, French firms preferred exporting to manufacturing abroad and France held the leading position in world exports of motor cars up to the First World War, with its exports amounting to some 44–50 per cent of the country's total car production. Exporting was particularly attractive as much of exporters' success stemmed from the autonomous initiative of importing agents of foreign birth, and from the influence of wealthy tourists who purchased cars in France and took them to their native country.[6]

As a result, only a few, generally larger, firms (Panhard, Renault, Darracq), became multinational, and even they devoted only a limited part of their capital and manpower resources to foreign investments.[7] They developed in four successive and complementary directions.

Permanent networks of dealers were created abroad to find markets and simplify supply. Corporations which entered the motor industry from other sectors, like Panhard,[8] first used their existing foreign agents. By 1914 Renault had 31 foreign agents, Panhard 26, and Unic, the ninth largest motor car company, 20.[9] Most of them were foreigners.[10]

In addition, to supply the most important markets, the major French car makers found it necessary and profitable to have their own sales branches. Panhard paved the way in the early 1900s with its New York Agency, which in 1906 accounted for a fifth of sales.[11] Renault was more extensive and more systematic. It opened branches in Great Britain, the United States, Germany, Spain, Hungary and Russia. In most cases, the management came from France and the capital from Renault, although in Britain the senior management was British. In some branches Renault welcomed minority capital from other French investors and even from foreigners.[12] Yet often agents and sometimes the branches themselves complained they were not sent enough units despite their energetic requests.

Some French car makers went further and bought the capital of existing foreign car manufacturers. Two French firms took over Austro-Daimler in 1906, and in 1907 Lorraine-Dietrich bought a majority interest in the Isotta-Fraschini motor car company of Milan, subsequently disposing of it in 1911.[13]

In a limited number of countries assembly plants were established. French manufacturers hoped by this strategy either to serve more quickly the growing markets, or to fight on equal terms with local industry. Italy was their favourite target. In 1905 Clément established a subsidiary for assembly and ultimately manufacture of cars. In 1906 both Peugeot and Darracq formed car-assembly companies with the help of Italian investors, the former in Turin, the latter in Milan. Darracq also went into Spain in 1907, but its subsidiary failed within a year.[14] In Great Britain, Clément had formed in 1903, with a few English partners, Clément-Talbot Ltd to assemble and eventually manufacture his cars in London. Lorraine-Dietrich established a factory of its own in Birmingham in 1907, with a British board to manage it.[15] In Russia Renault built a factory to assemble cars at St

Petersburg during 1914, and Panhard made the necessary preparations for the opening of an assembly plant in 1915 in the same city.[16] The level of custom duties was the main reason for the establishment of small assembly plants in the United States, by de Dion-Bouton, CGV and Panhard. Renault also considered this strategy in 1902, but did not proceed.[17]

Most of these foreign plants produced only small numbers of vehicles and fell into financial difficulties. Except for Lorraine-Dietrich, French car manufacturers did not commit themselves sufficiently in foreign ventures to enable them to succeed and to acquire the specialised know-how required for multinational operations.

Yet foreign business taught them lessons. Renault created sales branches at home after the success of its own foreign branches, using its American branch to improve its industrial organisation in France. The same thing happened in Italy, at Fiat which also learnt to produce cars fulfilling the special requirements of foreign markets.[18]

The First World War reduced this early multinationalisation to a minimum, except in Britain and Russia. In central Europe French property was sequestered; everywhere tariff duties were raised. France limited drastically its home production of motor cars but Renault Limited started manufacturing operations in Britain, as the Royal Flying Corps urgently needed spare parts for aviation engines.[19] In Russia, Renault's Petrograd factory made trucks and armaments. In 1916 Renault established a new factory for automobile and aeroplane parts at Rybinsk, on the upper Volga. Louis Renault in Billancourt thought the expansion of both factories went too far, and came into conflict with their (French) manager, Sicault. The upshot was the working out of a kind of primitive multinational circuit, as the Russian Renault bought American machine-tools in the United States through the Renault sales office in New York. However, the seizure of power by the Bolsheviks in October–November 1917 settled the matter: both factories were nationalised without compensation.[20] Renault's experience as a whole was in marked contrast to that of the American Ford Motor Company, which was able to benefit after the war from the intense wartime development of its subsidiaries in Canada and Britain.

1919–1945: Fewer Exports and Further Multinational Growth

Here it is necessary to distinguish between two very different periods: before and after 1926.

From 1919 to 1926, French motor companies were keen on exports. They not only wanted to win back foreign markets lost during the war, but they also wished to profit from the comparative advantage created by the depreciation of the French franc.[21] As a result, exports of French

159

car firms rose from 20 per cent of their production in 1922, to 30 per cent in 1925.

Nevertheless French car makers had to overcome new obstacles to their penetration abroad such as higher tariff walls, taxes penalising foreign vehicles, and strong American competition. They reacted in two ways.

On the one hand, they resorted to direct investment on a larger scale than before the war. Peugeot, which had been contemplating such a move since 1920, struck first, setting up an assembly plant in Milan in 1925, together with the Italian company Isotta-Fraschini, and another in Mannheim in 1927, together with the German firm Richard Kahn. Renault took the same course, establishing a factory in Belgium in 1926 and another in England in 1927. These ventures, however, were little more than finishing workshops.[22] Citroën was bolder. After considering a factory in the United States in 1923, they created in 1926 assembly plants in Germany, Britain, Belgium and Italy.[23]

On the other hand, French car manufacturers doubled the number of their sales offices abroad, as they found new agents in other cities and created new branches, often with the help of foreign capital. They also replaced former agents. The pre-eminence of Citroën, which led in French motor car exports, was supported by their eight foreign subsidiaries, which were very active. Europe was the centre of this offensive, together with the French colonies; pre-war shares of the American market could not be recovered. By 1926 French exports and assembly plants represented 40 per cent of motor car production.[24]

After the stabilisation of the French franc in 1926, the exchange rate advantage which had benefited French car makers disappeared. Simultaneously, their American counterparts developed their exports considerably, and other European countries raised their tariffs. As a result, French motor car exports declined, first in percentage terms, then in value. Britain climbed in 1929 to the position of being the largest motor car exporter in Europe. The first reaction of French producers was to establish new sales offices abroad, but this tactic failed to halt their decline. Moreover, most of the foreign assembly plants were in financial trouble. Peugeot even had to wind up its Italian and German factories.

During the world depression the situation worsened. According to Louis Renault, foreign business was maintained by car makers 'to recover their working costs, but without any profit'. Citroën's financial results abroad 'had no relationship with the invested sums, and it had to close down its Italian plant. Renault closed its English plant temporarily for three years. However, it would not be fair to suggest that no positive initiative was taken during the depression. Citroën established an assembly plant in Poland, followed by assembly workshops in Holland and Sweden. Renault tried (though in vain) to get its vehicles produced in Austria and Romania.[25] Every car maker developed its sales network in the French colonies.[26] At the end of this period, two different policies emerged. Citroën, after its takeover by Michelin in 1935, closed down its German, Polish and Czech subsidiaries. It reorganised all the others 'on more modest bases', because of the difficulties in importing assembly parts, in repatriating profits and in finding adequate markets. From then on foreign business played a secondary role in Citroën's policy. Renault, on the other hand, became the leading French car multinational. Between 1935 and 1939, it enlarged its British factory, developed that in Belgium, arranged for a Romanian company to produce its tractors and tanks, licensed production of its trucks in Poland and its cars in Japan, and undertook to build a truck factory in China.[27]

Although this multinationalisation remained on a small scale compared with American car manufacturers, it still exceeded the French firms' own resources. Citroën had to finance its British investment by borrowing from two commercial banks, Lloyds Bank and the Commercial Bank, and two merchant banks, Guinness Mahon and Schröder. Similarly, Renault Limited received a loan from the Midland Bank in 1925. In the United States, Renault, to keep its sales office in business, had to borrow from the Morgan Bank.[28] Nevertheless, the French motor industry on the whole had committed itself to multinationalisation much more than any other European competitor, apart from Italy, and had thereby incurred many losses. With the single exception of Renault, multinational networks were more limited in 1939 than in 1930.

The Second World War confirmed the evolution which had been taking place since 1926. In the case of Citroën, its Belgian, Dutch, Danish, Norwegian and Tunisian subsidiaries soon ceased their normal activity. The Spanish, Portuguese, Swedish and Swiss subsidiaries focused on motor car repairs and on the setting up of gazogenes. Only the British subsidiary kept growing, developing the production of spare parts for Great Britain and also for Algeria, Egypt, Madagascar and Portugal, assembling trucks and making munitions for the British. Similarly, Renault's subsidiary in Britain assembled navy engines. On the other hand, its Belgian plant was seized by the Germans and partly destroyed by Allied bombs.[29] While American motor car companies' overseas operations remained profitable during the war, the fortunes of the French subsidiaries were much more mixed.

1945–1979: Renewal of Exports, Expansion of Multinationalisation
During these years the dual process of renewal of exports and the expansion of multinational growth went through four stages. From 1945 to 1951, the French government, like its British counterpart, encouraged motor car firms to increase the share of their production reserved for exports. It was hoped thereby to improve the French trading balance, and also to bring in some of the foreign currency needed to buy new materials, machines and elementary products in this era of reconstruction.[30] Exports soared in these early post-war years. By 1947 they represented 57 per cent of French motor car production. As in the 1920s, Citroën became the major exporter. However, from 1949 onwards, prospects for exports declined, as the devaluation of sterling made British firms more competitive, and German manufacturers returned to export markets. Multinationalisation did not progress at the same pace as exports, because of the French car makers' lack of available capital. Citroën created two sales branches abroad. Renault rebuilt and soon enlarged its Belgian plant, and developed its sales office with the help of the Société Belge de Banque. It enlarged the British plant too, which exported to the Commonwealth, as well as to Thailand and Spain, in a pattern which obviously followed Ford UK's traditional practice. In 1949, Renault concluded agreements with foreign firms to have its vehicles assembled by them in Australia, India, Ireland and Mexico. These firms produced only a small number of cars.[31]

Between 1951 and 1965, French car makers considerably developed their foreign business (Table 9.1). The dominant feature of this period was the institution of an international network of assembly plants on a world-wide basis. This time Renault led the way. In 1951 such plants were established in South Africa and Spain, where Spanish interests held the majority of capital. In 1953 they concluded a licensing agreement with the Japanese firm Hino Motors. The pace of international growth accelerated after 1955. There were six new plants or agreements between 1955 and 1960, and nine plants between 1961 and 1965. By 1965 Renault had 23 plants abroad, in Africa, Latin America and Europe. All of them used a growing number of locally produced parts, as demanded by the various States whose trade barriers and markets had partly prompted this building of plants and agreements. The sales offices simultaneously became more numerous. There were 11 in 1955, and 25 in 1960. Other car makers followed the trend, but on a much smaller scale. Citroën, for instance, created during these years only four assembly plants, and entered into licensing and producing agreements in six other countries.

Table 9.1: Percentage of Total Citroën and Renault Production Manufactured Outside France

	Citroën (%)	Renault (%)
1955	3.94	7.76
1961	14.79	25.37
1965	18.80	28.07

Citroën, like Renault, established new sales branches, five being created between 1952 and 1963. French firms were limited, however, in their industrial development abroad by the lack of spare capital. This explains why they invested less in Latin America than Fiat or Volkswagen.[32] To mitigate this drawback, they used several devices. In many cases they concluded agreements with local producers, or took shares of their capital. They also concluded agreements with other French producers, or with other European producers (on joint ventures for the production of trucks, for instance). Renault went further, and offered to Fiat and Volkswagen a permanent agreement jointly to make parts and components. They refused. Renault also made the most decisive move to solve the financial problems. It created two financial subsidiaries in Switzerland. Renault Holding (1964) was to borrow on the international capital market to finance part of Renault's foreign business; Renault Finance (1969) was to finance the working capital of the sales subsidiaries abroad and centralise their funds.[33] Yet it should be remembered that Europe remained in the mid-1960s, after the failure on the American market, the most important outlet for French motor multinationals, and the models remained identical to French models, with a few exceptions such as Citroën UK. And more and more subsidiaries began to export the vehicles they had assembled.[34] As a result, exports rose from 28.3 per cent of the production in 1951 to 39.6 per cent in 1965.

From 1965 to 1978 there was a rationalisation of the foreign subsidiaries and their total number ceased to increase. Some were closed down, because their costs were too high compared with direct exports or with their competitors. This was not a new decision in the post-war period. After all, Renault (in 1960) and Citroën (in 1965) had had to close their English plants, but these decisions now occurred on a much larger scale. Nevertheless, some new plants were created. These were more orientated towards manufacturing than their predecessors, and were designed to achieve a larger volume of production. As a general rule, the whole international network of French motor car companies was reorganised to yield economies of scale. All these changes required larger investments, and the French companies increased their share of the capital of their subsidiaries. The better organisation of the subsidiaries on the one hand, and the constant pressure of foreign countries for the development of manufacturing on the other, made it possible for the foreign subsidiaries to produce parts and components formerly made in France and to export them to France. This time the product itself became international. Spain, Eastern Europe, Latin America became purveyors to the parent companies. European subsidiaries began to export entire vehicles to France. Special models for manufacturing abroad were slowly developed, such as the Renault Site in Spain from 1975 onward. The policy of compensation, initiated in the early 1960s at the request of less-developed countries, traded motor cars and trucks for coffee (Columbia and Ivory Coast), onions (Egypt), tobacco (Bulgaria), oranges (Spain), petroleum (Algeria). The know-how which was gained was used to sell turn-key plants, mostly to Eastern European countries, and to internationalise other products made by the motor car groups (i.e. machine-tools and roller bearings). The complexity of international operations had thus reached a level which entailed a reshuffling of the structures of parent companies. For instance, Renault created in 1971 a Division of International Affairs. However, the most efficient move in this direction was initiated by Ford, when it launched Ford of Europe. French exports (including assembly) climbed from 39.6 per cent of total French production in 1965 to 53.5 per cent in 1975, a percentage which was not exceeded until 1979.[35]

In 1978–9 French car makers took a new direction. They bought existing companies in developed countries to increase their penetration into profitable markets. Peugeot-Citroën bought Chrysler's European subsidiaries in 1978. Renault acquired a minority share of Volvo in 1979 and, the same year, shares in American Motors and then Mack, and produced a specifically American model for AMC. Bernard Hanon, who had suggested these American investments to Renault's chairman, became in 1981 Renault's new chairman. He had started his career at Renault Inc., near New York, around 1960. He was the first 'human product' of the multinationalisation to reach senior management in the French motor industry. Yet by 1984 Peugeot's chairman declared that the acquisition of Chrysler's western European interests had been 'an error'. He acknowledged that his company lacked the human and financial resources to absorb them properly, all the more as Chrysler's subsidiaries were in bad shape. While Renault's American investments were a success, they slowed down the modernisation of factories and models in France. It can be argued that the eyes of both French car makers were bigger than their bellies.[36] Indeed, foreign investments had come to represent 30–35 per cent of their total investments.

Conclusion

Even if the multinationalisation of French car makers proceeded at a slower pace and in a more Eurocentric way than that of their American counterparts, it had only one equivalent in Europe before 1939: the Italian Fiat. German manufacturers made up for lost time only after 1949, at the same time as they took the lead among European exporters. In fact, after World War II three strategies of multinationalisation became visible. One was principally marketing-orientated, and limited therefore the establishment of industrial plants abroad. It was adopted by Peugeot, by Japanese car makers and by those European producers centred on large cars like Daimler-Benz, BMW and, for most of its export range, Citroën. A second strategy was production-orientated and aimed at economies of scale by focusing on a few centres of world industrial development and fast-rising markets. This was the case of Volkswagen in Brazil and in the United States and also the major thrust of Fiat's international policy in the 1970s. A third strategy was orientated towards diversified industrial expansion. It was followed by Renault and, during many years, by Fiat. It may have been adapted from the American pattern.[37]

The growing multinationalisation of French car makers should also be analysed from the point of view of its social costs. It was often felt by the firms to be a process which laid constraints upon them in terms of such costs. One of them was the allocation of production between foreign and home markets. Foreign agents and subsidiaries kept complaining between 1900 and 1926 that they were not sent enough vehicles to sell, a complaint which reappeared in some countries during the 1950s and 1960s. In the years 1945–50, the French motor industry deeply resented 'the export policy forced on the industry by the authorities', and declared that 'it can only develop normally on the basis of a sufficient domestic market', partly because 'French purchasers would be willing to pay much higher prices than are possible under present conditions'.[38] The French shared with other European car makers the view that profit margins on exports were generally lower than on home markets.[39] Another constraint of multinationalisation was the necessary emphasis on marketing investments. To French managements whose chief interest was directed toward refinements in the product itself and the expansion of their production capacity, the proportion of investment allocated to sales abroad often seemed excessive. Renault's Chairman observed that the priority in the development of the European network in his five-year investment plan of 1965 'thrilled' most executives of the company.[40] A final constraint was that multinationalisation might strain the relations with the labour force in France, as the unions and the left-wing parties sometimes challenged its necessity.

On the other hand, multinationalisation offered new opportunities to French motor car companies. It gave the possibilities of more diversified careers to executives, some of whom specialised in working abroad whereas others had mixed careers, partly abroad, partly in France. The majority of the managers of foreign operations remained French. It enriched the managerial abilities of the companies. It slowly induced them to differentiate their product lines, and they gained competence in new fields such as engineering, dispatching, transportation, banking and international trading. It made them able to collaborate on joint ventures with foreign producers, a change which was pioneered by the French and the Italians.[41]

As a result, foreign production accounted for 15 per cent of French vehicle production in 1979, which put them in third place behind the Italians (33.8 per cent) and the Americans (34.1 per cent). In view of recent trends it was still too European and too much dispersed on small plants.[42] The problem of being able to conduct simultaneously an active direct export policy and a more and more integrated internationalisation of production had become the central challenge for the managements of the French motor industry.

Notes

1. A. Okochi and T. Inoue (eds), *Overseas Business Activities* (Tokyo, 1984).
2. M. Wilkins and F. Hill, *American Business Abroad: Ford on Six Continents* (Detroit, 1964). G. Maxcy, *The Multinational Motor Industry* (London, 1981).
3. G. Horras, *Die Entwicklung des deutschen Automobilmarktes bis 1914* (Munich, 1982) pp. 9–10. J.P. Delaperrelle, 'Amédée Bollée Père, *Cénomane* (Spring 1984), pp. 17–19.
4. G. Maxcy, op. cit., Chapter 1.
5. V. Castronovo, *Giovanni Agnelli* (Turin, 1971).
6. J.M. Laux, *In First Gear. The French Automobile Industry to 1914* (Liverpool, 1976), pp. 71–2, 75, 98–102, 116, 142, 203, 209.
7. J.M. Laux, 'Les capitaux étrangers et l'industrie automobile' in M. Lévy-Leboyer (ed.), *La position internationale de la France* (Paris, 1977), pp. 372–3.
8. M. Flageolet-Lardenois, 'Une firme pionnière: Panhard et Levassor jusqu'en 1918', *Le mouvement social* (October–December 1972), pp. 31–3, 39–41.
9. *Annuaire de la Chambre Syndicale des Constructeurs d'Automobiles* (Paris, 1914), p. 74. P. Fridenson, *Histoire des Usines Renault*, vol. I (Paris, 1972), p. 143. D. Dubarry, *Unic* (Paris, 1982), p. 42.
10. P. Fridenson, 'Les débuts de Renault en Belgique', *De Renault Frères Constructeurs d'Automobiles à Renault Régie Nationale* (December 1984), p. 223–5.
11. C.W. Bishop, *La France et l'automobile* (Paris, 1971), pp. 278–306; J.M. Laux, *In First Gear*, p. 116.

12. H.O. Lukes, 'Renault au Royaume-Uni (1902–1913)', *De Renault Frères* (June 1978), pp. 141–7; P. Fridenson, 'Les premiers contacts entre Louis Renault et Henry Ford', *De Renault Frères* (December 1973), pp. 247–50; Fridenson, *Histoire*, pp. 53–5, 66–8.

13. G. Maxcy, op. cit.; J.M. Laux, *In First Gear*, pp. 165–7.

14. Società Anonima Peugeot-Croizat, *Assemblea straordinaria del 26 giugno 1907* (Turin 1907). Officine Meccaniche Torinesi e Brevetti Automobili Peugeot *Assemblea generale straordinaria del 20 maggio 1908* (Turin, 1908). My thanks to Duccio Bigazzi for sharing with me these documents. J.P. Bardou, J.J. Chanaron, P. Fridenson, J.M. Laux, *The Automobile Revolution* (Chapel Hill, NC, 1982), p. 36. Laux, *In First Gear*, pp. 104–5.

15. J. M. Laux, *In First Gear*, pp. 44, 165–6.

16. P. Fridenson, *Histoire*, pp. 67–8. M. Flageolet-Lardenois, op. cit., p. 41.

17. *Annuaire de la Chambre Syndicale des Constructeurs d'Automobiles* (Paris, 1914), p. 72; Renault Archives (Billancourt), business correspondence, letters to Mr Neubauer, 18 and 19 April 1902, and contract with Paul Picard, Chicago agent, April 1902; C.W. Bishop, *La France*, pp. 290, 300. F. Roe, 'Some Still-unanswered Questions', *Automotive History Review*, (Summer 1984), p. 16–17.

18. P. Fridenson, 'Les premiers contacts', p. 248–9; J.M. Laux, *In First Gear*, p. 142.

19. H.O. Lukes, 'Renault au Royaume-Uni (1914–1939)', *De Renault Frères* (December 1978), pp. 210–11.

20. French Army Archives, Vincennes, 10 N 73, correspondence with Roussky-Renault, 1917; Renault archives, note on the Russian subsidiaries by chartered accountants J. Doyen and J. Gauchet, 5 June 1928.

21. B. de Jouvenel, 'Interview d'André Citroën', *L'Europe Nouvelle* (12 January 1924). D. Henri, 'La Société Anonyme des Automobiles Peugeot de 1918 à 1930', M.A. thesis (University of Paris I, 1983), p. 94.

22. D. Henri, 'La Société Anonyme', pp. 97–9; H.O. Lukes, 'Renault au Royaume-Uni (1914–1939)', pp. 213–14. E. Quackels, D. Wafellman, 'Renault en Belgique', *De Renault Frères* (December 1983), pp. 89–90.

23. *Detroit Times*, 15 April 1923. Archives of the commercial court of the Seine, Paris, 'rapport à Messieurs les créanciers de la Société André Citroën' (1935), p. 19.

24. P. Fridenson, *Histoire*, pp. 143–5, 158–71, 322–3. C. Rocherand, *L'Histoire d'André Citroën* (Paris, 1979), pp. 87–92. J.L. Loubet, 'La Société Anonyme André Citroën 1924–1968', PhD dissertation (University Paris X-Nanterre, 1979), pp. 159–63; F. Sabatès and S. Schweitzer, *André Citroën: les chevrons de la gloire* (Paris, 1980), pp. 257–61. D. Henri, 'La Société Anonyme', pp. 94–101.

25. D. Henri, 'La Société Anonyme'; also H.O. Lukes, 'Renault au Royaume-Uni (1914–1939)', p. 216.

26. P. Pellé, 'L'industrie automobile française et l'Empire colonial durant le crise des années trente', MA thesis (University Paris VIII, 1978).

27. J.L. Loubet, 'La Société Anonyme des Automobiles', p. 299. P. Fridenson, *Histoire*, pp. 276, 280; H.O. Lukes, 'Renault au Royaume-Uni (1914–1939)', p. 216–17; E. Quackels, D. Wafellman, 'Renault en Belgique', p. 90; Renault Archives, Pain Papers, agreement with Etablissements Teissier, 18 October 1938; Daladier Archives (Paris), 2DA4 dr8, letter from Calinesco to Daladier, 14 July 1939.

28. H. Bonin, 'Les banques face au cas Citroën (1918–1930)', *Revue d'histoire moderne et contemporaine* (January 1985). H.O. Lukes, 'Renault au Royaume-Uni', p. 213; P. Fridenson, *Histoire*, p. 171.

29. J.L. Loubet, 'La Société Anonyme des Automobiles', pp. 354–6; H.O. Lukes, 'Renault au Royaume-Uni (1940–1957)', *De Renault Frères* (June 1979), pp. 281–2. E. Quackels, D. Wafellman, 'Renault en Belgique', p. 91.

30. P.M. Pons, *Le programme quinquennal de l'industrie automobile française* (Paris, 1945), p. 7; Commissariat Général au Plan, *Rapport de la commission de modernisation de l'automobile* (Paris, 1948).

31. J.L. Loubet, 'La Société Anonyme des Automobiles', pp. 371, 379, 381–2, 396; M. Freyssenet, 'Les processus de l'internationalisation de la production de Renault (1898–1979), *Actes du GERPISA* (October 1984), p. 31. E. Quackels, D. Wafellman, 'Renault en Belgique', p. 91–2; H.O. Lukes, 'Renault au Royaume-Uni (1940–1957)', p. 283–4.

32. S. Soares Ferreira, *Caractères des exportations de l'industrie automobile française* (Montrouge, 1974), p. 7–83; M. Freyssenet, "Les processus de l'internationalisation', pp. 32–38; J.L. Loubet, 'La Société Anonyme des Automobiles', pp. 515–25; L. Franko, *The European Multinationals* (London and New York, Harper and Row, 1976), p. 116, 118, 128–9; G. Maxcy, op. cit., Part II, Chapter 4.

33. P. Dreyfus, *La liberté de réussir* (Paris, 1977), p. 188, 198–200; P. Bercot, *Mes années aux usines Citroën* (Paris, 1977), p. 149–72; J.L. Loubet, 'La Société Anonyme des Automobiles', p. 465; P. Bairati, *Vittorio Valletta* (Turin, 1983), pp. 322–40.

34. 'L'automobile à la conquête des marchés fermés', *Entreprise* (21 January 1961), p. 15; F. Picard, 'Histoire de la Dauphine (suite)', *De Renault Frères* (June 1983), p. 13–20; E. Quackels, D. Wafellman, 'Renault en Belgique', pp. 92–3.

35. 'La D.A.I. ou Renault dans le monde', *Renault Informations Publicité* (September 1973); P. Dreyfus, *La liberté*, p. 158, 162; J.L. Loubet, 'La Société Anonyme des Automobiles', pp. 521, 524–5; P. Joffre, 'Stratégies commerciales des exportateurs de produits de consommation', PhD dissertation (University Parix IX, 1978), p. 120–177, 178–191. S. Soares Ferreira, *Le commerce extérieur et la production française de véhicules utilitaires* (Paris, 1975); G.D. Holliday, *Technology Transfer in the U.S.S.R., 1928–1937 and 1966–1975: the Role of Western Technology in Soviet Economic Development* (Boulder, Colo., 1979).

36. S. Lall, R. Jenkins, *Transnational Corporations in the International Auto Industry* (New York, 1983), pp. 46–47, 88–91, P. Romon, 'Renault aux Etats-Unis: la petite dans la cour des grandes', *Libération* (27 March 1984), p. 23; E. Seidler, *Le défi Renault* (Lausanne, 1981), pp. 231–5, 237, 241–2; article by V. Maurus, *Le Monde* (23 August 1984), p. 16; K. Shimokawa, 'New Developments in International Cooperation within the Motor Industry', *The Wheel Extended* (January–March 1983), pp. 15–23; P. Fontaine, *L'industrie automobile en France* (Paris, 1980), pp. 158–77; Statement by Jacques Calvet, Radio Europe I (7 October 1984).

37. G. Volpato, *L'industria automobilistica internazionale* (Padova, 1983), pp. 361–414; P. Joffre, 'Les stratégies commerciales', pp. 128–130; A. Okochi, T. Inoue (eds.), *Overseas Business Activities*, pp. 7, 59, 128, 168–9, 195.

38. See report from the Economic Section of the US Embassy in Paris: H.C. Bell and F.C. Grant, 'On French Automobile Industry and Export Policy', US National Archives, Suitland depot, 286 AID, Box 3 (23 August 1948).

39. P. Dreyfus, *La Liberté*, p. 193. Dreyfus was the chairman of Renault from 1955 to 1975.

40. P. Fridenson, 'French Automobile Marketing, 1890–1979' in A. Okochi, K. Shimokawa (eds), *Development of Mass Marketing* (Tokyo, 1981), p. 127; P. Dreyfus, *La Liberté*, p. 190; E. Seidler, *Les grandes voix de l'automobile* (Paris, 1970), pp. 45, 103–4.

41. J. Hartley, *Management of Vehicle Production* (London, 1981), pp. 120–1; G. de Bonnafos, J.J. Chanaron, L. de Mautort, *L'industrie automobile* (Paris, 1983), pp. 28–9.

42. L. De Mautort, 'Concurrence internationale et norme de production dans l'industrie automobile', *Revue d'Economie Industrielle* (January–March 1982), pp. 10–11.

10 The Multinationalisation of the French Electrical Industry 1880–1914: Dependence and its Causes

Albert Broder

French dependence on foreign influences was as strong in the electrical sector as it was in the field of organic chemicals. This is reflected in the declaration of the founders of the Compagnie Générale d'Electricité (CGE) in the introduction to their prospectus in 1898: 'As far as lighting and the manufacture of electrical components are concerned, we have been left so far behind that there are very few firms now in France which are not dependent on foreign initiative or capital.'[1]

This dependence, the disadvantages of which were to become abundantly clear during World War I, was not the result of an initial French backwardness in scientific development. From the 1860s to the 1880s, the decades when the earlier scientific discoveries were 'industrialised', France played a leading role in their development. Certain sectors like electrochemistry and electrometallurgy were developed so effectively that they were regarded as being in the forefront of international technological progress and production. The scene changed dramatically, however, and the international exhibitions of the period provided ample evidence of this. Whereas British and French achievements were foremost at the exhibitions of Vienna (1873) and Paris (1881), at those of Paris (1889) and Chicago (1893) the tide had turned in favour of the Germans and the Americans. Their technical and industrial lead quite dominated the great Paris exhibition of 1900. At this time, power stations in France, both thermal and hydroelectric, even though employing equipment produced mostly in the country, were based upon the patents of Edison, Thomson Houston, Westinghouse, AEG or Brown Boveri. When after a long history of conflict between the State and the city the first underground line of Paris (Maillot-Vincennes) was built for the great exhibition, the engineering was done by the Empain group of Belgian origin and the locomotive system was of the Sprague type, to patents held by General

Electric. Motors were built in the factories of the Compagnie Française Thomson Houston.

France and American industry
The Failure of the First 'National' Initiatives

It would take too long to list all the attempts to create new firms in the last quarter of the century, but the general situation is illustrated by the two most important. The Compagnie Générale pour l'Eclairage Electrique (1880), although sponsored by two of the main banking groups[2] was not able to assemble the 8 million francs required for its initial equity capital. The same was true of the Compagnie Générale d'Electricité,[3] which needed 10 million francs and gave up, partly because of the obstacles raised by the municipality of Paris to the integration of electrical networks in the French capital. At first sight the failure can be put down to a simple set of adverse conditions, notably the power of the gas companies and the general situation in regard to capital availability. At the beginning of the 1880s, the only serious market that seemed promising was the electric lighting business, yet in most French towns and above all in Paris, gas lighting had a near monopoly. Concessions had been granted by the municipalities on a long-term basis and, in the case of Paris especially, ties between the city administrators and the gas companies served to reinforce the opposition to 'electrification'. Moreover, contrary to what was happening elsewhere, the French gas companies showed no inclination to add turbo generators to their gas plants.[4]

Turning now to capital availability, between 1871 and 1890[5] private enterprise was not among the favourites of bankers and the stock exchange. The scene was dominated by public funding: to pay back loans placed abroad to cover the 1871 war indemnity, to finance the Freycinet plan for re-equipment (which strengthened established industries to the detriment of innovative industries), to cover the mass issue of railway bonds necessary for the construction of the new network, these all drained the market.[6] Even neglecting the impact of foreign demand, internal public capital borrowings bore clearly a smaller risk and promised higher profit margins for the banker. Further, one has to add the hangover from the 1881–2 economic crisis which reduced for a long period and in a decisive way the industrial ambitions of the banks. Admittedly, France seemed to remain a highly important capital market, but its part in the overall volume of issues in Europe was shrinking whilst its own market was being fed by a considerable number of foreign investors, especially from Belgium and Switzerland.[7] Moreover, one should not make the mistake of judging the Paris capital market on its foreign issues. An important fraction of these issues was bought back at the end of the 1870s by nationals of the debtor countries, especially Italians and Spaniards, who thus reacquired their own public and private debt (in the latter case, particularly railway debentures).

Despite all these factors, this is not sufficient to explain the situation completely since the capital needed for investment in the electricity sector was at the beginning rather modest. The 8 million francs capital with which the Compagnie Générale proposed to start was already in excess of the initial capital of the Deutsche Edison-Gesellschaft of Emil Rathenau, so it would have been theoretically possible to have started business with less. We must therefore look outside the known reserves of French bankers *vis-à-vis* innovative change for the main reason for this action.

The background is the crisis of the French economy between 1881 and 1905. The evidence provided by the indexes calculated by Crouzet and Levy-Leboyer is clear.[8] From 1875 to 1895 Crouzet's index of industrial production grew by a mere 1.9 per cent per annum, the engineering sector increased by 3.15 per cent, while the 'new industries'—including electricity production—grew by only 2.95 per cent. These figures demonstrate that the French performance was distinctly worse than the German (not to mention the British).[9] The deep crisis in French agriculture exercised an influence on capital flow in the financial markets. At the same time, and for diverse reasons, traditional French exports met with growing difficulties,[10] while demographic stagnation depressed the growth in demand. As a result, industrial investment suffered. French industry modernised very slowly, and before 1895 it provided only a modest demand for electricity.

The demographic and industrial stagnation led to a slow rate of urbanisation and daily commuting between home and work increased more slowly in France than in Germany. Consequently, in addition to the difficulties met by the attempts to install electric lighting, one has to add the limited growth of public transport. This, in turn, led to a long amortisation time for such important investments as electric tramways. Only under the stimulus of the 1900 Paris exhibition coupled to some economic recovery was the large-scale electrification of Paris tramways undertaken. Urban electrification progressed slowly. In Paris, which should have been the most important urban market, the city administration subdivided the territory into sectors, at the same time attributing concessions that did not exceed 30 years. The limited market that a single sector comprised and the time that could be counted for amortisation precluded major investments which would have induced economies of scale and a growth of the market. It was only in 1907 that the constitution of the Compagnie Parisienne de Distribution d'Electricité led to the concentration of all concessions in a single one which was then extended to 99 years.

There is a final influence which could explain the absence of a national French industry that was able to compare in growth with its German neighbour. France did not have an investment goods industry which was at the level of its position in the world economy. Since the 1880s, a growing dependency *vis-à-vis* foreign producers on investment goods became a noticeable feature of the French industrial structure. German and American industry acquired a clear lead over their French, as well as their British, competitors.

This technical and organisational lead was also seen in the origin and growth of the electrotechnical sector. Moreover, the movement of the frontier that made Alsatian Mulhouse German was a heavy blow to future French development in engineering and electrotechnology. This weakness caused a considerable sectoral deficit in the balance of trade. Tables 10.1 and 10.2 show the situation in 1902.[11]

Table 10.1: French Engineering Imports, 1902 (in millions of francs)

Category	Total	From Germany
Various machines	30.97	5.6 (a)
Textile machines, printing machines and machines for paper production	3.10	2.5
Agricultural machines	21.00	(b)
Sewing machines	14.40	5.6 (c)
Dynamos and other electric machines	2.40	0.5 (d)
Machine tools	9.40	4.4
General engineering equipment	9.70	5.2
Total (not including components or spare parts)	90.97	23.8 (= 25.9%)

(a) 15.00 from Great Britain
(b) 17.8 from the USA
(c) 7.9 from Great Britain
(d) 1.3 from Switzerland

Leaving aside colonial trade, only 19.1 million francs of imports, or some 21 per cent, were covered by exports. Furthermore, one should note that total French exports of machinery corresponded more or less to German exports of these products into France. As no investment goods industry (except the American) could survive without exporting, the above-mentioned foreign trade figures are significant.

At the same time, capital requirements for the creation of foreign manufacturing, trade or service affiliates were still small, which meant that investigating foreign firms could easily gain access to the French (or British) capital markets.

American Investment
There is as yet insufficient evidence to be dogmatic on the early strategies of the American electrical industry in Europe. It seems to be clear, however, that Great Britain and its Empire was considered as a separate entity right from the beginning. Consequently the British Empire markets, with the exception of Canada, were handed over to

Table 10.2: French Engineering Exports, 1902 (in millions of francs)

Category	Total	To French Colonies
Various machines	4.0	
Textile machines	3.1	
Printing machines and machines for paper production	1.1	
Agricultural machines	4.5	(1.6)
Sewing machines	0.6	(0.4)
Dynamos and other electric machines	1.9	(0.5)
Machine tools	3.8	(0.5)
General engineering equipment	5.4	(2.3)
Total (not including components or spare parts):	24.4	(5.3)

affiliates established in London. With one exception,[12] neither the European continent nor Latin America were served from there. For the latter region, and the Far East, the American parent companies collaborated with German partners who were neither their licencees nor completely independent from them. In Europe, France became the legal and industrial seat of their operations. On the occasion of the 1881 exhibition, the Edison group created three firms: Industrielle Edison for the production of incandescent lamps, Electrique Edison which was supposed to produce power equipment for small urban or industrial plants and, third, Continentale Edison, a finance company which administered the European patents of the Edison group. Not much capital was required for the last of these, but even if one keeps that in mind, the total input of capital—$0.65 million or 3.5 million francs—was still not impressive.[13]

As the archives of the Edison company are not accessible, it is difficult to sort out the motives which led to their investment. If it had been solely for the sale of licences in Europe, the financial strength of Continentale Edison would have been sufficient. The existence of the other two Edison affiliates seems to indicate a rather hesitant or unclear strategy. The firm may have wanted to attack European markets using France as a base, given France's financial, and to a certain extent also technical, reputation on the European continent at that time. This was possible at minor cost since the capital for the French affiliates came from bankers which had not been involved with the Edison group before, some of whom were American.[14]

The sudden reversal of the situation, to the profit of the German side did not, however, result from the feeling of the American Edison group that they had been deceived by the French bankers, as Mira Wilkins has suggested.[15] It came from an appreciation of the limitations to growth in France and the dynamic action of Emil Rathenau who was allied to Siemens and a certain number of important German banks.[16] The incandescent lamp patent, the most important one, had been assigned to Rathenau by Continentale, for exploitation in Germany. Rathenau, however, succeeded in dealing directly with the American group, leaving aside its French affiliate. Moreover, by selling in central and eastern Europe, he violated the contracts made with Edison, but the American company did not intervene being apparently disappointed by the rather passive attitude of its French affiliates.

These French companies had to face a market which grew only slowly. Once inaugurated, the lamp factory's production remained at a low level, and power equipment did not find a rapidly expanding market. This meant that the establishment of a larger production unit could not be envisaged. Consequently, production was entrusted to a subcontractor, Ateliers Postel Vinary. Even so, losses mounted. As a result, the whole system was restructured, and the patents were ceded to the manufacturing companies. The Americans abandoned Continentale which subsequently became one of the concessionaries of electric power distribution in Paris.

Two years after the arrival of Edison, another American company, Thomson Houston, came to Europe with a much more elaborate strategy. International Thomson Houston was established in Paris in 1883 with a field of activity that comprised France, her colonies and the Mediterranean basin excluding the Ottoman Empire. The American firm also had a British affiliate, and a partner in Berlin, Ludwig Loewe, with whom it created the Union Elektrizitäts-Gesellschaft. The firm's activity in France remained modest, especially since the main Thomson Houston products (turbines, dynamos and above all the Sprague electric traction system) found only a limited market there until the turn of the century. In contrast, the firm found various markets outside France far more rewarding, and affiliates were established in Egypt, Spain, Greece and Italy. Even more than in the case of Edison, the American stake was a technical one while the entire capital investment came from the French side.

This situation could have continued as new French competitors did not materialise. 'National' firms were established, but they moved into electrometallurgy or electrochemistry and stayed out of electro-technology.[17] There were French-owned electrical firms like, for instance, Fives Lille, but they remained rather small and did not possess the resources necessary for rapid expansion. The situation changed, however, as a consequence of the Edison-Thomson merger of 1892 which, because of the complex relationship between these two groups in Europe, led to the establishment of a new equilibrium. In Germany, AEG and the Union Elektrizitäts-Gesellschaft, which held the Thomson Houston patents, merged in 1903, while in the Mediterranean countries the situation between the Thomson Houston affiliates and AEG interests remained rather confused.[18] In France, partition had to be reconsidered both in France itself and in the Mediterranean countries. In Paris, the interest of the two parent companies was Houston (CFTH) which, in contrast to previous practice, was provided with a significant amount of capital, some 40 million francs. American financial participation was rather weak, but what really counted were the American patents and the fact that even if there were only two Americans, C.A. Coffin and E. Griffin, on the board, they nevertheless held key positions in the main company, General Electric.[19] The importance given by the Americans to their participation was further underlined by the nomination of Frederic Parsons as a deputy director. AEG's interests were, on the other hand, guaranteed by provisions concerning the the French company's activities abroad.

The new company created in this fashion proved to be far more ambitious than its predecessors. Foreign competition and the financial problems of the consumers of electrical equipment (producers and distributors of electric energy, tramways) induced CFTH to introduce into France the financial model which had been applied with so much success in the United States and in Germany.[20] Majorities of shares or controlling minorities were acquired in consumer companies and this in turn led to the purchase of equipment and, in particular, the electrification of the tramways. At the same time, CFTH could guarantee loans, and in most cases it was able to create intermediate financial holding companies which united CFTH with local entrepreneurs and the banks. A large market was guaranteed for the necessary future issues of shares and bonds.

The economic revival that set in in the middle of the 1890s helped to make the development of this firm a true success, the most spectacular manifestation being the creation of the Energie Electrique du Littoral Méditerranéen (EELM), which was founded in 1902 in a joint action by CFTH, the Société des Grands Travaux de Marseille and the Société Marseillaise de Crédit. In 1905 the merger of EELM with the Forces Motrices des Alpes Maritimes was financed by a group of participating banks, the Comptoir d'Escompte, the Crédit Industriel et Commercial and the Banque Française pour le Commerce et l'Industrie. The foundation of the Forces Motrices de la Haute Durance in 1908 gave EELM the leadership in electricity production and distribution in the southern part of the French Alps and in the Mediterranean coastal zone east of the Rhône river. Moreover full employment of CFTH's factories for heavy electrotechnical equipment was guaranteed from 1898 by the new Paris metro to which it supplied motors and by the electrification of the tramway system of the capital.[21]

Ten years after its foundation, the French affiliate of General Electric possessed an impressive portfolio and by the start of the war controlled directly or indirectly 40 per cent of French electricity production and supplied 60 per cent of all electrical equipment installed in France.[22] Potential competitors, such as the Compagnie Générale d'Electricité, found it difficult to attack this quasi-monopoly, particularly since international patent sharing contracts tended to cut them off from foreign markets. It is in these markets that the merger of Edison and Thomson Houston took effect. To coordinate the interests of AEG and the Union Elektrizitäts-Gesellschaft, the Paris-based International Thomson Houston had to disappear without offending public opinion and the political authorities. Consequently, in Brussels Thomson Houston de la Méditerranée (THM) was founded under the auspices of the American parent company.[23] THM received the patents of

International Thomson Houston registered in Mediterranean countries and took over the Mediterranean Thomson Houston holdings. CFTH as well as General Electric and AEG became shareholders of the newly created THM and provided it with cash (see Table 10.3).

Table 10.3: Capital Structure of Thomson Houston de la Méditerannée[24]

1898: 10,000 shares of 5 million francs	
CFTH received for its patents and concessions	2,500 shares
CFTH received as capital	2,985 shares
CFTH and General Electric (USA) jointly received as capital	1,515 shares
Foreign holdings of capital	
	3,000
1900: Capital increased to 60,000 shares of 30 million francs	
CFTH and private French shareholders	47,690
CFTH and General Electric (USA)	2,945
German (AEG) and Belgian shareholders	9,365

Despite the fact that the majority of THM's capital and all patents were held by CFTH, the statutes of THM provided for an equal division of orders between CFTH and AEG. In any case, THM was only given the functions of a commercial affiliate. As soon as the position of AEG and Union in Germany and Belgium had been clarified and coordinated, the affiliates of AEG and CFTH in Italy, Spain, and Greece were merged; the merger conditions, however, safeguarded up to a certain extent the pre-eminence of the German side.[25] As soon as the merger operations were finished and THM's patents and concessions had been transferred to the AEG-CFTH affiliates in the Mediterranean countries already mentioned, THM was liquidated in Belgium and its assets were taken over by CFTH. *Inter alia*, this action provided for the increase of the General Electric quota in CFTH, and at the same time it allowed AEG to become a shareholder without too much publicity. The German participation opened also the possibility of regulating the problem of eventual competition between CFTH and AEG in the French market.[26] As a result, the German firm abandoned all direct commercial activity in France in exchange for a participation, guaranteed by the statutes, in all contracts which the Paris company would obtain in France and her colonies.

When all these different operations had come to an end, one could say with certainty that General Electric, despite its recent foundation, was well able to handle all the devices of transnationality. The initiative in Belgium, mentioned above, demonstrated a community of interests of the American group and the firm of Rathenau. Besides their common affiliates in Latin America, the two groups came in close touch via their common shareholding in CFTH and in the Mediterranean affiliates. These links were further strengthened in Europe and Latin America by the foundation of the Société Financière de Transports et d'Entreprises Industrielles (SOFINA) in Brussels.[27] Both the development of the group as such and the strong ties between General Electric and the Germans were detrimental to the French side, whose factories were prevented from exporting, whilst reserving part of its internal market for its German partner.

The presence of an AEG representative on the CFTH board and of a CFTH representative on the AEG board did not lead to any reciprocity in the commercial field. It is furthermore characteristic that none of the financial holdings created by CFTH brought in business outside France. In contrast, one might note, however, that the Compagnie Générale d'Electricité, when it came into being, was not prevented from being active in the markets, notably in Italy, where Swiss and German companies had interests.[28]

German firms and the French market

Unlike the Americans, German firms did not need to found manufacturing affiliates in France and there seemed to be no tendency to move into licensing. AEG did not possess its own patents during the first years of its existence and the other producers preferred exporting as a strategy with the exception of special cases such as in the Russian or the Austro-Hungarian market.[29] There can be no doubt that the French market and its tariff protection favoured the establishment of manufacturing units, but AEG was not free in its decisions and from 1898 it certainly profited from the expansion of the French Thomson Houston company; Siemens on the other hand remained sceptical after the failure of its attempt to get into electricity production and distribution in Paris in 1879.[30] One should also add that German industrialists did not appreciate the rather narrow-minded and hesitant mentality of French State bureaucracy.[31] It was therefore only from 1898, when the general climate had regained some of its vitality, that the Germans envisaged going beyond mere exports to include France in their foreign direct investment strategies. Even then AEG preferred simply to increase its shareholdings in financial holdings and in the hydroelectric companies created by CFTH, thereby guaranteeing growing sales at minimum risk.

It was Schuckert of Nuremberg—the least active in exports of the three big German electrical producers—which first established itself in France where it bought, in 1898, the firm of Dayde et Pillie. This was certainly not a very well-managed firm and there was little it had to offer technically, but its activities in the different sectors promised to make it an interesting investment for Schuckert as soon as organisational and technical problems could be resolved. The known financial difficulties which beset Schuckert itself in 1901–2 and which led to its merger with Siemens have to be held responsible for a certain neglect suffered by the French affiliate. When Siemens, or rather the newly founded Siemens-Schuckert, took it over in 1902 and changed its name to Société Générale d'Electricité de Creil its operations still brought annual deficits. One of the first actions undertaken was to begin eliminating the French members of the board and the French managers and replacing them with Germans sent from Berlin. In the French market CFTH dominated the scene, and this meant that the Creil firm was only second best alongside Fives Lille, the emerging Compagnie Générale d'Electricité and the French affiliate of the Swiss Brown Boveri company.

This situation certainly motivated the German group to specialise in a market sector where it held a clear technical advance, namely railway electrification. There Siemens and AEG had worked together founding a common *Studiengesellschaft* (research and development company) in 1899.[32] The Americans were less advanced and the French—especially Fives Lille as well as Escher Wyss and Westinghouse—lacked production capacity despite their being technically up to date.[33] In order to become active on the French market Siemens must have consulted AEG because of the patents they held in common. There may also have been decisions to divide the French market between Siemens, with its future involvement in railway electrification, and AEG which, through CFTH, was already established in a strong position in other sectors of the electrical business. Moreover, the two German firms had a common stake in the French production of Osram light bulbs. With its factory at Creil and its technical and financial potential, Siemens had a good starting position. Railway electrification, however, was also a strategic matter and, in consequence, there were military considerations quite apart from the need for direct financial aid from the State. This meant, of course, that a foreign firm, and above all a German firm, could not act alone in the nationalistic climate prevailing in those years. A joint venture together with the Schneider-le Creusot group promised to be a viable solution. In the electrical sector, Schneider had not operated with much success but it was the leading French supplier of locomotives and a metallurgical producer of great importance.

The new alliance might have seemed rather strange to those who recall the chauvinistic tone adopted by the Schneider company and the bitter battles fought against its German competitors in the business of heavy armaments. In the railway sector, however, a clear division of labour with Siemens seemed to be the most profitable solution: Siemens would provide the parts that were needed for traction: electric motors, the aerial lines and the whole system of electric energy supply; Schneider would construct the mechanical parts of the locomotives and the pylons for the supply lines. If it had worked, this common venture would have practically monopolised an entire sector and would have excluded all other French firms from this profitable business. In order to avoid negative reactions on the part of government authorities or public opinion, the arrangement with Schneider was made through the British branch of Siemens, Siemens Bros. London, which was legally autonomous from the Berlin firm. In all this, the French affiliate at Creil was not consulted; the last Frenchman left in its management protested against the decision and resigned. The arrangement became effective and a common company, the Société des Applications Electriques à la Traction,[34] was founded in 1912 by Schneider on the one side, and Siemens Brothers and the Compagnie Générale d'Electricité de Creil on the other. Its activity remained rather modest since the French railway companies continued to hesitate over investments which to them seemed not really profitable. During the war the company was liquidated.

Apparently more modest although equally camouflaged seems to have been the establishment of an affiliate by the Mulhouse Société Alsacienne de Constructions Mécaniques in Belfort in 1889. The capital of the new firm in Belfort, which lay just over the border on French territory, was only 900,000 francs, but it held an exclusive licence for producing Siemens electrical equipment in France. Things become clearer if one looks at the statutes, which show that the Belfort enterprise was to construct plants for public and private lighting using the steam engines made by its Mulhouse parent company and the electrical equipment delivered by Siemens. In addition a cable factory was installed at Belfort with Siemens Berlin, Siemens London, and the Société Alsacienne Mulhouse as partners.[35]

French Industry and the Multinationals
'National' Firms and the French Market
From the figures cited in Table 10.4, it can be seen that the nominal capital of French electrical firms amounted to only 0.25 per cent of the nominal value of all French shares. It is furthermore of interest that

Table 10.4: Capital Assets of the Main French Electrical Industry Companies at the End of 1902 (in millions of francs)

	Shares		Bonds	
	Nominal value	*Quoted value*	*Nominal value*	*Quoted value*
Compagnie Générale d'Electricité	15.0	12.45	14.3	13.5
Société des Applications Industrielles	5.0	4.5		
Eclairage et Force	10.0	9.5		
Générale Electrique et Industrielle	12.5	14.75		
Industrielle d'Energie Electrique	10.0	10.0	Founders' shares=0.75	
Breguet	4.0	3.1	0.9	0.8
Gramme	2.3	2.5		
Travaux Electricité et Force	3.0	1.5		
Mors	2.0	3.4		
Compagnie Française Thomson Houston	40.0	50.6	28.4	27.9
Générale de Traction	30.0	5.7	11.3	5.5
Industrielle de Traction	5.0	9.3	Founders' shares=2.9	
SIT	18.0	18.6	10.0	9.9
Compagnie des Compteurs	7.0	43.4	4.3	4.9
Total of firms selected	163.8		69.2	

Total issued capital in the electricity sector (manufacturers of electrical equipment and of energy, distributors of energy):
393.9 shares + 363.0 bonds.
Total of all French securities listed at the stock exchange:
60,132.1 million francs.

CFTH, which used foreign technology and which, despite the importance of the French participation in its capital, could be regarded as a multinational enterprise, held first place with 24 per cent of the nominal capital of the whole sector; it was followed by the Compagnie des Compteurs, on the basis of current market value, but this firm belonged only marginally to the electrical sector.

Table 10.4 does not give an exhaustive picture but there are three reasons why one should consider it at least as indicative: firstly, the main activities of other firms with electrical interests (for example, Schneider, Fives Lille) lay in other sectors and the importance of the electrical side remained limited; secondly, the Paris stock exchange on whose figures Table 10.4 is based, covered more than 80 per cent of the capital issued on the national financial market; and thirdly, although certain firms, such as the Société Alsacienne de Constructions Mécaniques or the Société Générale de Creil were not quoted on the stock exchange, their opportunities for expansion—except through the participation of foreign shareholders—were limited because they did not get access to the bond market. There might have been the possibility of using a holding company as an instrument of finance but at least in the electrical sector such holding companies did not exist in France.

One must compare the assets of the French companies with those of the American and German competitors. Calculated in francs, General Electric disposed in 1900 of a nominal share capital of 217.1 million; the corresponding figures for AEG were 75 million, for Siemens 67.5 million, and Schuckert 52 million. For 1908 the *Bulletin Financier Suisse* indicated a total capital of 1,200 million francs for the two German groups that remained—AEG and Siemens.

French industry in the electrical sector, it would seem, was badly equipped to fight its formidable foreign competitors which already occupied most of the field. Neither a recovery of the national market nor a strong participation in the expansion process that set in at the end of the 1890s seemed to be possible given the general reluctance of the large industrial groups and particularly of the important banks.

Concentration on specific new areas of technology did not yield results. For railway electrification, as we have seen, the collaboration between Schneider and Siemens threatened to exclude French suppliers. Similarly in the telephone sector, SAT did not carry much weight compared with Siemens or the Swedish firm of Ericsson and still less compared with American industry which had already introduced automatic exchange systems. To a large extent responsibility for this particular backwardness must fall on the administration of the postal services. It is just one example of the negative influence of the public sector and of State bureaucracy on the French economy since the end of the nineteenth century.

The Compagnie Générale d'Electricité, 1898–1913

The development of the Compagnie Générale d'Electricité (founded in 1898) demonstrates how the inferiority of French industry in the electrical sector could, in practice, be overcome: by responding to the market expansion and drawing from this growth the means for a gradual reduction in the influence of foreign multinational groups. The role of Paul Azaria, the founder of the new firm, was a determining factor. It is, however, also interesting to note that right at the beginning there were links and contacts with two multinational businesses. One was Brown Boveri, which assigned some minor business to the newly founded French firm and was for a short time represented on its board. This short-lived cooperation seems to have been the consequence of personal contacts between Azaria and the Swiss company, but there is very little documentary evidence on the motivations. Possibly Brown Boveri looked for an electricity producer to which it could sell its equipment, and was prepared for the new French firm to profit from its technical know-how. We have no better information on the reasons for the contacts that were established with another multinational, Metallgesellschaft of Frankfurt, which held the leading position in the world-wide business of non-ferrous metals. It could have been an attempt to obtain CGE's market for copper and tungsten.[36]

In any case, CGE followed the example of CFTH by acquiring minority holdings in electricity producing firms and tramway companies in order to create a market for its electrical equipment. Soon, however, this business reached its limits. Normally CGE could only deliver part of the equipment needed, and in the case of tramways it frequently had to buy it from CFTH. In other cases it was the lack of financial backing which forced it to hand over important contracts to its competitor either because a profit could be guaranteed only over a long run or because the overall financial volume of the operation was too big. It was for this reason that the electrification of the Rouen tramways ended up with CFTH, which took over the Société Normande d'Electricité, the parent company of CGE and one of its major shareholders.[37] During the fifteen years before the outbreak of the First World War CGE followed a policy of continually buying and selling holdings, trying to adapt constantly its ambitions to its relatively scarce means. This permanent search for financial stability contrasted strongly with the comparative ease with which its foreign-based competitors could get financial support. It also explains why after the war CGE chose to operate as through a holding company (without

183

setting up the corresponding legal structure); this was an attempt to get control of its own financing and its own industrial activity.

The Cartelisation of Heavy Electrical Equipment, 1893–1913

The process of concentration in US industry during the 1890s and the outcome of the 1900–1 crisis which led to a major remodelling of the German electrical industry left the world market dominated by four industrial groups tied together two by two: General Electric and AEG on the one side, Westinghouse and Siemens on the other.

An important outsider was the Swiss Brown Boveri group which AEG unsuccessfully tried to incorporate. Founded by a British technician, Charles Brown, and a German businessman, Walter Boveri, their common enterprise soon concentrated on highly specialised machinery which could meet very specific requirements. Whereas the big firms were increasingly engaged in mass production of a broad range of standardised electrical products, Brown Boveri succeeded in particular sectors such as, for example, the market for high power turbines. Switzerland being a rather small market, the firm was forced to look for expansion abroad right from the beginning. Before 1914, this expansion remained, however, essentially limited to Western Europe through the French CEM, the Deutsche Brown Boveri, and the Tecnomasio Italiano Brown Boveri.

The two American groups dominated the scene in the United States and Canada through their control over their customers and the influence of bankers like Morgan. The adoption of technical standards (in this context the technical decisions taken for the Niagara Falls project cannot be overestimated) and the handing over of certain patent rights to overseas partners reinforced their position. Both agreements—the one between General Electric and AEG and the one between Westinghouse and Siemens—set clear territorial limits to the use of American technology by the Germans. Still more restrictive were the constraints imposed on those British and French firms which were directly controlled by the Americans, and the example offered by Thomson Houston de la Méditerranée illustrates this point particularly well.

There were regions excluded from these partitions: the Scandinavian countries, Austria-Hungary, the Tsarist and the Ottoman empires, the Far East and Latin America, but penetrating these zones was not easy for companies based in France. In Russia and Austria-Hungary Siemens had been well established since the beginnings of the telegraph. These countries, as well as Italy, could also have been promising markets for AEG and for the French producers, but while AEG was financially and legally an independent firm, the only French enterprise that could have become a successful exporter, the French CFTH company, remained under American technical control. AEG and its principal bankers, the Deutsche Bank and the Berliner Handels-Gesellschaft took advantage of this situation and founded financial holding companies; thus it was possible to control the customers and finance their purchases of electrical goods supplied by the parent company. Among others this led to the creation of the Banque pour Entreprises Electriques (Bank für elektrische Unternehmungen) in Zurich which, at least at the beginning, was directed at central Europe, Spain, and Italy. Two other important holdings were the Brussels-based SOFINA and the Deutsche Überseeische Elektricitäts-Gesellschaft destined to operative above all in Western Europe and Latin America respectively.[38] The lack of substantial financial support must certainly be considered to have been one of the principal reasons for the weak presence of the French producers in these markets; a characteristic example is offered by the Compagnie Générale d'Electricité retreating from Catalonia, where it occupied quite a favourable situation, in favour of Siemens.[39] The case already mentioned of Thomson Houston de la Méditerranée provides convincing proof that southern Europe was firmly in the grip of German producers. Furthermore, the same concept of a territorial partition of markets explains the Latin American situation where Westinghouse and Siemens were less active but where General Electric and AEG ended up with clear agreements dividing up certain markets and cooperating in others so that it becomes difficult not to draw a parallel with the well-known treaty of Fordesillas. Ottawa and Brussels served as starting points for this type of common operation. Ottawa was chosen above all for legal reasons.[40] Brussels because it was the seat of SOFINA where German and American interests met; again the French branch remained in a minority position and whilst receiving its due share of profits was excluded from any influence in entrepreneurial decision-making.[41]

On the eve of World War I the world market for heavy electrical equipment was thus effectively dominated by four groups.[42] Competition between them was rather limited; there were agreements on common research programmes and joint ventures in these fields,[43] and certain patents were exchanged. France and Britain and their colonial empires, however, were not included in these formal market partitions, but even there the big firms did not really wage war against each other. The weight of General Electric in both countries and the particular relationship established with AEG prevented the latter from becoming very active, while the other groups—Westinghouse and Siemens—produced in more specialised sectors. Despite the economic and financial potential of Britain and France their purely 'national'

185

electrical firms were more or less successful only within their national boundaries and even there the German and American groups were sufficiently superior to limit seriously the growth of native enterprise.

The Effects of Multinational Predominance on French Industry

There is no inevitable progression in the way international groups take control of an industrial country's markets. We have tried to show the extent to which economic but also political and social conditions prevailing in France acted as primary causes for the failure of an industry which, in a number of sectors, was as technically competent as its principal competitors. Once the process had started, however, the situation became totally different. The establishment of powerful foreign firms on the French market above all came about because the market was slow to expand and there were insufficient industrial and financial means to support the investment. None of those factors can alone be considered determinant, as illustrated by the success of Brown Boveri. The expansion of large enterprise is not initiated by concentrating on market control or on protectionist policies but these go together with expansion.

Most revealing in this respect is a comparison of the electrical and chemical industries. No tariff protection whatsoever and no other form of state intervention could prevent the world-wide dominance of the German organic chemical industry before 1914. There was comparatively little direct investment abroad by the Germans, who concentrated on exports; the plants of their foreign subsidiaries were relatively small and often limited to the final stages of production. The electrical industry, on the other hand, owed its precocious multinational structure to a number of essentially technical influences: while the chemical industry progressed by multiplying the number and the types of its products, the electrical industry combined this with a high degree of accelerated obsolescence. Whereas know-how in the sector could be disseminated more easily than in chemicals, the costs of transport and especially of the after-sales service (both maintenance and spare parts delivery), proved to be very high. In order to succeed, firms had to meet a true technical and financial challenge since research and development of new products demanded efficient laboratories backed up by production units capable of switching over to mass production. This in turn required a corresponding demand for the products which, in fact, only two national markets were able to offer—the American and the German.

Growth and concentration of firms seemed to be the logical answer, not only to the leaders of these firms but particularly also to their financial backers, such as the American Villard and a group of Berlin bankers. Unlike companies in the chemical industry, the electrical firms needed to build up a powerful and costly technical and commercial environment if they were to export on any scale. This obliged them to go abroad and set up units of production or take control of eventual users in order to assure a market for their goods. It was therefore the internal logic of this branch of industry which drove the American and the German firms into multinational expansion. The fact that this process proved to be a success was then responsible for the tendency to diversification into the low-current sector or simply into mass consumer goods like records, radios, light bulbs, and so on. The temporary lack of capital, distance and ignorance of markets can explain the choices made by the Americans between the establishment of subsidiaries, the granting of licenses or exporting through taking control of customers. With the principal exception of Austria-Hungary, the Germans seem to have preferred the second solution, and this is proved by the examples already mentioned of the Zurich Banque pour Entreprises Electriques and the Brussels-based SOFINA. The establishment of foreign manufacturing subsidiaries was then more of a sop to the political authorities in order to defend existing market positions. Siemens for instance did this in Russia after the 1850s, first with the telegraph business, and later with heavy high-voltage material; AEG followed this lead but without much conviction.

In the French case, less importance should be attached to the concept of a conflict between the strategy of multinational enterprise and the interests of the French government and administration. Although multinational enterprise tries to follow its own logic, which does not necessarily coincide with the will of national governments, this was a minor aspect. The volume of direct foreign investment, notably in CFTH, whose holdings gave control over a number of producers of electricity, as well as the restrictions which accompanied the handing over of patents limited the growth of technically and financially 'native' firms like Fives Lille or the Compagnie Générale. Moreover the restrictions also blocked the multinational affiliates like CFTH which would have had the capacity and the means for expanding abroad. Progressively, because of the predominance of the 'band of four' and their control of the world market, efforts to combat their hold became even more difficult. Moreover, customers used to American or German products hesitated to switch over to new suppliers as that would increase their problems of maintenance and spare parts.

Obviously the supplier of the first equipment remained in a priority position, and the French had to learn this lesson when they tried to conquer new markets in central Europe during the 1920s. More complex, and so far insufficiently studied, is the role of technical standardisation in which the German DIN seems to have been the leader. The latecomers, and among them the French, were forced to adapt themselves or to lose markets. The four large groups forced the others to accept German and American technical standards and were thus able to create virtually protected markets in central Europe and Latin America.

Conclusion

American and German multinationals became established in France after the 1880s not least because for them this was only a secondary market, while it was of course of the greatest importance to the native electrical industry. In this respect, the contribution of foreign groups was definitely positive since it procured the high technology which native firms could not or would not invest in. On the other hand, the nature of the system and the behaviour of the big electrical groups rapidly changed France into a technically and industrially dependent country.

One must, however, recognise that the Schneider group, for example, showed an ambiguous attitude in its relations with Siemens over railway electrification, and there were firms in small countries, for example, Philips and Brown Boveri, which were highly successful. It is not easy, therefore, to avoid placing a great deal of the responsibility at the door of French entrepreneurs and managers. Elsewhere we have called in question the attitude of Paul Doumer, future President of the Republic when he was president of the Compagnie Générale in 1913.[44] Somebody like Ernest Mercier, whose reputation seems to us exaggerated, was never a real industrialist and never took into account the possibility of building an export-conscious industry.

Multinational enterprises were at one and the same time motor and brake of the growth electricity in France, so they cannot carry all the blame for the poor performance of the native competitors. The reasons for their success in France as well as for the origins of the backwardness of French industry must be found in the social and economic structure of the country itself, and neither Hilferding's finance capitalism nor Lenin's concept of imperialism can explain this phenomenon. Too many examples show that the situation was by no means irreversible, that 'new combinations'—those founded, for example by Brown Boveri—were not tried. In any case, the analysis of the electrical industry in France between 1880 and 1930 offers rich material for the study of the early phase and of the strategies of multinational enterprise. In addition, it can throw new light and raise new questions on the economy of the Third Republic.

Notes

1. Compagnie Générale d'Electricité, information notice of 1898, Archives Nationales (AN) Paris, 65 AQ G 160.
2. Founded to exploit the patents of Janin and Gramme (the latter became a member of the board and was paid in shares of the new company). The bankers were Durrieu, President of the Crédit Industriel et Commercial, Rostand, President of the Comptoir d'Escompte, Lehideux (Private Banker), de la Bouillerie. See ibid.
3. Founded on 23 May 1881 for the exploitation of the patents of Reynier and Werdemann, an Englishman. The banker involved was Durrieu. See ibid.
4. This would, however, be the case with the Lebon group, first in Spain, then in North Africa and later on in the small stakes it had in France. A. Broder, 'L'Industrie Electrique Française dans le Contexte International 1881–1930', *Congrès du Centenaire de la Société des Electriciens*, (Paris, December 1983), to be published.
5. A. Broder, *Le rôle des intérêts étrangers dans la croissance de l'Espagne 1768–1920*, (Lille, 1984).
6. Neymarck, *Finances contemporaines*, vol. 2 (Paris, 1911) pp. 257–9.
7. Ibid., note 5.
8. F. Crouzet, 'Un indice de la production industrielle française au XIXè siècle', *Annales, E.S.C.* 25 (1970), pp. 70–99; M. Lévy-Leboyer, 'L'héritage de Simiand. Prix, profits et termes d'échange au XIXème siècle', *Revue Historique* 493 (1970), pp. 77–120.
9.

Industrial production	Germany	France
1875–84	100	100
1885–94	137	116
1895–1904	209	141
1905–13	303	171

B.R. Mitchell, 'Statistical Appendix 1700–1914' in C.M. Cipolla, *Fontana Economic History of Europe*, vol. 4 (London, 1973).
10. A. Broder, *Histoire Economique de la France* (Presse Universitaire de France) 1976, vol. 3/1, pp. 305–346.
11. *Tableau Général du Commerce et de la Navigation*, (Imprimerie Nationale, 1902 (vol. 1) and 1903).
12. British Westinghouse had the right to sell in France the same products which were manufactured by the French affiliate. While the French affiliate could be active only in France and her colonies.
13. L'Industrielle Edison was founded with a capital of 1.5 million francs, the other two with 1 million francs each. See, for example, *Gaz et Electricité: La cote des valeurs*, (1893) p. 12.
14. These were Speyr Brothers and Drexel & Harjes. On the French side participated Seligmann Frères, the Banque d'Escompte de Paris and the Société Centrale de Banque. *Almanach Financier* (various issues).
15. M. Wilkins, *The Emergence of Multinational Enterprise. American Business Abroad from the Colonial Era to 1914* (Cambridge, Mass., 1970), p. 53ff.
16. A. Broder, 'L'expansion internationale de l'industrie electrique allemande', *Relations Internationales*, 29 (1982), pp. 65–87.
17. See on this subject the contributions made by H. Morsel, especially *Congrès du Centenaire de la Société des Electriciens*. World-wide the French electrometallurgical industry had a clear technical lead.
18. A. Broder, 'Le rôle des intérêts étrangers', pp. 1837–43.
19. Coffin was chairman of General Electric, Griffin was President of International Thomson Houston.
20. Either control of or a minority position which could block others in the companies

producing or distributing electrical energy. For AEG see A. Broder, 'L'expansion internationale'. For the United States see, among others, *U.S. Senate Hearings*, Document 46–70, 1 (1928).

21. CFTH: *Rapports des Assemblées Générales*, for example that of 13 April 1905.
22. A. Broder, 'L'industrie électrique française dans le contexte international 1881–1930. *Congrès du Centenaire de la Société des Electriciens*.
23. A. Broder, 'Le rôle des intérêts étrangers', pp. 1728ff.
24. Ibid.
25. For Spain see ibid.
26. Ibid.; for details see particularly the act of liquidation of the Société Thomson Houston de la Méditerranée. An (alternating) member of the AEG's supervisory board (*Aufsichtsrat*) had a seat on the board of CFTH. The CFTH *administrateur délégué* Ernest Thurnauer sat on the AEG board without any practical consequences, however, since CFTH had no prerogative in the contracts concluded by the German firm.
27. Ibid.
28. Especially the financial holdings Franco Suisse and Italo Suisse. See A. Broder, 'L'industrie électrique française', and K. Hafner, *Die Schweizerischen Finanzierungsgesellschaften für Elektrische Unternehmungen*, (Geneva, 1912), Pollux les Electroholdings en Suisse; SLND.
29. Tsarist Russia demanded for the equipment delivered to the State that it be manufactured in the country itself, and, in practice, all important projects were State contracts.
30. Siemens had constructed the power plant at Passy in 1879 but it was sold during the following year.
31. See, for instance, the correspondence of Thyssen concerning the purchase of iron ore deposits in Normandy and the construction of steel works in the same region: A. Broder, 'L'industrie électrique française'.
32. A special track was constructed near Berlin where locomotives reached a maximum speed of 210 km/h. From 1912 special endurance tests were started on the line Dessau-Bitterfeld. On the other hand, in France the Army hierarchy were against a technology which, according to their views, would have increased the vulnerability of rail transport in time of war; that is why they remained completely indifferent when the Midi railway company started to electrify its network in the Pyrenean region.
33. See Joseph Dubois, *Les locomotives du Nord. Histoire de Fives Lille Cail* (Lille, 1983).
34. It was the foundation of this firm which was responsible for the resignation of the French members of the board of the Compagnie de Creil. The press did not fail to mention ironically that on other occasions Schneider counted among the most fervent defenders of the boycott of German products. These comments, however, appeared only in the specialised financial publications, such as *La Journée Financière* (23 April 1914). Interestingly enough neither the big newspapers nor the important economic papers (*Economiste française, Economiste européen, Réforme économique, Le Globe*, etc.) had mentioned the purchase of Creil by the Germans.
35. See the statutes of the Alsacienne de Constructions Mécaniques, Belfort. It specialised in thermoelectric equipment. At the beginning cables and conductors were furnished by Mulhouse, in special cases by Siemens Berlin or even by Siemens Brothers London. By statute Mulhouse supplied boilers and steam engines, Berlin the dynamos (AN Paris, 65 AQ M415–6).
36. See the statutes of the Compagnie Générale. The archives of the firm have so far not supplied any further information on the origins and on the contents of the stipulations with the Metallgesellschaft (sources CGE, AN 65 AQ G160).
37. Ibid.
38. A. Broder, 'Le rôle des intérêts étrangers'; A. Broder, 'L'expansion internationale'.

39. A. Broder, 'Le rôle des intérêts étrangers'.
40. Ibid. Companies established in Canada but not active there were exempt from taxes. See also International Court of Justice, case concerning Barcelona traction application (1958) and new application (1962), in particular Belgian annexes and appendix, The Hague, SD.
41. Ibid. German and French banks were present in Belgium (on the French side for instance the Banque de Paris et des Pays-Bas and the Crédit Lyonnais, on the German side among others the Banque de Bruxelles and the Banque Internationale de Bruxelles). Besides, Belgian legislation was extremely liberal in regard to the manipulation of capital.
42. Apart from the provisions between Westinghouse and General Electric for the partition of patents (US Senate, Document 46–70, 1, 1928), Siemens and AEG being, of course, independent companies collaborated in several joint ventures.
43. See the example quoted above in note 32. Other cases would be Osram, Telefunken, Deutsche Tudor, Deutsche Grammophon.
44. Doumer yielded all the participations which his group held in Catalonia to Siemens suggesting the opposite to the alarmed French government (for the details see A. Broder, 'Le rôle des intérêts étrangers').

Index